ADVANCE PRAISE

"This book is a powerful clinical support to anyone who works with individuals or couples who experience ongoing systemic trauma. Riley-Richardson expertly interweaves neurobiology, our own embodied wisdom, and vivid clinical examples to help all of us face the reality of relational privilege and partner with our clients to help them thrive. If you want to support your clients to build their self-trust and feel empowered in their relationships, this book is a must-read!"

—**Juliane Taylor Shore, LMFT, LPC,** author of *Setting Boundaries that Stick*

"If you work with couples, this book belongs on your shelf. *Marginalized Couples in Therapy* by Akilah Riley-Richardson goes beyond technique, showing how systemic trauma and oppression shape intimacy for BIPOC and LGBTQIA+ partners. With practical interventions, case examples, and the groundbreaking PRIDE model, this book gives therapists concrete ways to help couples heal and thrive. It's both a call to action and a roadmap for more just, inclusive therapy."

—**Shane Birkel, LMFT,** host of *The Couples Therapist Couch* podcast, creator of training programs on couples therapy intensives

"Fact: If you are a therapist of any sort, this book belongs in your library! True relational security demands recognizing systemic context, yet because most of our training is imbued with the white, Western lens, we rarely get a glimpse beyond that perspective. Akilah Riley-Richardson walks you through developing that wider perspective and delivers exactly the kind of accessible approach that should be required reading. Poignant stories, diverse voices, and her clear, concise writing make this important work my favorite couples book of all time."

—**Sue Marriott LCSW, CGP,** coauthor *Secure Relating: Holding Your Own in an Insecure World*, host of *Therapist Uncensored* podcast

"Akilah Riley-Richardson's work is a timely and essential contribution to the field of couples counseling and therapy. She offers practical guidance while deepening our understanding of the multisystemic dynamics that shape intimate relationships. By centering individuals and communities who have historically been marginalized, her text invites a more inclusive, socially responsive approach to relational work. I look forward to including this book as required reading for my doctoral students in clinical psychology."

—**Cynthia Lubin Langtiw, PsyD,** professor, The Chicago School of Professional Psychology, Chicago Campus

MARGINALIZED COUPLES IN THERAPY

MARGINALIZED COUPLES IN THERAPY

Interventions for Healing From Systemic Trauma

AKILAH RILEY-RICHARDSON, MSW, CCTP

Norton Professional Books
An Imprint of W. W. Norton & Company
Independent Publishers Since 1923

Note to Readers: This book is intended as a general information resource for professionals practicing in the field of psychotherapy and mental health. It is not a substitute for appropriate training or clinical supervision. Likewise, any member of the general public who is not a professional practicing in the field of psychotherapy and mental health, should regard the recommendations in this book as suggestions only and any such recommendations should not be seen as a substitute for obtaining professional advice. Standards of clinical practice and protocol vary in different practice settings and change over time. No technique or recommendation is guaranteed to be safe or effective in all circumstances, and neither the publisher nor the author(s) can guarantee the complete accuracy, efficacy, or appropriateness of any particular recommendation in every respect or in all settings or circumstances.

Any URLs displayed in this book link or refer to websites that existed as of press time. The publisher is not responsible for, and should not be deemed to endorse or recommend, any website other than its own or any content that it did not create. The author, also, is not responsible for any third-party material or any content that appears on third-party websites.

Copyright © 2026 by Akilah Riley-Richardson
Foreword copyright © 2026 by Resmaa Menakem
Foreword copyright © 2026 by Rae Alibey

All rights reserved
Printed in the United States of America
First Edition

For information about permission to reproduce selections from this book, write to Permissions, W. W. Norton & Company, Inc., 500 Fifth Avenue, New York, NY 10110

For information about special discounts for bulk purchases, please contact W. W. Norton Special Sales at specialsales@wwnorton.com or 800-233-4830

Manufacturing by Versa Press
Production manager: Gwen Cullen

ISBN: 978-1-324-08296-5 (Paperback)

W. W. Norton & Company, Inc., 500 Fifth Avenue, New York, NY 10110
www.wwnorton.com

W. W. Norton & Company Ltd., 15 Carlisle Street, London W1D 3BS

Authorized EU representative: EAS, Mustamäe tee 50, 10621 Tallinn, Estonia

1 2 3 4 5 6 7 8 9 0

For Brandy Rodriguez, Colin Robinson,
and Eswick Padmore aka Gaynor De Gaye Foster

CONTENTS

Acknowledgments	xi
Foreword by Resmaa Menakem	xv
Foreword by Rae Alibey	xvii
Introduction	xxi

PART I. When the Outside Violence Seeps In: The Wider System Affecting Our Inner Relationships — 3

    CHAPTER 1. A Prison With Invisible Bars: The Impact of Systemic Trauma on BIPOC and LGBTQIA+ Individuals and Relationships — 5

    CHAPTER 2. Intimacy Has a Context: Exploring Relational Privilege — 24

PART II. The Clinical Is Political — 37

    CHAPTER 3. The Therapeutic Stance: Becoming the BIOME — 39

    CHAPTER 4. Building PRIDE — 50

PART III. Facilitating Healing: Working With Marginalized Couples — 59

    CHAPTER 5. Relational Curiosity — 61

    CHAPTER 6. Responsible Externalizing and Setting Intentions — 93

    CHAPTER 7. Continuous Trauma Work — 109

    CHAPTER 8. Building Liberatory Connections — 129

    CHAPTER 9. Reclaiming Lost Spaces — 164

    CHAPTER 10. Conclusion: Reflecting on the Path Toward Liberation — 173

References — 177
Index — 185

ACKNOWLEDGMENTS

I am filled with gratitude as I reflect on the many individuals who have supported me. Each person mentioned here has played an important role in my path, and their encouragement has been invaluable.

To Franka Philip, thank you for always believing in me during difficult times. Your unwavering support at the beginning of my journey provided me with the strength I needed to carry on. To my husband, Damian Richardson, your flexibility and willingness to create space for my growth have been the backbone of my progress. I am eternally grateful for your love and understanding. To Mzuri and Osei Richardson, my children, who inspire me to look closely at my own relationship with power and responsibility. Thanks for challenging me fiercely.

A special thanks to Ronald Richardson, whose interest in reviewing my work helped me to feel supported. To Amrika Siewdass, my personal assistant, your support for me and my children has made this journey much easier. I deeply appreciate Juliane Taylor Shore, Terri Delaney, and Rebecca Wong—your encouragement through tears and turmoil has kept me afloat, reminding me of the importance of sisterhood and solidarity.

Zach Taylor, Lauren Dockett, and Livia Kent from Psychotherapy Networker, your platform has been a beacon of opportunity and exposure, allowing me to share my work with a wider audience. The experience of writing for the Networker has been transformative.

To Brian Gibney and Lou Hanson, thank you for seeing me and loving me for who I am. To Stan and Tracey Tatkin, your excitement for my work and opportunities is uplifting and heartwarming. Resmaa Menakem, your witnessing the joy I feel when discussing the PRIDE model reminded me of my true purpose.

To my brother-in-law, Nigel Richardson, you've constantly reminded me to "keep doing the work." Because of you, I stayed grounded and focused.

Andrew Mac Intosh, I'm grateful for your unwavering support and for standing by me when I had so many questions. Your guidance has steered me. Thank you, Dana Kanhai, for your steadfast belief in my capacity. Where would I be without you there cheering me on?

To Tracie Rogers, my dear friend who always champions my endeavors with love, and to Rae Alibey, my chosen sister and steadfast advocate, your bravery has encouraged me tremendously. Thank you to my cousin Adele Beckles, who always wanted to see me grow, and to my aunt Marjorie Beckles, for your unwavering support and encouragement. Joe Winn, your teaching that the clinical is political has always remained with me. Cynthia Lubin Langtiw, thank you for promoting my work and the belief you have in my voice. To Ardene Sirjoo, your support during the writing of my book proposal has been invaluable, and to Carla Watkins, your excitement for me always means the world to me.

Brian Spielmann and the Academy of Therapy Wisdom, thank you for providing a platform for my work and fostering my growth. Franklyn Dolly, you reminded me that my skill level surpasses my self-belief, and for this, I am incredibly thankful. To Jennifer Holder Dolly, your generous opportunities have encouraged me to pursue my passions, even when I was unsure of myself. Thank you, Brent Pereira and Nkechi Dolly for allowing my authenticity.

Glenda Hinkson, your leadership, friendship, and advocacy will never be forgotten. You fought for the space I needed to write this book. Linda Thai, the knowledge I've gained from you has enriched my perspective immensely. A heartfelt thank you to Isaiah Alexander and Bokie Joy—your expertise has opened my eyes in so many ways. Nikki Shaheed, your inspiring graphics support my work in ways that I never imagined. To Hayden De Four, my cousin, thank you for sitting with me through hard times, sharing in both joy and harrowing fear. Keron Niles and Nova Reid, in the beginning of the process, you wanted to make sure that I was protected and fairly treated. Thank you!

Jamie Marich, you remind me constantly of the complexity and uncertainty in therapy. Thank you for grounding me. Wanda Chesney, you are the first academician I met whose excitement for grounded epistemology actually matched mine. I am so deeply appreciative of your presence. To Chantella Richardson and Katinka Kundler, your unapologetic natures have inspired me to embrace my whole self, and Anastacia Richardson, your humorous remark that my "brain is different" has reminded me to celebrate my unique perspective.

Acknowledgments

To Jennifer Mullan, who answered countless questions about this process and always held space for me. You are fierce. To Angela Lin and, Laura Walsh, and the entire team at Collectively Rooted, I would be nowhere without you! To my colleagues at Caiso Sex and Gender Justice, thank you for allowing me to work with a community that has enriched my existence! To the folks of Friends for Life, the immense lessons I learned from you were pivotal for me.

To my editor, Jamie Vincent, your zeal, encouragement, and commitment to this work have made me a better human and professional. To Deborah Malmud, your decision to make this happen has changed my life. To W. W. Norton and Company, your decision to give voice to this work in these most difficult times in our world is a powerful emblem of courage. I am happy to have walked this journey with you!

To Zola Phillips, Dionysia Browne, Sanaa Hyder, Libby Sinback, Akiel McLeod, La Shanda Sugg, Jay Sugg, Conrad Mitchell, Alana Lum Lock Cardinez, Sasha Massiah, Darcel Guerra, Jade Woodroffe, Anthony Woodroffe, J'élle Valdez, Amy Leigh Curry, Shad Seaton, Shelley-Ann Tenia, Mikhail Woodruffe, Kernita-Rose Bailey, Chanelle Fingal-Robinson, Joanne Modeste, Jason Arthur, Bayo Akomolafe, Krystal-Jane Verasammy, Andrea Bellerand, Maureen Murray, brunson, Victoria Dos Santos, Fritz Galette, Laura Reagan, and Anika Nicholas—your unwavering support has been a constant source of strength.

To the many LGBTQIA+ and BIPOC individuals and couples who allowed me in their space and have taught me so much, and this would never have been possible without you. I am forever grateful.

FOREWORD
BY RESMAA MENAKEM

Akilah Riley-Richardson's work isn't simply another book on couples therapy, it's a visceral necessity. In a world grappling with the long shadows of systemic racism, the insidious tendrils of oppression, and the ever-present threat of feral division, this book arrives not as a manuscript, but as vibratory *resonance*. It is a repetitive inquiry into the enduring power of love and communal connection, illuminating a path toward a more just, equitable and generative world.

For years, I've dedicated my work to helping people understand how racial trauma manifests in the body, shaping our perceptions and interactions, leaving us wounded, disconnected, and struggling to find our footing in a world that often refuses to acknowledge our pain and contributions to human existence. Akilah's work speaks directly to this understanding in ways that are both powerful and profoundly moving. It is a reminder that the work of liberation is not a luxury, but a fundamental human reclaiming.

This isn't just about techniques, it's about a fundamental shift in *cultivating consciousness*, a radical reimagining of how we approach tending and justice. Akilah grasps an important truth: For many—especially Black, Indigenous, and Bodies of Culture (BIBOC) and LGBTQIA+ individuals—the very definition of intimacy has been warped, distorted by centuries of systemic violence. Relational curiosity, responsible externalizing, and the creation of liberatory connections aren't merely therapeutic tools; they represent acts of creational emergence of radical self and communal care.

The power of this work lies in its unwavering commitment to *bodies* and to the lived experience of those who have been systemically and philosophically marginalized. It isn't solely about techniques or methodologies; it's about the *energy*, the rhythm, the *vibrations* that pulse through our relationships. It demands that we—as practitioners—show up fully and vulnerably, with a willingness to confront our own limitations that lie hidden in our virtues and to hold space for the messy, unpredictable truth of our clients' experiences.

This book offers a global perspective, looking at couples from all corners of the world, recognizing the universality of human connection while honoring the unique cultural contexts that shape our intimate lives. It is a reminder that we are all interconnected, that our struggles are intertwined, and that our liberation is bound together.

Akilah's development of the PRIDE model is a significant contribution to the field. Having seen her work in action through demo videos, I recognize the potential of this approach to offer an effective tool for liberation—a pathway toward healing and transformation that extends into the broader world. It is an attestation to Akilah's vision, her dedication, and her unwavering belief in the power of tending and kinship care.

The PRIDE model isn't a rigid set of instructions; it's a framework for exploration, a guide for navigating the complexities of systemic trauma, and an invitation to practitioners to embrace their own creativity and intuition. It invites us to slow down, to listen deeply, to honor the wisdom of our clients' bodies, and to create spaces where they can reclaim their narratives and redefine their relationships on their own terms. It is a reminder that healing is not a destination, but a journey, a continuous process of growth, discovery, and transformation.

I see Akilah's emphasis on *relational privilege* as particularly vital in these times. As she so powerfully illustrates, intimacy itself can often be experienced as a privilege, shaped by the forces of power and oppression that permeate our society. This understanding challenges us to move beyond individualistic approaches to therapy and to recognize the systemic factors that shape our clients' experiences.

Akilah centers the voices of marginalized couples, amplifying their stories and experiences in a way that is both empowering and transformative. Through carefully crafted case studies, she illuminates the unique challenges these couples face and the resilience they demonstrate in navigating a world that often seeks to silence them. These stories are not merely illustrative; they are a testament to the power of human connection and a call for practitioners to create spaces where marginalized voices can be heard, honored, and celebrated.

Akilah's work is a tribute to the resilience and strength of those who continue to fight for love, connection, and justice, even in the face of unimaginable adversity and ferality.

FOREWORD
BY RAE ALIBEY

When Akilah approached me to write a foreword for this book, I was both humbled and honored. As a person of trans experience from Trinidad and Tobago, and after decades spent in the trenches providing casework support, researching the life stories of our LGBTQIA+ elders, and fighting for basic human dignity, I have learned to recognize those who genuinely understand and connect with our struggles as a marginalized and invisible population. Through my own experiences with Akilah and the safety I feel recommending her services to other community members, I know that she has an uncanny way of seeing, hearing, and understanding the toll marginalization places on minority population, as individuals and as couples. Akilah's instinctual ways of knowing and connecting makes the least among us leave her presence with a strong sense of validation. Akilah is not just an ally; she is one of us.

Marginalized Couples in Therapy is more than another academic exercise. It is a lifeline thrown to therapists, social workers, and anyone brave enough to walk alongside couples navigating the minefield of systemic oppression. It is a testament to the power of bearing witness, of truly seeing and hearing the stories that the dominant society so often tries to erase. Akilah refuses to flinch from the hard truths—the ways our very systems, meant to help, often deepen our wounds. She bravely confronts the uncomfortable realities of systemic trauma, internalized oppression, and the unique burdens carried by BIPOC and LGBTQIA+ individuals and couples.

I have experienced firsthand the ways in which these burdens manifest. The constant vigilance, the hyper-awareness of potential threats, the exhaustion of navigating a world that often feels hostile—taking a toll on us, not only as individuals, but on our most intimate relationships. Personally and professionally, I know the trauma of couples torn apart by the weight of societal expectations, by the lack of legal protections, by the constant barrage of microaggressions and outright discrimination. And rest assured that there is *nothing* "micro" about the impacts of these aggressions.

What resonates most deeply is Akilah's unwavering commitment to centering the voices and lived experiences of those most often pushed to the margins. She understands that our stories are not just anecdotes; they are data, they are evidence, they are the foundation upon which we must build a more just and equitable world. Without offering simplistic solutions or dull answers, she gifts us a framework—the PRIDE model—that enables practitioners to cultivate bravery, intimacy, openness, microliberatory movements, and epistemic embracing. More than concepts; these are the essential tools for creating a therapeutic space where marginalized couples can finally be seen, heard, and validated in their full humanity.

As a foot soldier who has spent years on the ground, I know that theory is not enough. What is needed are practical tools—strategies that can be implemented in the real world. Akilah provides these in abundance, offering concrete guidance on everything from responsible externalizing to building liberatory connections. She challenges us to move beyond traditional therapeutic approaches and embrace a more holistic, justice-oriented framework.

I have always believed that the personal is political, and Akilah's work embodies this principle. She understands that our relationships are not separate from the wider world; they are deeply intertwined with it. The challenges that marginalized couples face are not simply individual issues; they are the result of systemic forces that have been shaping our lives for generations.

Akilah challenges us to examine our own biases, to interrogate our intimacy stories, and to take relational risks to create a therapeutic space where marginalized couples can truly heal. These challenges demand that we acknowledge the weight of history, the impact of societal norms, and the ways in which power and privilege shape our relationships. We are asked to be vulnerable, honest, and willing to step outside of our comfort zones.

This book is not for those seeking easy answers. We are required to confront our own privilege, to challenge our assumptions, and to lean into our discomforts. And the rewards are immense! When we embrace the principles outlined in this book, we can create a world where all couples, regardless of their race, gender identity, or sexual orientation, have the opportunity to experience love, intimacy, and connection in its fullest expression.

I think about the elders in my community; those who paved the way for us, fought for our rights, and endured so much pain and suffering. They did not do it for us to simply survive; they did it for us to thrive. This book is a tribute to their legacy, a call to honor their sacrifices by creating a world where all couples can flourish.

As I reflect on my own journey, I am filled with hope and gratitude for Akilah's work. This book is a testament to her unwavering commitment to social justice and her profound belief in the power of love to heal and transform. I urge you to read it, to study it, and to put its principles into practice. Together, we can build a world where all couples can thrive.

INTRODUCTION

I want to gently invite you to imagine with me. Picture yourself traversing the wonderful yet tumultuous waters of love and intimacy under the relentless pressure of societal discrimination and oppression. Visualize the experience of sitting with a practitioner—the weight of confusion and overwhelm resting heavily upon your shoulders—attempting to dissect the disruptions in your relationship, while grappling with external forces that seem largely beyond your control. Now imagine being in a therapeutic space with a practitioner, whose efforts are not targeted to address the real cause of your pain: the system that inflicts it. For many BIPOC (Black, Indigenous, and people of color) and LGBTQIA+ (lesbian, gay, bisexual, transgender, queer/questioning, intersex, and asexual) folks, this is the disconcerting reality. These folks are marginalized, which means that they are disempowered, excluded, denied basic rights, oppressed, and treated as if they are insignificant.

There was a stage in my practice when I reached a pivotal point. I realized that I wasn't thoroughly prepared for working with clients who walk this painful truth every day. I was versed in various modalities, but I was not holding enough space for the assault my clients faced from the wider system. I needed to look not just deeper but wider. There was a dire need to broaden my lens. It was this quest that birthed this book, which illuminates the intersections of systemic trauma and relational privilege, specifically as they affect marginalized couples.

I view this book as a fulfilled commitment. The experiences of marginalized people are often devalued, even by helping professionals, and this text is my dedication to carving a space where we, as practitioners, can ensure that we are of service in a way that is rooted in the realities of our people. It is also a reflection of my obligation to marginalized couples and individuals. My sincere wish for them all is that they are never harmed in therapy but instead uplifted.

As a Black Caribbean woman who hails from Trinidad and Tobago, I also know that my decision to write is an important statement. So often, voices from this part of the world are dismissed or relegated to lesser platforms. I have had the privilege of being able to serve clients from the Caribbean and from many other parts of the world. All of those voices have informed this work, and as I occupy this body, battling the ravages of postcolonialism, xenophobia, and racism, I am reminded of the importance of my voice in this world.

Divided into three parts, this text begins by exploring systemic trauma in Part I. Here, we discuss the pervasive effects of discrimination and marginalization on intimacy. Part II invites us to consider how to build a transformative therapeutic posture via the BIOME (bravery, intensity/intimacy, openness, microliberatory movements, epistemic embracing). The PRIDE model of intervention is also introduced in this part of the work. In Part III, you are escorted through distinct phases of working with marginalized couples. You are furnished with actionable methodologies, which are all supported by case examples and quotes in order to enrich your understanding and application of the work. In order to respect the privacy and anonymity of my past and present clientele, these case examples represent an amalgam of cases I have worked with over the years and pseudonyms have been used. The amalgam is deliberate so that stories are not identifiable. Additionally, pseudonyms have been used for some of the other direct quotes throughout this text. Essential concepts, such as relational curiosity, responsible externalizing, and building liberatory connections, are examined to equip you with what you need to support your clients. Finally, you are gently encouraged to sit in the discomfort we feel when some of our strategies do not work.

I have designed this book to provide guidance for therapists, social workers, counselors, and practitioners who either work with marginalized couples or wish to in the future. This book can also be used by current students of the aforementioned disciplines. It can support us all in appreciating the unseen complexities of intimacy that operate under the surge of systemic oppression. I hope that this book enhances your work and deepens your commitment for advocacy for social justice.

As a social worker, educator, trainer, and therapist, I have dedicated much of my practice, research, and teaching to address the needs of the communities I have written about in this text. My work in this field is ongoing and constantly unfolding. You are meeting me and this work in one phase of my journey. I am delighted to know that as I continue my work with so many communities,

I will continue to be nourished by additional insights. Some of these insights will shake the very foundation of where I am now. I am ready for that. I am also deeply grateful for the ways in which the voices of my clients have already had such a profound effect on my work. Their stories, which are highlighted in this text, have deeply inspired the body of work that I share with you now.

Please embark on the journey within this book in a way that feels right for you. Engage it with an authentic heart. Allow yourself to think critically about the work and to feel your own creativity. It is my sincere hope that this book emboldens you to do that. Be brave! Find and use your voice!

Together, let's explore the power that lies in humbly and wholeheartedly connecting with marginalized people. Together, let's work *with* them to create steps toward liberation and authentic relationship building.

Let's begin!

MARGINALIZED COUPLES IN THERAPY

PART I

When the Outside Violence Seeps In: The Wider System Affecting Our Inner Relationships

Welcome to Part I of this journey toward supporting marginalized couples and partnerships! I am truly delighted that you are open to exploring the context that marginalized people occupy before we take a deeper dive into the ways that we can support them. Understanding their reality is a crucial step to doing the work. When we do not appreciate this, we run the risk of intervening in ways that are unhelpful and even harmful. As such, it is our responsibility to be with their reality from a place of deep reflection and curiosity. You will be supported in these reflections throughout this book.

This part contains two chapters. In Chapter 1, we discuss the nature of systemic trauma itself and its general impact on marginalized people, while in Chapter 2, we focus specifically on its effect on relationships. Chapter 2 also introduces the concept of relational privilege, which is a significant idea in this text. This idea is offered to help you frame your work every step of the way. I welcome you to this process so that we can truly be with clients in meaningful and authentic ways.

CHAPTER 1

A Prison With Invisible Bars
The Impact of Systemic Trauma on BIPOC and LGBTQIA+ Individuals and Relationships

It is not one moment. It is all the moments, and it is a system. It is a system of questions because you are never really sure what is happening to you.
—Yara, on dealing with racism and xenophobia in the United Kingdom

It is hard, every single day. It is like every single day, this is the fight. When you get up in the morning and you get dressed, it is a struggle to dress a particular way or look a particular way. It is exhausting.
—Jay, on facing homophobia in Trinidad and Tobago

Since transitioning, I've noticed a lot of people think I have a personality disorder. None of these people have ever been a therapist who has supported me, but they all know I am trans. So many people think I am a "crazy tranny." I've noticed that it's much easier to be taken seriously at work and in everyday life if people don't know that I am trans. I'm afraid of disclosing. I'm proud of who I am, but I am sick of being discriminated against.
—Elena, on being a trans woman in the United States

I remember what it felt like to sit with the three clients quoted above. I could sense their stifled, anxious, hypervigilant, and weary states. They were living in prisons with invisible bars, struggling to live fully, freely, and wholeheartedly. Their bodies were heavy with grief over the reality of a field that, even in its aim to be therapeutic, inflicts harm by not appreciating the true genesis of their painful narratives. For these clients, sitting with clinicians was difficult and often, horrid. They were experiencing a profound sense of trauma, but often, their therapists did not understand how to provide support. Clinicians became additional perpetrators of harm, with assessments and treatment plans that paid tribute to the therapist's comfort and narrow etiologies.

We, as practitioners, sometimes ask the wrong questions when working with many of our clients. There is a deeper dive to be taken. There is a need for a wider scope and a form of clinical curiosity that stretches beyond the microcontexts of our clients. Referring to the work of Thema Bryant, Linda Thai (trainer, mental health practitioner, and storyteller) notes: "Traditional psychology asks 'What's wrong with you?' Trauma-informed therapy asks 'What happened to you?' Culturally informed psychology asks 'What happened to your people?' Liberation psychology asks 'What continues to happen to you and your people?'" (Kelley & Marriott, 2023).

We are not doing the work if we are not asking the last two questions!

WHAT HAS HAPPENED AND WHAT CONTINUES TO HAPPEN? AN EXPLORATION OF SYSTEMIC TRAUMA

Systemic trauma can be defined as harm that emerges from components of the *wider* environment, cultural norms, and institutions. Perpetrators of systemic harm often include educational systems, economic structures, criminal justice systems, and religious institutions. For example, in Australia, a 2024 research report from the National Indigenous Youth Education Coalition School Exclusion Project points to the exclusion of Torres Strait Islander and Aboriginal people from the 19th century to present day in the country's public school system. The report goes on to demonstrate how Indigenous students are also treated differently in the educational system. Almost 7% of all expulsion is meted out to Indigenous children though they only represent approximately 2% of the student population. The criminal justice system has also presented its own challenges to marginalized people. Throughout the world, this system continues to horribly fail lesbian, gay, bisexual, transgender, queer/questioning, intersex, asexual, and other (LGBTQIA+) people. At the time of writing, in countries such as Trinidad and Tobago, as well as South Africa, many LGBTQIA+ complain about the lack of responsiveness from police to their various complaints of homophobic and transphobic violence (Naidoo et al.,

2023). The challenges that Black people in the United States experience at the hands of the police are also well known. This felt so vivid for me as I listened to the story of Lincoln, a Black man living in Florida. While discussing his experience of the police system as a taxpaying citizen in America, he said, "I'm paying them to kill me." Sadly, the horrors do not end there for marginalized folks. Even religious institutions have been sources of harm. African slavery and genocide against Indigenous people are but two examples of the ways in which religious dogma has contributed to harm marginalized groups. For LGBTQIA+ people, there are countless stories of religious-based conversion practices as well as a loss of connection from their religious communities (Jones et al., 2022).

Features of Systemic Trauma

Why do we need to pay so much attention to the role of systemic trauma in the lives of marginalized people? Why do we need to pause and be with this type of trauma differently? It's because there are four specific features of systemic trauma, which actually make it difficult to treat in therapy. Systemic trauma is *chronic and pervasive*, *disenfranchised*, *system induced*, and *unpredictable*. Its chronic and pervasive nature is evident by the fact that it continues to persist across time and space despite many efforts. Day by day, marginalized people have stories to tell about numerous microaggressions or larger infractions inflicted on them by those who hold more power in the world. From shopping in a store to navigating the judicial system, they live in a state of unsafety, surrounded by callous and unjust acts. Sadly, much of this is ignored or even invalidated by others who refuse to believe the experiences of marginalized people. The result of this lack of acknowledgment is disenfranchised pain, as their claims are often dismissed by those who hold more power and privilege in the world. Over time, this degree of systemic invalidation becomes self-invalidation, where marginalized people begin to doubt themselves and their experiences. As Jamie, a 25-year-old Asian transwoman shared:

> *"You are always asking yourself, 'Did that just happen? Did I imagine that? Did they mean that or am I too sensitive?' It destroys your nerves—always having to be on guard for harm, and then always wondering if you are perceiving the world right."*

Michael, a Caribbean immigrant living in Florida shared:

> *"After a while, you live in questioning. Questioning your sanity, questioning your thoughts."*

Sitting in the above realities results in persons living out of alignment with their own understanding of the world. This is one of the most violent pieces of systemic trauma: the way in which it forces you to step outside of your own reality in order to survive. Living your own truth becomes a privilege, accessed by those who hold power in the world. We explore more about this later in this chapter.

The unpredictable nature of systemic harm means that persons are often hypervigilant and are deeply concerned with survival. Irritability, mood disturbance, and changes in sleeping patterns present for persons who are always on the lookout for harm. In some cases, effects on the brain itself have been noticed. Research done by Fani et al. (2021) noted that Black women who indicated more experiences of racism also had more responsivity in brain regions that were responsible for vigilance and threat detection. Additionally, it was observed that there was greater response within the threat-inhibition networks in the brain, which indicates not only greater vigilance but "suppression of the threat response" (p. 1010). In other words, systemic trauma not only affects how vigilant one must be, but in order to survive this degree of harm and keep safe, one must overregulate how one responds to perceived threats. To gain a clearer understanding of how systemic trauma is truly unique and different from other types of trauma, see Table 1.1.

TABLE 1.1 The Difference Between Systemic Trauma and Single-Incident Trauma

Type	Systemic trauma	Single-incident trauma
Source	Ongoing, pervasive, societal structures	Singular event (e.g., accident, assault)
Onset	Often insidious, cumulative, may go unnoticed	Sudden, clear onset
Impact on nervous system	Chronic dysregulation, hypervigilance, etc.	Acute stress response, posttraumatic stress disorder (PTSD) possible

Impact on emotional regulation	Difficulty regulating emotions, emotional numbing	Difficulty regulating emotions, flashbacks, nightmares
Impact on identity	Erosion of sense of self, shame, internalized oppression	Shock, confusion, potential for identity shift
Examples	Racism, sexism, homophobia, poverty, discrimination	Car accident, natural disaster, violent crime

Systemic harm causes considerable emotional, psychological, sexual, spiritual, financial, and physical distress to persons who are considered minoritized or marginalized in our societies. Let's discuss these further.

Psychological and Emotional Harm

I feel like I am in an aquarium. I feel like I am behind glass in a museum. They are looking at me, just for their own entertainment. They are judging and laughing.
—Yara, on being Black in the United Kingdom

I'm tired a lot. Part of my battery gets used just existing, and part of that fatigue is because my nervous system is active all the time. Existing in this space is hard.
—Steph, on being Black in the United States

I sometimes find myself going into derealization. I feel like I often have to control who I am. For most of my life, I had to play a part because my gender expression was policed.
—Jess, on being a trans woman in the United States

Living in constant watch for harm is an unimaginable pain. Persons who exist on the margins of our society also *exist outside of the margins of the possibilities for their lives.* Being constantly vigilant places their nervous system in states that are not optimal for imagination, growth, creativity, flexibility, self-regulation, and coherent thinking. The state of the nervous system that allows for this is what I call the "window of possibilities," an adaptation of the beautiful concept known as the "window of tolerance" developed by Dan Siegel (2020). I say "possibilities" because I believe that trauma traps us in a narrow range of outcomes for our lives. It is a violent stripping of different ways of being in the world. Our repertoire of behaviors, ideologies, and decisions becomes smaller, or perhaps more restricted to our survival and not our growth. To understand more about this, let us look at the way that the autonomic nervous system (ANS) works and the impact of systemic trauma on the ANS. We will then look at the window of possibilities and Siegel's window of tolerance.

The human nervous system consists of two major parts: the central nervous system and the peripheral nervous system. The brain and spinal cord make up the central nervous system; the peripheral nervous system is composed of nerves that travel from the spinal cord and extend to the rest of the body. The ANS, which is a significant part of our upcoming discussion, is considered part of the peripheral nervous system. Consider the diagram in Figure 1.1 for further understanding.

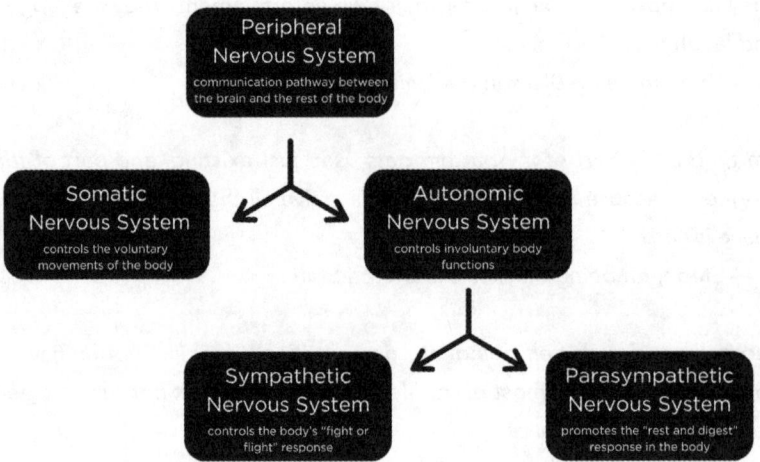

Figure 1.1: Understanding the components of the peripheral nervous system. Illustration by Nikki Shaheed.

The ANS helps us regulate our automatic bodily processes, such as breathing, sexual arousal, blood pressure, urinary functions, heart rate, and digestion. It also controls the involuntary responses of our muscles and glands to our internal and external environment. Additionally, as we live in the ever-changing realities of our environment, the ANS is one of the systems that assesses how best to enhance our well-being and safety. When certain environmental cues are presented, this system organizes actions according to the cues.

There are two branches of the ANS: the sympathetic nervous system (SNS) and the parasympathetic nervous system (PNS). We will first spend some time discussing the PNS by leaning on the Polyvagal Theory by Stephen Porges (2011). According to this theory, there are two branches of the PNS: the ventral vagal branch and the dorsal vagal branch. When we feel safe within our bodies and in our environments, the ventral vagal branch—which is connected to many body parts including our larynx, face, inner ear, and neck—is activated. Our inner middle ear muscles become engaged, which increases our ability to hear the human voice and filter it out from other background sounds. Our facial muscles also have increased capacity to make communicative expressions, and the larynx is able to produce a soothing vocal tone and a modulated vocal patterning. These changes support our ability to rapidly communicate our internal state of calm and security, as well as our availability for connection to others and social engagement. Perhaps this is the state we often notice when marginalized persons are in safe affinity spaces. These spaces are designed for persons with shared identities to feel a sense of ease while sharing stories, ideas, and connection.

However, these spaces exist because so much of our reality extracts us from this state of calm. The rest of the world is often a space of both real or imagined threats. These threats lower our vagal tone. Our SNS is activated to prepare for defense. When this happens, we can begin to feel immense panic and possibly, even rage. The body is preparing to fight or run. In order to facilitate these responses, the heart rate quickens and the pupils dilate. More blood is steered to parts of our body that need oxygen so that we can protect ourselves from danger. The muscles in the middle ear lose their tone and perceiving the human voice becomes difficult. Instead, we become more responsive to high- and low-frequency sounds, which essentially are predatory sounds. The nerves that manage our speech are inhibited and so there is less regulation of tone or voice pattern. *This is not a state of connection.* In this state, connection and bonding behaviors are not physiologically supported. In fact, as the presence of threat continues with no relief in sight, this can move from fight and flight to a state of terror and freeze, which is actually a blend of responses from two separate systems: the SNS, and now, the dorsal vagal system, which activates to support additional strategies for protection. We turn now to understand more about this branch: the dorsal vagal branch.

The body cannot sustain that degree of terror and freeze for a long time. As such, if the threat continues, the dorsal vagal system eventually takes full control. When we perceive danger that is inescapable, this branch, which is another part of the PNS, activates to support immobilization. This increases the possibility of survival. When the body is in this mode, other changes are noticed. This could include a flatter facial expression, less access to vocabulary, and less vocal prosody. Persons in this state experience fatigue, incoherent thinking, and numbness. They feel less connection to their emotions, to other people, and the environment. Often, people in this state have reported experiencing despair and shame. We speak more about the impact of shame on marginalized partnerships in Chapter 2.

The activity of the ANS can also be easily understood, using Dan Siegel's window of tolerance. The window of tolerance refers to an optimal zone of ANS arousal, in which we can experience the state of connection described earlier. Siegel notes that when there is increased activity of the SNS, which is known as hyperarousal, we are taken outside of our window of tolerance. In this state, we experience hypervigilance, anxiety, and anger. Conversely, we can also experience hypoarousal, which is the dorsal vagal state mentioned earlier. It protects us through numbness, flat affect, and feelings of despair. Because the window of tolerance is the space where we feel safe, curious, and open, I also refer to it as the window of possibilities. An image of the window of possibilities is shown in Figure 1.2.

In the window of possibilities, people experience more creativity and imagination. They live in the fullness of their human potential, and can engage in human relationships with flexibility and depth. Because of the chronic nature of systemic trauma, marginalized people are often not allowed to live the true breadth of their lives. Their psyches are battered, torn, and worn by living in a world that considers them less than human. As such, many of them battle intense mental health challenges. As one Black woman living in Portugal once said to me: "It feels like I am always at war!" Indeed, this sounds similar to the phenomenon of racial battle fatigue, a concept that explains the psychophysiological reality of Black people who move through White spaces (Smith et al., 2011). From anger, shock, depression, and anxiety, Black adults in the United States live in psychological realities that make them more likely

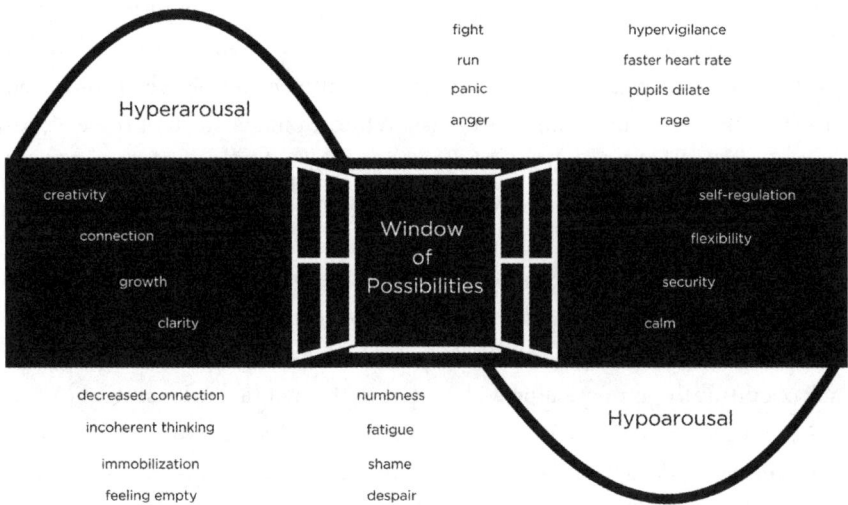

Figure 1.2: In the window of possibilities (inspired by Dan Siegel's window of tolerance), people experience more creativity and imagination. They live in the fullness of their human potential, and can engage in human relationships with flexibility and depth. Illustration by Nikki Shaheed.

to report psychological distress than White adults (U.S. Department of Health and Human Services, 2025). Other racial minorities also face a dismal reality. According to the American Psychiatric Association (2017), American Indians and Alaska Natives experience disproportionately higher rates of mental disturbance than the rest of the U.S. population. In the mid-17th to early 20th centuries, they were removed from their lands and had to endure government-run boarding schools. This removed them from their families and spirituality, which has contributed to higher rates of suicidality, substance abuse, and traumatic stress. Within the U.S. Latinx community, adults are more likely than youth to experience psychological distress due to acculturation and immigration in the United States.

In the United Kingdom, people from Black and minority ethnic groups are more likely to have psychotic symptoms than other racial groups (National Health Service, 2016). In fact, Black men present a higher likelihood of experiencing psychosis than any other group. This startling reality, which presents in both African and Caribbean men in the United Kingdom, does not occur for Black men in predominantly Black spaces. This clearly suggests that this is due to the context of feeling unsafe in largely White communities (Khan et al., 2017). Additionally, Black women in the United Kingdom experience a greater likelihood of having common mental health challenges when compared to White British women and non-British White women. Much of these aforementioned challenges can be attributed to racism, which has been connected to an increased probability of developing delusions, hallucinations, depression, and posttraumatic stress.

The relative lack of access to support exacerbates the reality for Black, Indigenous, and people of color (BIPOC). For instance, Asian American and Pacific Islander communities face obstacles such as language barriers and the lack of culturally competent providers within the mental health system (Mok, 2023). There are also considerable financial barriers. Almost 10% of African Americans do not possess health insurance when compared to approximately 5% of non-Hispanic White persons (Keisler-Starkey & Bunch, 2020). This severely compromises the ability to access counseling support and/or pharmacotherapy. Additionally, issues such as a lack of transportation and not knowing where to go to access care reduce the ability and willingness to obtain care (Alang, 2019). Furthermore, there is growing fear and mistrust of treatment as engaging with the mental health system can sometimes lead to involuntary hospitalization and inclusion of the criminal justice system (Alang, 2019).

Fear of experiencing discrimination, experiences of actual harm and microaggressions within the system, as well as high levels of internalized queerphobia are just a few of the factors that prohibit the LGBTQIA+ community from accessing services. Horrific experiences, such as being misgendered or being asked invasive and inappropriate questions about their sexual practices, also deter LGBTQIA+ folks from reaching out. These experiences are dehumanizing and further traumatizing. What results is a reluctance to engage the system or early dropout. This is unfortunate given that members of the LGBTQIA+ community experience high rates of mental health concerns. In 2021, a study conducted by Ramchand et al. revealed that gay, lesbian, and bisexual individuals have increased suicide risk in the United States. Furthermore, LGBTQIA+ persons are more than twice as likely as heterosexual people to suffer with depression, anxiety, and substance abuse. Similar findings also exist in countries such as New Zealand. Stats NZ (2021), an official database agency in New Zealand, revealed that people who were LGBTQIA+ were over twice as likely to experience day-to-day feelings of depression and anxiety than their non-LGBTQIA+ counterparts. These statistics also revealed considerable physical health disparities as well.

Physical Harm

I try my best not to go to the doctor. I only go if I absolutely have to.
—Samuel, a 57-year-old gay man in Florida

The sentiment expressed above represents so much about how queer people feel when interacting with the health care system internationally. There are also many reports of being harmed by nurses and pharmacists, whose glaring blind spots show up as systemic violence of the highest order. When compared to non-LGBTQIA+ adults, LGBTQIA+ adults in the United States report adverse health care experiences at a higher rate (Montero et al., 2024). Furthermore, 6 in 10 LGBTQIA+ adults admit that they prepare themselves to be insulted by medical practitioners when seeking medical care. Many also believe that they must alter their physical appearance to receive just treatment in the health care system (Montero et al., 2024). Similar reports pervade in the Caribbean. Many members of the LGBTQIA+ community can attest to the struggles while accessing health care. According to 33-year-old Femi, a gay man living in Trinidad who refused to access care: "I was afraid of being made a spectacle, of being laughed at." Shanti, a 40-year-old trans woman in Trinidad, echoed similar sentiments as she divulged: "Accessing health care is a ritual that I never want to perform!"

It is heartbreaking to acknowledge that so many health care providers provide such a tiresome experience for the LGBTQIA+ community. Some of this is spurred on by a lack of awareness. Clients who I have interacted with have shared that some health care providers do not even understand the difference between sex and gender, while others evade the issue of gender altogether. Some professionals also ask invasive and irrelevant questions about the clients' sex lives, gender transitioning, or their physical bodies. All of these gruesome occurrences serve as undeniable hindrances when community members need help.

And their need for help is quite real! LGBTQIA+ people are disproportionately affected by many illnesses, such as cervical cancer, anal cancer, and breast cancer (Baker, 2020). Specifically, same-sex-loving women and bisexual women are more susceptible to cardiovascular disease and obesity whereas bisexual men report a higher degree of diabetes (Fredriksen-Goldsen et al., 2013). Aging LGBTQIA+ persons face higher rates of disability and HIV diagnoses when compared to their heterosexual counterparts (Emlet, 2016). Perhaps the most disheartening point to note is that in many cases when LGBTQIA+ persons are diagnosed with various conditions, there is also a lack of culturally appropriate responsiveness by medical professionals. In addition, LGBTQIA+ people also lack the financial resources to care for themselves in many of these circumstances.

Financial Harm

> I am so tired of this, being unable to find work. No one wants to employ you when you are dressed like this. So just to find work, I have to betray who I am and wear a suit and pretend.
> —Clara, on trying to find employment as a trans woman in the Caribbean

The economic and employment barriers faced by racial and sexual minorities are unfathomable. Even in countries that have shifted away from institutionalized segregation in so many ways, these are sizable impediments to economic inclusion. Black and LGBTQIA+ South Africans can attest to this harm. In a 2022 World Bank Report on inequality in Southern Africa, South Africa was deemed to be the most unequal country in the world, with its Black populace being the poorest group in their society (United Nations, 2024). This report notes that income disparities are directly attributed to race and racism in South Africa. The United Kingdom shows a similar reality where there is a large income inequality between ethnic groups. In the United Kingdom, Pakistani, Bangladeshi, and Black persons have the lowest median household incomes (House of Commons Library, 2020). In the United States, White people still have far more wealth than their Black counterparts. According to the Federal Reserve Survey of Consumer Finance (2023), though there has been growth in income for Black households, their income still is just a fraction of that of White households. In Australia, Aboriginal and Torres Strait Islanders have lower employment rates when compared to non-Indigenous people (National Indigenous Australians Agency, 2022). Significant barriers to education, as well as entrenched discrimination in the criminal justice system, all contribute to these.

In many ways, this is also the reality for queer folks: Lack of access to formal education or rampant discrimination in the education system often render them with limited opportunities in the job market. I have heard so many stories of young LGBTQIA+ individuals who were unable to complete their high school education due to disturbances in their adolescence and early adulthood that were directly tied to their sexual orientation or gender identity. For example, Luke, a 40-year-old LGBTQIA+ activist from Guyana openly noted: "From an early age, my parents put me out of the house when they realized I was trans. Who could find the time to study or become anything when you have nowhere to live and nothing to eat?" Additionally, being on the receiving end of merciless taunting and homophobic discrimination by school colleagues and faculty makes it very difficult for many queer persons to thrive academically and become qualified in their desired fields.

Even when fully qualified, LGBTQIA+ persons are often denied full participation in their economic environments and job markets, as they are denied jobs or promotional opportunities. So attests Videsh, a 47-year-old Indian gay man from Trinidad and Tobago. In one of his sessions with me, Videsh disappointingly shared, "I was in line for the promotion, but they called me and let me know that I couldn't get the job, because they knew about my orientation, and they were afraid of how that would look!" His is one of many stories of rejection and injustice that goes unnoticed and unnamed.

Another form of harm that is often invisible is the effect on human relationships. We turn our focus here now, which is the central essence of this book.

Relational Harm

After a while, you don't even want to be touched.
—Stacy, a Black woman, on the impact of racism on her relationship

As a Black Guyanese migrant in London, Stacy began to realize that her interactions with her male partner, Shaun, were slowly shifting. She was becoming hypervigilant, less interested in sex, aggressive, and even withdrawn at times. She struggled to connect with Shaun and didn't always understand the reasons for this. However, she did indeed sense that something else was at play.

She understood that her inability to be emotionally and physically intimate was because her body was being assaulted in other ways. This Black woman was under the onslaught of racism and xenophobia, and there was little to no redress for this degree of harm.

Despite this, Shaun didn't comprehend Stacy's behavior toward him at all. He found her temperamental, and he was becoming impatient with her low sexual interest. When she complained about her daily experiences of race-based prejudice and discrimination, he just saw her as being overly sensitive and belligerent. During one of his declarations that she was unnecessarily reactive, he complained, "She is beginning to see things that don't even exist." She felt gaslit and not seen. He felt helpless and believed that he could do nothing right to appease her.

Neither of them could effectively name what was destroying their relationship, though Shaun felt that it was all due to Stacy's trying personality. This is how he understood it. In his eyes, she was just *difficult*. Racial activist and somatic abolitionist Resmaa Menakem often says that trauma that is decontextualized can look like personality (Fragoso, 2020). And here it was, decontextualized trauma, masking itself as personality and ruining meaningful connection. Their love was not playing by the rules. Despite all the insight they had into each other's own foibles, preferences, and familial traumas, they could not seem to shift what was really happening to them.

The same degree of despair was felt by Jay and Ronnie, two men who had been romantically involved for 10 years. As Jay noted,

> "I don't understand this cowering thing. He never wants to hold hands. He hides me. I get no affection in public. He lets other people determine how we live. I want to live together, and he is rejecting me. Even that he doesn't want!"

Ronnie perceived Jay to be unreasonable and ridiculous. He lamented over Jay's lack of consideration and the fact that Jay seemed to not care that Ronnie would lose his family, friends, and community from being open about his orientation. Here were two men who desperately wanted to make their relationship work, but they were managing the impact of queerphobia quite differently. In fact, they were also destroying each other emotionally in the process.

I've been with many of these stories, both directly and indirectly. I've sat with BIPOC and LGBTQIA+ partners who are struggling with the impact of racism and queerphobia, respectively, or in some cases concurrently. When systemic trauma seeps into relational dynamics, it leaves a trail of chaos. So many of us have been taught that there is a clear path to intimacy. This path includes trust, accountability, responsiveness, compassion, and interdependence. However, systemic trauma disrupts this path because it muddles these very components that we need to enable true connection. These seemingly attainable components are, in fact, tied very closely to our social location in the world. In other words, the characteristics of intimacy in our *private* relationships are affected by the amount of power and privilege that one holds in one's *wider context*. Intimacy, as we currently understand it, does not operate outside of one's wider economic, educational, legislative, judicial, religious, and cultural contexts.

It is important to note here that the harmful relationship between marginalized couples' intimacy and the wider social system is not just a contemporary phenomenon. It is also not an accidental connection. There have been well-organized mechanisms that have deliberately harmed the relationships of those who hold less power in our world. Such was certainly the case for African slaves in the Americas. Hill (2005) asserted:

> Slavery destroyed the African heritage of blacks, claims Kenneth Stamps, and left them living in "cultural chaos" since the family patterns of whites were "meaningless and unintelligible" to them. Moreover, the definition of slaves as property was one of many efforts to negate their humanity and deny the significance of their personal and family lives. Slaves' property status precluded them from entering a legal marriage contract, as the law recognized no form of marriage among slaves, "whether they 'take up' with each other by expression of their owners, or from mere impulse of nature, or in obedience to the command to 'multiply and replenish the earth.'" With no standing before the law, slave marriages could be and were ended at any time at the discretion of slave owners. (pp. 58–59)

Though same-sex marriage is, at the time of this writing, legal in 36 countries in the world, there are still many spaces where this is not so. In countries where there are well-entrenched and established systems that formally diminish, and in many cases, criminalize same-sex relationships, there is undeserved strain on these partnerships. In my practice, I have seen the different ways in which the nonrecognition of these unions cause breakdowns and conflict.

Delegitimizing same-sex love forces many partners to view intimacy as risky and unsafe. In addition to a fear of public displays of affection, the strain placed on the relationship to maintain safety even stifles the partners in the privacy of their own homes. Jacinth, a 56-year-old lesbian woman, notes, "It's like a noise in my head. I can't turn it off, and so even when we are trying to be intimate, I just can't. It's right there . . . between us." The challenges are further amplified if both partners have different assessments of risk. Many arguments ensue over safety measures, with one partner often deeming the other to be either too uptight or restrictive, while the other is accused of being reckless. Additionally, many of these relationships are not entitled to the same privileges of heterosexual couples. For example, social security "spousal" benefits are typically nonexistent for persons who exist in illegitimate unions. This adds additional fears about financial safety and security. In some countries, even being able to find housing for partners can become a harrowing and daunting experience, often with no real success in the end. Living in this constant state of disquietude does not augur well for connection.

We cannot forget that it is not only our ability to be connected and intimate that is affected by our systemic reality. Our capacity for navigating the vagaries of intimate relationships on a whole is compromised by systemic harm. Yes, being in a romantic relationship necessitates deep intimacy. However, relationships also require the partners to know how and when to practice healthy boundaries, when to engage in deep self-trust, when to be one's own advocate, and quite frankly, when to disconnect. Due to structural oppression and systemic discrimination, marginalized people do not always have experiences that foster what is necessary to maneuver the ebb and flow of intimate relationships. As Ola, a 25-year-old nonbinary client shared, "I learnt from my experiences in the world that I should not trust myself. If I begin to trust myself, then I would be angry all the time, so I just can't do that."

The belief that one is not worthy of one's own trust in the wider system can certainly spill over to other domains in one's life. This lack of self-trust can prevent major life decisions that are critical to preserving well-being during difficult moments in intimate relationships. Additionally, marginalized people do not always have the resources required to seek their own interest when relationships are either harmful or no longer desirable. For example, some partners find it practically impossible to end relationships that they no longer wish to be in because they do not have sufficient financial resources to be alone and independent. This limits their relational possibilities. Caribbean sex and gender analyst Isaiah Alexander, who is also a gay man, shared:

> *"Sometimes, it is hard leaving a relationship because being in a relationship with a good-looking man gives you social capital that you just don't have as a queer person. Sometimes, you even put up with an abusive relationship because you have no financial security, and financial security overrules emotional security. Standing on your own is scarier than existing in a loveless relationship."*

In fact, some even believe that finding happy relationships is extremely rare. James, a same-sex-loving male client in Jamaica confessed: "I was in love once, and for me that was like a needle in a haystack. There is no way that I can find that love again, not in this country!" A similar sense of despair is felt by some clients of color. When speaking of his relationship with his White female partner, 37-year-old Tahj admitted, "The truth is that this relationship's been over a long time ago, but where will I go?" His experience is one of many stories that indicate the severe limitations placed on marginalized people.

Oppression can place unique stressors on relationships as partners may experience both *individual-level* and *couple-level minority stress*. Individual-level minority stress refers to extreme levels of stress experienced by minoritized people that are directly tied to their wider social reality. This type of stress usually results in adverse physical and mental health outcomes. Couple-level minority stress, on the other hand, refers to hardships that couples and partnerships face because the *relationship form* itself is marginalized. This is often the case for interracial or same-sex partnerships, whose relationships undergo considerable devaluation, discrimination, and painful scrutiny (LeBlanc et al., 2015). As you will see ahead, current literature gives us critical insight into the impact of both individual- and couple-level minority stress on couples.

Lavner et al. (2018) investigated the relationship between racial discrimination and couples' relational health. In their study, which focused on 344 rural, low-income heterosexual African American couples, they found that partners who experienced high levels of racial discrimination outside of their relationship reported increased physical or psychological aggressive tendencies between them. Other research has presented a similar picture. In a sample of 330 Latinx newlyweds, it was revealed that male partners' experience of discrimination negatively affected wives' marital quality (Trail et al., 2012).

These findings suggest that BIPOC partners construe their relational experiences within the context of their systemic reality (Goldberger & Veroff, 1995). LGBTQIA+ couples also report the same challenges. Some research in this area has indicated that increased experiences of minority stress are connected to lower relationship quality for same-sex partnerships (Doyle & Molix, 2015; Frost & Meyer, 2009; Otis et al., 2006; Todosijevic et al., 2005). This is undoubtedly heightened when these partners experience couple-level minority stress where their relationship form is stigmatized, thus leading to additional strain on the relationship (Frost et al., 2017).

The impact of systemic trauma on these relationships can be understood using the concepts of stress spillover and stress crossover. The spillover of stress from one facet of an individual's life to another is known as "stress spillover," whereas stress crossover refers to the crossover of stress from one person to another (Bolger et al., 1989). Martin, 26 years old, can certainly vouch for the experience of stress spillover. As a Black man in America, Martin often felt that he was "being drowned." He wasn't just drowning. He was *being* drowned by something outside of him that he could identify but couldn't shift. "I can't pull myself up," he cried. He said that he felt his relationship with his wife, Leanne, was becoming "a lot" because that was the way everything felt. There was no distinction for him, and even being asked to construct one felt unfair and tedious. He experienced night terrors and would yell at Leanne often. She bore her pain in silence, though noticeably aching in session. As the stress crossed over to her, Leanne became a shadow of herself. She lost her sense of interest in life, invested only in ensuring that Martin was okay.

I want to be clear though, that not every single marginalized person experiences the circumstances described above. I am not attempting to universalize or generalize the experiences of minoritized people. We are quite vast and different. We are not all having the same experiences. There are, indeed, many individuals who withstand the pangs of daily prejudice and harm, and still have healthy relationships. There are many who are able to trust themselves, maintain a sense of ego integrity, and develop beautifully intimate and resonant interactions. However, if we are to stay true to the integrity of the helping profession, we must be with the fullness of *all* experiences. We must hold, with tenderness and deep curiosity, the realities of those for whom the system has anchored its weight. This helps us truly be of service.

All of the stories above point us to a need to widen our understanding of intimacy, and to excavate the definitions of intimacy and relationality from homogenizing forces that do not hold the myriad circumstances of LGBTQIA+ and BIPOC partnerships. When we truly grapple with this, we can provide services that are authentic and most importantly, not damaging. It was this quest to serve in this way that drove me to conceptualize the idea of "relational privilege," a concept that we explore further in Chapter 2.

Practitioner's Reflection
This is an invitation to reflect on the four features of systemic trauma and the many ways in which marginalized people are harmed. As you process how these features can show up for your clients, what are you noticing within you? Take note of any feelings, images, thoughts, sensations, or joint and muscle activation that may result. As you sit with these, reflect on your current ways of working with trauma. What would you like to continue doing? What would you like or feel the need to change given how systemic trauma is experienced for marginalized people? Can you think of any other features of systemic trauma that may be useful for you to reflect on?

CHAPTER RECAP

- *Systemic trauma* can be defined as harm that emerges from components of the *wider* environment, cultural norms, and institutions. Perpetrators of systemic harm often include educational systems, economic structures, criminal justice systems, and religious institutions.
- Marginalized people, such as LGBTQIA+ and BIPOC individuals, disproportionately experience systemic harm, which affects their psychological, physical, and financial well-being.
- The intimate relationships of BIPOC and LGBTQIA+ folks are negatively affected by systemic trauma. Systemic trauma disrupts their ability to stay connected.

CHAPTER 2

Intimacy Has a Context
Exploring Relational Privilege

Intimacy has a context. Our degree of power and privilege in the wider world determines the relational themes that sit in our bodies. Experiences connected to our status in the world can often lay fundamental messages in our bodies about how we should function and are seen in all relationships, even romantic ones. These messages outline how much we can trust, be accountable, depend on others, and be responsive to needs outside of our own. Additionally, we learn how much risk we can take in our romantic relationships as a result of how much power we generally hold in the world.

Intimacy is risky. Every decision about how we should interact with our partners is deeply connected to our ability to do so safely. These decisions sit in a context, feeding on the amount of agency we experience every day and the cost of exercising that agency in all our relationships.

What intimacy means, how it is understood, and the ability to fully explore it is situated in the wider structure that holds it. Intimacy cannot be understood outside of the system. Intimacy is a relational privilege.

I define *relational privilege* as one's ability to navigate intimate relationships based on one's own social location, power, and privilege in the world. Being in relationships from a place of true connectedness and self-trust is *facilitated by one's systemic context*. There are specific experiences required to cultivate this type of privilege, experiences that are often denied to LGBTQIA+ and BIPOC individuals. They are *living your truth*, *protection*, *social welcoming and belonging*, and *self-worth*. These can be seen in the relational privilege wheel shown in Figure 2.1.

Intimacy Has a Context

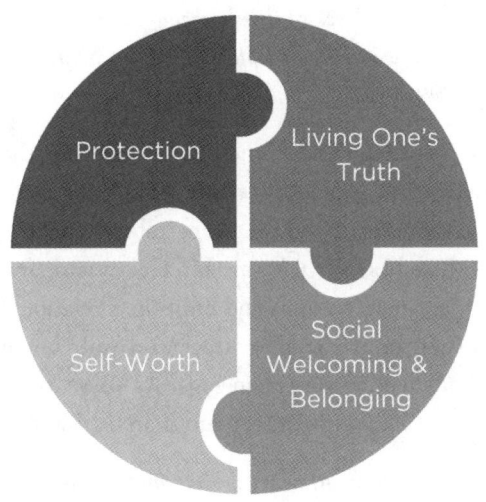

Figure 2.1: The relational privilege wheel.
Illustration by Nikki Shaheed.

These areas are certainly not mutually exclusive components. They interact with and reinforce one another. Their overlap is natural as these parts of relational privilege actively affect intimate partner relationships.

PROTECTION

Experiencing physical protection, psychological protection, and even financial protection allows us to move through the world with more ease, and allows us to feel safer to connect with those around us. I want to emphasize the value of the word "protection" here. Years ago, when I began this work, I used the term "safety" (instead of "protection") in my discussion about what was missing for many marginalized people. However, during my interaction with Tyson Yunkaporta's (2020) *Sand Talk*, which illustrates the value of Indigenous thinking, I experienced a huge wake-up call. The word "protection" (and not "safety") provides a more accurate description of what my clients were lacking. In his discussion about the word "safety," Yunkaporta notes that there is no "such thing as safety in Aboriginal worldviews" (p. 209). He added:

> *However, we have plenty of words for protection. Protection has two protocols. The first is to look out for yourself. The second is to look out for the people around you. This is such a wonderful way to live, knowing that you have the*

> power to defend yourself and the ones you love, while also being intensely aware that at any given moment there are dozens of people who are watching your back as you watch theirs. (p. 209)

And this is just it. For many BIPOC and LGBTQIA+, there is no sense that the systems around them are truly invested in protecting them. In fact, as mentioned earlier in Chapter 1, these systems are often the perpetrators. To navigate these spaces, the SNSs of BIPOC and LGBTQIA+ are often activated, and this can compromise their social engagement systems and limit their relational possibilities. Dealing with chronic and unpredictable attacks on your being with no recourse can result in the body feeling always on edge. As 44-year-old Mirabel, who is a Caribbean immigrant living in Amsterdam shared:

> "I don't feel safe at all here. We live in an apartment building and we are the only immigrants here, and I always have this thought that if the place is caught on fire, they will leave us here to burn. It's just so much. I don't know how to take off my sense of fight. Even my hearing is off. Every time he chews, the noise is so loud. We lived together in the Caribbean before and I never heard everything so loudly. I feel like my senses are opened up and there is no sense of rest. It is hard to be near him, to be intimate with him. All I know is my guard is up. I have to fight."

In my practice, I have also noticed that the fawn response that often shows up when racial minorities are interacting with the police or other powerful White figures, can become a feature of intimate relationships. This is amplified if one partner holds a privileged identity while the other does not. In this case, the sense of not being protected in the wider system is also felt within the confines of the relationship. John, a White trans man, confessed during a joint session with his nonbinary Black partner, Elle, that he was often seen as "the face of oppression in the relationship." Inevitably, when they had disagreements, Elle would try to appease John in order not to upset him so that they (Elle) could feel safe. From shaking to stuttering, Elle struggled to be able to speak truth without fear to John. Rae Alibey, president of Trinidad and Tobago Transgender Coalition, noted that for LGBTQIA+ partnerships, fawning can also sometimes be quite apparent. She shared:

> "As queer people, we learnt that speaking truth to power in the system can get you in a lot of trouble, so you have learnt to go along to get along. Fawning

> *is the path of least resistance. It's second nature. You don't want to run the risk of a breakup. The consequences can be high."*

As Yunkaporta (2020) also noted, an important part of protection involves your ability to protect another. When this too is restrained, the experience can also lead to behaviors that are deleterious to the attachment. Such is the case for Davis, a 35-year-old Black man in New York who divulged:

> *"I've found myself yelling at my wife more. I just feel like we need to keep safe and she doesn't understand that. There is really danger to us. I am a Black man in America. I say the wrong thing and the police are gonna attack me. She doesn't get it, but this madness is real. They will come after you. I know what can happen to me . . . to her!"*

It is not only a lack of physical protection that evokes such responses but also a lack of psychological protection. Having psychological protection entails a knowledge that there are resources within and outside of oneself that can be used to safeguard and restore mental well-being. While so many marginalized people develop internal protective factors and even affinity spaces that enrich their sense of happiness, ease, and comfort, the bombardment of subtle and overt harm is still undeniably potent. It becomes very difficult to manage this and its impact on intimate bonding. Frank, 22 years old, in his discussion on being a gay man and relating to his partner, sadly confessed: "It's the judgment and the criticism. I'm always thinking about the fact that someone thinks I am filthy or dirty. It's in my head all the time, even when we are intimate. I can't get it out."

In his discussion about financial protection and relational privilege, sex and gender expert Isaiah Alexander averred, "Protection, at the end of the day, is what we are all looking for." He added that with the lack of financial protection that queer persons have, there is an increased vulnerability that limits the ability to clearly state one's needs and desires in the relationship. You cannot erect healthy relationship boundaries when you are literally trying to survive.

In reality, your survival may also be contingent on performance and abandoning your own truth just to have some sense of well-being and to stay alive.

LIVING ONE'S TRUTH

> *I keep being pulled out of the truth of my experiences.*
> —Abi, a Black middle-aged woman during couple therapy with her White husband in Ghana

> *It's exhausting being yourself and it is exhausting sifting through the bull to find someone who will accept you for you.*
> —Josiah, on being a gay man in the Caribbean

> *When I am interacting with someone romantically, I often ask myself how much do I have to cut out or hide so that the person doesn't reject me because of femme-phobia. Sometimes when I do things that other men see as being too girly, I am not seen as a viable partner.*
> —Allan, 30 years old, in a discussion on starting new romantic relationships in the United States

> *Homophobia stole him from me.*
> —Randall, 22 years old, reflecting on the end of his last relationship

To sense and be yourself both privately and publicly is a true gift to every human being. To be yourself is also a gift to your intimate interactions. However, this gift is often denied to persons who experience systemic trauma. The mechanisms of systemic trauma unleash an unyielding attack on the identities of marginalized people, and it is these identities that then walk into relationships, massacred, yet tethered to ideologies of those who oppress and commit harm.

Let us explore how this psychological violence happens.

An Assaulted Sense of Self

Ken Hardy (2023), in his profound work on racial trauma, noted:

> *It is difficult to possess a clear, cogent, and healthy sense of self when one is consistently on the receiving end of devaluation and acts of racially based psychological domination. Consistent and prolonged exposure to racial oppression and the subtle forms of psychological domination it usually entails*

> *assaults People of Color's sense of who they are and their perceptions of who they can ultimately become. (p. 180)*

Hardy explains this as an assaulted sense of self. From the slavery plantation to the modern-day television advertisements that summon bodies of color to adopt White standards of beauty, the attack on the BIPOC sense of self is relentless. Slavery and colonialism were contraptions designed for the erasure of non-White ways of being in the world. Their apparatuses were calculated and overt. On the plantation in the Caribbean and Americas, Black men and women were violently forced to surrender their language, spiritual practices, and ways of understanding their world in order to adopt European ways of being. This is also true for other racial groups, such as Indigenous children in Canada who were forcibly placed in residential schools during the 19th and 20th centuries. The schools violently indoctrinated these young ones into European-Canadian ways of knowing the world.

For some of us, there is a sense that we have two identities. W. E. B. Du Bois shared the idea of "double consciousness" in 1903 (Du Bois, 2007). He noted that this is the feeling you have when you hold more than one identity. This can make it very difficult to have a true sense of self. In the opening essay of *The Souls of Black Folk*, he shared: "It is a peculiar sensation, this double-consciousness, this sense of always looking at one's self through the eyes of others, of measuring one's soul by the tape of a world that looks on in amused contempt and pity" (Du Bois, 2007, p. 8).

People of color learn that they must abide by the White-centered norms and standards in order to progress. Deceased American novelist and editor Toni Morrison described this as living under the White gaze (American Masters, n.d.). Whether we like it or not, the White gaze is present everywhere. For example, in the workplace, Whiteness is often touted as professionalism, and your inability or unwillingness to perform this is either punished by non-advancement, pay cuts, or unemployment. Many men and women who have experienced hair discrimination can attest to this.

White values are dominant even in countries that are predominantly populated by people of color. Even as I write this text as a native of Trinidad and Tobago, a small twin island state in the Caribbean, I know that I have to ensure that my White English is perfect. Even as I reside here in these Caribbean shores, filled with diverse ways of knowing the world, I have been trained in therapeutic models and frameworks that are created by White men from Europe and North America. When I sit and chat with my brothers and sisters in parts of Africa, they inform me of the dominance of White ideologies. I walk around some parts of the world where darker-skinned bodies are still on an unabating search for lighter skins, using bleaching to accomplish this goal.

Several BIPOC have also learned that when they speak up against White bodies, there is a price to pay. A Black man knows that speaking truth to a White police officer may be the last day that he ever sees his family. A woman of color learns that speaking truth and naming harm to her White boss may be the end of her career. I have lived through this fear and felt its tentacles in my bones. You then learn to perform, whether you like it or not. You learn to hide how you feel. You sometimes feel forced to erode your own boundaries and sense of being in the world, just to not be on the receiving end of harm.

And yet, in intimate partner relationships, you are required to be quite the opposite. You must be able to identify your likes and dislikes, as well as articulate your longings, joys, and desires. You also must be aware of your boundaries, and communicate to your romantic partner(s) what is non-negotiable for you. In order to fully *share* who you are with another human being, you must be truly *aware* of who you are and living from this place. Self-knowledge and awareness are critical to relational health. This is, however, often eroded for BIPOC bodies, and the erosion can filter into their intimate relationships. As Huei, a 37-year-old Korean man, said to me in therapy, "We are not allowed to trust our voices, and this is due to racialized trauma." Contemporary couple therapy needs to make room for this systemic reality and for the ways in which this can show up in relationships.

Hardy's notion of the assaulted sense of self is also quite glaring for many LGBTQIA+ persons. In fact, one of my female clients, Hannah, explicitly stated:

> *"I was punished for being gay, and so, when I eventually would have sex with women, I would never connect emotionally. All of this because my parents punished me for being gay. I would have sex with women and then feel like 'I never want to see you again.'"*

Hannah could not experience the emotional fullness of relationships because she was not comfortable with the essence of who she was. Julius, a 55-year-old gay man, also shared about one of his earlier relationships:

> *"My partner felt repulsed by me. Touch and connection became something he felt remorseful for. Like he would always shower after sex because he felt dirty when he screwed me. Sex sucked! I knew it wasn't his fault that gay sex was laced with shame but that didn't help. I ended it."*

Many other LGBTQIA+ individuals can also attest to the impact that being unable to live in their truth has on their relationships. In many countries where sex and gender diversity is largely frowned upon, the pressure to remain invisible and exist inauthentically severely restricts LGBTQIA+ couples both publicly and privately. The need to hide or to not be "out" means that the modes of public expression afforded to cisgender and heterosexual couples are not enjoyed by LGBTQIA+ couples. Restricting levels of "outness" also places strain behind closed doors. For some couples, their discord has been rooted solely in the different ideas about how to manage the public face of their relationship. Tulsa and Sanaa, a queer couple, struggled with this intensely. Though both were queer, Tulsa was femme presenting (feminine presenting) and was able to "pass" as heterosexual, while Sanaa was nonbinary, masc presenting (masculine presenting), and did not have passing privilege. Sanaa argued in one session:

> *"We would be much more at peace if Tulsa would just stay invisible. People like us have to deal with questions and explanations to other people that I don't want to have to deal with. This could be solved if she would just be like me—invisible!"*

Their divergent views on this matter were so potent that it limited their ability to be with each other fully, as much of their relationship was focused on how to keep safe, instead of how to actually *be* with each other. Their connection was waning due to the systemic stress, and the tensions between them were soaring because they were experiencing different degrees of relational privilege. Tulsa had more *physical* and *psychological protection* in the world as she was femme presenting. Sanaa had considerably less. This prevented them from being able to enjoy their relationship openly. Experiences such as this are common as noted in a study by Reeves and Horne (2009, as cited in Hartig, 2019). They found that a "discrepancy in the level of outness between partners predicted less relationship satisfaction compared to those partners who were similarly to equally out" (p. 6). Hartig continues by indicating that "being out" and living your truth openly indicate the amount of comfort and certainty that an individual has in her, his, or their sexual identity. This "comfort or certainty may then extend to their intimate interactions with their partners and facilitate a rewarding sexual relationship with their partners" (p. 6).

The above stories present a harrowing reality for these partnerships. Furthermore, for many, they are met with daily reminders that attempt to convince them that they do not belong.

SOCIAL WELCOMING AND BELONGING

> Marginalized folks do not get to decide what is socially acceptable. We don't make up the rules. We are accepted on cis–het White people's terms.
> —Carleen, a queer Asian client on the discussion of relational privilege in therapy

In a 2020 speech by actor John Boyega in Hyde Park, London, during a George Floyd protest, he emphatically stated: "I need you to understand how painful it is to be reminded every day that your race means nothing." Marginalized people don't simply lack acceptance. They lack a sense that they are truly welcome and belong in the world.

This sense manifests itself in both race and sex discrimination. These are forms of social rejection that present an extremely gut-wrenching reality. It also can lead to a chronic fear of rejection, otherwise known as rejection sensitivity, a phenomenon that is no stranger to BIPOC and LGBTQIA+ persons (Calhoun, 2018; Feinstein et al., 2012; Pachankis et al., 2008). Sadly, as noted by various studies and research papers, the impact of social rejection on intimate partnerships is apparent (Downey & Feldman, 1996; Hammond & Overall, 2013; Levy et al., 2012; Meehan et al., 2018). In interpersonal relationships, fear of rejection leads to jealousy; an inability to open up; a hypersensitivity to rejection cues; controlling behavior; aggression; self-protective, interpersonal stances; and limited self-disclosure (Levy et al., 2012; Meehan et al., 2018). Additional work has proven that these experiences of social rejection can lead to low relationship satisfaction for members of the LGBTQIA+ population (Pereira & Esgalhado, 2021).

Michael, 50 years old, experienced the impact of this rejection sensitivity on his relationship. He recalled "feeling like" he "was in a fight every day" as he moved through his daily life. This "fight" was one for acceptance. He continued:

> "You know what rejection feels like, even if you can't name it. I felt this maddening fear of being left alone when I was with my ex. I couldn't feel safe to not be perfect. It was so much anxiety. I felt like I had to control everything around me because I didn't want him to walk out on me. I don't care who thinks I was overreacting. This was a real risk. This wasn't no pretend risk."

With his current male partner, Michael was becoming increasingly irritable, and often believed that he could never truly find a safe space with him. Additionally, he internalized homonegativity, which led to discomfort during emotionally and sexually intimate interactions with his partner.

Lydia, 34 years old, felt the pangs of rejection sensitivity in other ways. She was extremely reactive to conflict in her relationship with Gail, and all her wounds that were connected to systemic rejection would manifest intensely when Gail was upset with her. She mournfully revealed:

> "My identity was rejected in literally every sphere of my life. So somehow, I couldn't feel that our arguments were about anything else. If she got mad with me over dirty dishes in the sink, it never felt that it was really about the dishes. It felt like it was about ME! Look at me! The dyke that messed up again."

Creator of the STAIR (self-trust and integrated resilience) method, Juliane Taylor Shore notes that our day-to-day experiences carve the "psychological floor" that we walk on (Shore, 2025). Integrating the language of emotion-focused therapy's creator, Les Greenberg, it may be safe to say that one's psychological floor is one's "felt sense" of the world (Greenberg, 2010, p. 7). All our beliefs about how the world works and how to survive it reside in our psychological floor. Chronic rejection carves a floor that says to marginalized people: "You are not welcome, and you never will be!" This is what many without power walk on. This floor has been brutally instructive, and the learned gait is often carried into our intimate spheres.

SELF-WORTH

Shame is the deeply excruciating sense that one is not worthy of being cared for, loved, accepted, or welcomed in the world. In a beautiful piece of work entitled "The Wisdom of Process," Prentis Hemphill (2021) shares about shame as it is experienced for marginalized people. They note:

> *Shame is also the way that oppression becomes internalized. It is an emotional ritual for the marginalised [sic]. It is a practice necessary to maintain our already conditional belonging here. We feel shame for the aspects of ourselves that are most fundamental to who we are, that are tied not onto our actions, but to our essence. Our Blackness, our genders, our queerness and all the things that accompany them—our skin tones, our hair textures, our cadences, our desires. (p. 44)*

Our sense of self is "profoundly influenced by relational experiences" (Siegel, 2020, p. 64) and the relational experiences of marginalized people with the systems around them are usually characterized by harm, rejection, and discrimination. As such, a poor sense of self-worth and shame are well-known co-travelers in their life span. It is the result of holding a lot that is not ours to hold. It is the result of enduring harm and watching the perpetrators escape with impunity. It is the result of constantly being told or shown that one is not welcome. Slowly, we digest the message "I am not enough." These experiences diminish our capacity for self-acceptance, and shame becomes an adaptive response. This sense of shame silences us and doesn't allow us to show up fully in our families, in our communities, and in our interpersonal relationships. It limits the flow of love within us and between us.

Shame is also a tool of self-protection. As my client, Pedro, a middle-age second-generation Mexican once shared: "In America, being worthy is sometimes life-threatening." When you believe that you are worthy, you speak up. When you believe that you are worthy, you challenge. However, the persons in our world who consistently and flagrantly harm marginalized people have two main characteristics that can render confrontation unsafe. They often have *little accountability* and a *lot of power*. Accountability, in this case, refers to your ability to hold yourself responsible for the ways that you harm *and* to listen to the *fullness* of your harm's consequences. When there is deficiency in this area—while holding the power to punish those who challenge you or to inflict further harm on them—the emotional labor then passes to those who have been hurt to pacify, self-police, and to make themselves small to escape wrath. When it is not safe to hate "chronic harmers" (a term by Bokie Joy, a queer, Asian trauma therapist), we begin to despise ourselves. This self-hatred suffocates our relationships. This was the reality for Shannon, an African American woman living in Texas. Shannon experienced considerable racial harm at her place of employment. Despite her requests for accountability, none of this was granted. During a couple therapy session with me, she shared:

> "Over time, I learnt that I had to suck it up because they just wouldn't listen. They just wouldn't change. I couldn't cope and eventually I fell into a year of depression and left my job. I just feel so worthless though. I should be over this by now and I should be able to go back to work. It's my fault."

Her husband, Devaughn, sadly shared:

> "She became a turtle at home. She wouldn't speak to me because she hated herself. She wouldn't speak to our daughter, and to this day, she can't hear me or allow me to care for her when I say, 'It's okay and it wasn't your fault.'"

Shame can also cause partners to withhold affection from each other. Hence, those afflicted by shame may sometimes show up in relationships as a shadow of themselves. This seemed to be the dominant theme for Shane, who realized in his late 30s that he was battling gay shame, otherwise known as internalized homophobia. He struggled to connect emotionally to his partner, and they felt more like friends than lovers. Both parties were thus in a lot of pain and were dissatisfied. Over time, Shane's shame also showed up as aggression. Hatred for the system became displaced and expressed toward his partner.

In my work, I distinguish between individual-level shame and couple-level shame. Couple-level shame is a result of couple-level minority stress, and exists when partners become ashamed of the relationship itself. This too creates a lot of anguish. When reflecting on her 30-year relationship with Roxanne, Joy-Ann admitted:

> "There is a way you grow up thinking that God will never bless this relationship. It is almost as if it is cursed so that when normal problems come up, you believe that this is happening because of who I am and who we are. You are

> *trying to prove the wider society wrong, that it does work and can work, but that puts its own pressure on the relationship."*

It is incumbent on practitioners to help clients see when shame is altering the course of their relationships. In fact, this is the case for all components of relational privilege. It is important to name these and to show clients how all the components are interacting with one another and shaping their intimate interactions. Practitioners must also "out the system" and their (the practitioner's) own relational privilege. We share a bit more about this in the next chapter.

Practitioner's Reflection

What are the dangers of not considering relational privilege when working with minoritized people? How have we as practitioners probably harmed LGBTQIA+ and BIPOC clients by not considering the ways in which a lack of relational privilege was affecting their dynamics? What is your responsibility now as a practitioner?

CHAPTER RECAP

- *Relational privilege* is one's ability to navigate intimate relationships based on one's own social location, power, and privilege in the world. Being in relationships from a place of true connectedness and self-trust is *facilitated by one's systemic context*.
- There are specific experiences required to cultivate relational privilege, experiences that are often denied to LGBTQIA+ and BIPOC individuals. They are *living your truth*, *protection*, *social welcoming and belonging*, and *self-worth*.
- As practitioners, we must often think about the impact of ignoring relational privilege on our clients.

PART II

The Clinical Is Political

How are we to show up with and for our clients? Given the nature of systemic trauma and the ways in which it compromises intimacy, what type of relationship is needed between the clients and the practitioner? What do therapists need to be intentional about and mindful of in their work with marginalized couples? Part II of this text aims to answer those questions by taking a deep dive into a helpful therapeutic stance and orientation called the BIOME. Additionally, we deepen our discussion by initiating an exploration into the PRIDE model of intervention with couples.

CHAPTER 3

The Therapeutic Stance
Becoming the BIOME

When beginning therapy with marginalized couples, we need to understand the weight of the invitation to work with us. We are bringing people into a field that has preexisting definitions of relational health and intimacy that are not always appreciative of the historic and systemic realities of those who hold less power in our world. *The degree of relational privilege we hold in our bodies informs how we construct and define intimacy.* It also affects the degree of relational risk that we are willing to take. We share more about relational risks in this chapter.

As mentioned in Chapter 1, systemic trauma is induced by components of a person's environment. The educational, judicial, religious, and legislative systems are just a few of the culprits involved in this type of harm. But these systems are upheld by human beings, so in essence, systemic harm can also be understood as relational harm. It is executed in and through relationships, which dispossess, sideline, and wound specific groups of persons.

From this type of relational harm, marginalized people painfully learn about their place in the world. They learn that most of the world is not their safe space. This is vastly different from the experience of the world that is *deeply needed by every human being* in order to thrive. Leaning on the tenets of social baseline theory by Beckes and Coan (2011), human beings are supposed to be each other's *biome*. We need to be with each other for our own well-being. Interacting and being in close proximity with others allows us to be non-anxious, and reduces activation in parts of the brain that look out for threat. In essence, we need one another to feel safe and regulated. This regulated state of being is our baseline. However, when our relationships with the world are filled with subordination and rejection, we are removed from this baseline. Our health is at risk and we become stressed. All of this results from not having a safe biome.

Marginalized individuals experience this stress often, as they move through a world that does not often feel like a biome. When the systemic dynamics penetrate their lives, even their intimate partnerships do not always feel like safe spaces. This is why it is incumbent on the therapists who work with marginalized clients to take their role very seriously. The therapeutic relationship must *become a biome*, intentionally disrupting the daily harmful experiences that people face outside of the counseling room. When we as practitioners are able to do this, we are tending to our clients' nervous systems, and opening the opportunity for them to enter the window of possibilities that we discussed in Chapter 1.

To deepen an exploration of the therapeutic stance and presence that may be required when working with marginalized couples, I share how I have conceptualized the *therapeutic biome*. This biome can be understood by itemizing the components of this required stance via an acronym: BIOME (bravery, intensity/intimacy, openness, microliberatory movements, epistemic embracing). The BIOME image is shown in Figure 3.1.

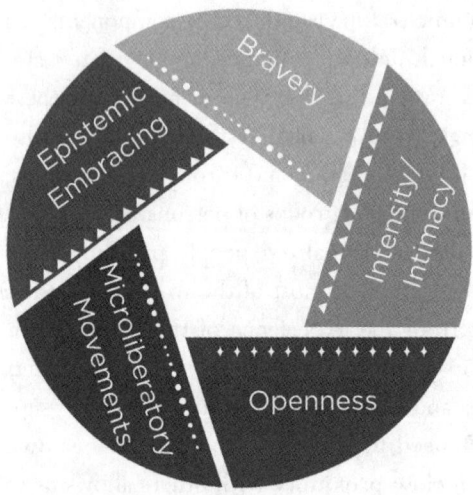

Figure 3.1: The therapeutic BIOME.
Illustration by Nikki Shaheed.

There is indeed overlap and continuity among these components, as they fortify one another in practice.

Let's begin.

BRAVERY

Being brave means that we as practitioners must be prepared to do the following:

1. Practice critical consciousness.
2. Pivot and interrogate our own assessments, imaginations, and stories about intimacy.

Practicing Critical Consciousness

Initially conceptualized by the deceased Brazilian educator and philosopher Paolo Freire, critical consciousness refers to a process wherein marginalized people are encouraged to analyze their social conditions and engage in action to transform them (Diemer, 2011). Diemer notes that there are three primary components of critical consciousness: *critical reflection*, *political efficacy*, and *critical action*.

When working with marginalized partners, we can use *critical reflection* to examine how the inequalities in the system are shaping their individual wellbeing and couple dynamics. We can shine a light on the elements of relational privilege and how the system impacts these components. During critical reflection, we also engage in responsible externalizing. This is explored more in Chapter 6. We are committed to showing clients the connections between their experiences in their relationships and the wider structure, and we are doing so slowly and judiciously.

When practicing critical consciousness, we, as clinicians, are also expected to examine our own role in systemic oppression. To do so, we must consider the following questions:

- Are there times when I am oppressed and other times I am not? Are there times when I am the oppressor?
- Do I use my practice to actively challenge systemic harm or am I complicit in harm? Do I speak up or am I silent?
- If I speak up, what feels easy for me to speak up about?
- If I stay silent, what do I usually stay silent about? What feels hard about speaking up?
- Which parts of my work with clients are helpful and which are harmful?

- When am I imposing notions of healing on my couples that may not align with their systemic experiences?
- How do I know when something in my process might be harmful to marginalized clients?

The second component of critical consciousness, *political efficacy*, is the capacity to make change by both individual and collective activism. As clinicians, we must believe in our own ability and our clients' ability to contribute to systemic change. Contributions do not need to be grand in order to be meaningful. In fact, we can help our clients see how even their attempts to address their relational dynamics are central to a wider shift in the world. By becoming aware of the ways in which systemic trauma is shaping their reality, they can become more mindful about ways to address these. By taking charge of their relationships in ways that feel in alignment with how they want to show up in the world, they are contributing to systemic change. Therapy helps them to expand their relational possibilities and as such, they enhance their *sense of well-being*, *agency*, and *groundedness* in the world. Walking in the world with this sense is the posture needed for systemic change! In fact, having this sense may even be described as *systemic change itself*! These expanded possibilities are in direct opposition to the oppressive forces that descend upon marginalized people daily.

The shifts in their relationships are a central component of *critical action*, which is the third component of critical consciousness. Some clients may also wish to do much more and we can support this. They may wish to see shifts in their wider environment as well. We discuss more about this component when we look at systemic intentions in Chapter 6.

Pivot and Interrogate Our Stories

We all live in our stories. These are stories about how the world works, and we make predictions about what will happen to us and others in various circumstances based on these stories. In these stories, we also determine how to keep ourselves safe. Our clients have these stories and so do we. These stories are influenced by our lived experiences, social location, and even our training.

One of the stories that largely impacts how we practice is our *intimacy story*, which refers to the way we define and practice intimacy in our lives. All our expectations about intimacy and how it should be experienced are interwoven within our intimacy story. Interrogating our intimacy story and how it was constructed is central to working with marginalized couples. Often, our intimacy stories may be very different from our clients, and if we are not brave enough to critically analyze these stories, we run the risk of imposing these stories on our clients. When working with practitioners, I offer them the following list of questions to support this type of introspection:

- How do you define intimacy?
- How do you seek intimacy?
- In what contexts do you feel safe to be emotionally and physically intimate?
- How do you communicate intimacy?
- How do you communicate vulnerability, empathy, safety, and accountability?
- How do you address moments when you harm people with whom you are emotionally or physically intimate?
- How do you address moments when you are harmed in intimate contexts?
- How does your social location affect your answers to the questions above?

It is also important to examine the intimacy story that directly guides your practice. It often sits in the modality that you use. Consider the following as a way to explore this:

- What is the definition of intimacy within your practice or the model that you use?
- How are your clients advised to seek intimacy or to create intimacy within the model that you practice?
- How are your clients advised to communicate harm or to address moments when they harm? What is the guidance provided by the model you use?
- How does your practice meet the needs of marginalized couples and their degree of relational privilege?

Considering these questions is one of the first steps to grounding your practice in the context of marginalized couples.

INTENSITY AND INTIMACY

What relational risks are you willing to take in your work? This is the first question I asked myself when I sat with the work of Ken Hardy (2016), a thought leader in the realm of social justice. Hardy advises us as practitioners to be intense and intimate in our practice and to take relational risks. These risks refer to the ways that we extend ourselves, possibly beyond the norms of conventional therapy and our comfort zones, so that we can show up for our clients in a way that is vulnerable and wholehearted (Hardy, 2016). To take these risks, we need to lean in with intensity and intimacy, sometimes bursting away from the harness of a practice that does not always sufficiently allow the true pain of LGBTQIA+ and BIPOC clients to be fully seen. In this type of engagement, we express to our clients the impact of their stories on our being. This does not mean that we grab the attention or switch the focus to us. It simply means that we express our emotions fully, while openly taking responsibility for our own self-care.

When we take these relational risks, we are directly confronting one of the more troubling characteristics of systemic trauma that we discussed in Chapter 1: its disenfranchised nature. Systemic trauma is seldom acknowledged and consequently, invisibilized. Lending our bodies in vivid ways so that we can make the invisible visible liberates our clients to see and acknowledge their own pain. Sometimes, the dominant notion of professionalism makes us less willing to display extreme anger or hurt when we listen to our clients' stories. However, this degree of containment upholds the oppression. This degree of containment sanctions harm! Clients must see through us that something is wrong! They must see through us the true violence of the system. The system suffocates their truth telling. It is we who must give voice to their truth through our relational risks. Our relational risks contribute to *their* relational privilege.

These risks, though, are not performative, inauthentic endeavors. We do not feign crying or rage with our people. We genuinely connect to their pain and ours, as we immerse ourselves in their stories. We slowly wade through all the voices in our head that scoff at emotionality in clinical practice, and recommit ourselves moment by moment to the responsibility of liberation in our work. When we feel afraid to emote, we greet this fear with compassion and with the watchful eye of a witnessing mind. And even with this, we must make bold decisions to be authentic. Each practitioner is different and we all have different comfort levels. It is important that we show up in ways that feel genuine and in alignment with who we are and what we want for our clients. Practitioners should not be bullied into emoting in particular ways. This, to be quite honest, is first an inner journey and we are all in different places.

Practitioner's Reflection

As you sit with the idea of relational risk taking, notice what feelings, sensations, or thoughts emerge. Does it feel scary in any way? What role does your own relational privilege play in the degree of relational risks that you are willing to take? What feels comfortable for you, and what does not? What tends to stop you from taking relational risks? What would make you want to take relational risks with clients?

OPENNESS

Who are we truly in this work? Are we prepared to be open to our clients about this? When we begin our process, are we open with them about the ways in which we may inadvertently harm them in the work we do with them? Do we let our clients know of their rights if we unintentionally harm them? When they confront us, are we prepared to listen and be candid about how our own gaps may have negatively affected them?

Additionally, do our clients thoroughly understand what we are doing with them in our therapeutic practice? Moment by moment, are we willing to share why we do what we do and how we are thinking through our intervention?

I am a cisgender heterosexual woman and I have worked closely with the LGBTQIA+ community for years. However, that, in no way, compares to the lived experience of those in the community. I understand much of the pain through wholehearted conversation. But that understanding *pales* in comparison to the reality that queer persons experience daily. As such, I will always have blind spots. I have to be open with my clients about this. I am also a Black therapist. My lived experience is different from that of other non-Black people of color. Being unmistakably clear about the ways in which both my similarities to and differences from my clients affect my practice is essential and ethical.

To foster a truly liberatory practice with marginalized couples, we as practitioners must be transparent about our social location and the ways in which it both strengthens and limits our ability to do the work. This degree of transparency requires setting a clear commitment to practice openness and to deal with the consequences of that degree of forthrightness.

We must let our clients know that we indeed have blind spots, and explicitly reassure them that they are not emotionally or mentally responsible for our practice oversights and faults. Early in our intervention and even throughout our journey with them, we can name these faults so that when we do err (*because we will*), our clients will be aware that the fault is not with them. We must let them know that they are free to hold us accountable. They can also decide how they wish to engage us or not. In a world with mortifying incidents of systemic harm, marginalized communities must take care of themselves in the therapeutic space in ways that feel right for them. This, too, requires our candor. Our clients must be informed of their right to feel, and to be in the fullness of their truth when we as clinicians mess up.

Therapists hold a lot of power in the room. We are often seen as authority figures, and that confers a great degree of privilege while working with marginalized couples, even if we share their social location. Once again, I am leaning on the work of Ken Hardy (2016). We must know that when harm is committed in therapy, the privileged and more powerful person must

> assume a greater degree of responsibility *to the relationship. In this regard, it is incumbent on the privileged to develop "thick skin," which is demonstrating the ability to and internal fortitude to* stay in *difficult conversations even beyond where it feels comfortable to do so. (p. 141)*

In no way do I support or endorse marginalized clients being abusive toward therapists. This is not acceptable. However, I do know that when we hold privilege in relationships with people who hold less power, this privilege requires us to stretch our capacities to listen and not police our clients' language so that our comfort is centered. There is certainly a bidirectional relationship between bravery and openness. The braver we are, the more open we can become, and our ability to tolerate the discomfort of openness helps us develop more capacity and courage.

Openness is not limited to sharing about our constraints and dealing with harm. We must also demystify our practice by being clear about our intervention steps, and the thinking behind why we do what we do. We allow our clients insight into our process. Every step is explained and we share power with them in the room. This cultivates an egalitarian and emancipatory ethos, where our clients feel empowered, a drastically different experience from the way they often feel in the world.

When we are open, our clients experience greater relational privilege. By declaring our truth, we cultivate space for our clients to *live their own truth*. By acknowledging our flaws, we *protect* them from internalizing responsibility, blame, and shame when we are the ones at fault. When we are explicit about our work and practice inclusion, we help them feel seen and *worthy*. This contributes to a sense of belonging. This degree of clarity is part of undoing systemic harm. Our clients develop *liberatory connections* with us. This idea of liberatory connections is examined in more detail in Chapter 8.

Showing up this way for our clients may disrupt our own comfort. Nevertheless, this is well worth it because it is one of many microliberatory movements that are needed when working with marginalized couples.

MICROLIBERATORY MOVEMENTS

In various contexts, I have learnt that the clinical is political (Erickson & Largent, 2024; Bodenheimer, 2018). Every clinical move is a political move. The decisions that we make in the therapeutic space either disempower or empower our clients. We must intentionally seek to create a voice for our clients, and support them to experience deeper somatic engagement with their personal truth. Connecting to your truth reduces the likelihood of self-marginalization.

Self-marginalization refers to ways that we deny parts of who we are or our entire selves. This is prevalent among LGBTQIA+ and BIPOC clients, who must often hide who they are to survive. As mentioned in Chapter 2, this shows up often as shame. If this is the case, then how can we create small and large moments in the work that reinstate power, self-worth, agency, and relational privilege? Clearly, we must be open, as discussed in the aforementioned section. However, much more is needed. We must be deliberate and we must structure or carve moments and exercises with this liberatory potential.

In Chapters 7 and 8, we speak more about how we can create these moments. We discuss how we can use processes, such as relational imagination and decolonizing the relationship, to reinstate power to marginalized clients. While doing these practices, we can integrate somatic engagement, which refers to work with the body. Our bodies are affected by the systems we inhabit. Because oppression can often manifest in the human body as muscle tension, breath constriction, increased heart rate, and many other unpleasant bodily sensations, it is important that as we do the liberatory work with our clients, they remain connected to their bodily experience and use their body to enhance their sense of liberation. As such, microliberatory movements are also physical movements. Clients complement the exercises mentioned above (relational declarations, decolonizing the relationship, etc.) with gestures, postures, and other forms of movement that nourish them and deepens emancipation. Being with the body in this attuned way is an anti-oppressive stance in the work. Historically, BIPOC bodies have not always been used as a source of wisdom, agency, truth telling, and power. Via chattel slavery, Black bodies have been exploited for profit. In the early 19th century, the bodies of Indigenous children were removed from their families to be bullied into ways of being that were not their own. LGBTQIA+ bodies, often deemed to be unholy and impure, are sometimes subjected to gruesome acts, such as genital mutilation. These horrific forms of conversion therapy are just but one way that queer bodies are violated and managed. Persons with more power see marginalized bodies as sites of control. Minoritized people must also be encouraged to see their bodies as sites for reclaiming power. We can facilitate that reclamation!

EPISTEMIC EMBRACING

There is beauty in a therapeutic practice that uses the worldview of the client as the *core* of its work. There is beauty in intervention that truly embraces the client's way of knowing the world. This is the practice of *epistemic embracing*. The word "epistemic" largely refers to the formation of knowledge. Embracing ways that our clients create knowledge and arrive at their subjective experiences of the world is central to a liberatory practice.

How do our couples define intimacy? How do they come to understand what it means to be in a relationship with others? What elements of this systemic reality inform this? How do our couples define conflict? How do they understand harm? Being with our clients as they share their epistemic pathways allows us to develop a healing relationship with them that privileges their concepts over our a priori assumptions of what relational health should look like. Liberation psychology is useful here. Developed by Spanish/Salvadoran psychologist Ignacio Martín-Baró, liberation psychology seeks to truly unearth how the oppressed understand the world (Sloan, 2002). Their definitions of the world have often been marginalized, and liberation psychology forces us as clinicians to ask ourselves, "What ways of knowing the world are being ignored here?" This pushes us to listen more to clients, and be with their stories as sources of experiential wisdom.

Practicing epistemic embracing prevents us from engaging in therapeutic gaslighting. I define *therapeutic gaslighting* as the process of overtly or covertly denying the experiences of clients in therapy. Covert and subtle gaslighting occurs when our interventions and assessments do not intentionally consider our clients' lived circumstances, and how these shape their understanding of what it means to be human, relational, intimate, and even healthy. This is more likely when working with marginalized people, as the social location of privileged (cisgender, heterosexual, and White) persons largely informs how therapy is practiced and how experiences are understood.

I admit that much of what I have shared in this text has been gained by sitting with marginalized people and learning. Being with them has helped me to birth my position about this work. Additionally, co-journeying with these clients has also propelled me to develop a practice model called PRIDE. We begin to delve into the nuances of this model in Chapter 4.

Practitioner's Reflection

As you reflect on the BIOME, how are you currently engaging in this way of being in your work? What are the specific actions you practice that allow clients to feel that they are in your therapeutic BIOME? What do you need to do to show up more as a BIOME for your clients?

CHAPTER RECAP

- Working with marginalized couples requires us to adopt a therapeutic stance that appreciates the painful reality of systemic trauma and facilitates liberation.
- Marginalized people do not always believe that the world feels like a safe place. The world does not always feel like a biome.
- In order to support marginalized clients, practitioners can practice *bravery, intensity/intimacy, openness, microliberatory movements*, and *epistemic embracing*.

CHAPTER 4

Building PRIDE

In *The Spirit of Intimacy*, Sobonfu Somé (1997) writes:

> When conflict shows up we may think that the best way to deal with it is to adopt an antagonistic stance toward the other person. But actually it is best to come together and tell spirit, "We've heard the words you sent to us. We may not know what to make of them, they are very hard, very painful for us to deal with. But we understand that it is through this trial that we will find our gifts and our wisdom. . . . But we are listening, and we are willing to get beyond our resistance." (p. 111)

I truly believe that we as practitioners can use our space to support marginalized couples in a process of moving with and through the impact of systemic trauma on their relationships. Our work with them may allow them to metabolize their gifts, intuition, and insight so that they can carve something that is redemptive and powerful. Facilitating this type of practice for people who are continuously disempowered in our world is a revolutionary exercise, rooted in an appreciation of the unique responsibility of the practitioner to fully integrate critical consciousness and liberation into their intervention.

Nonetheless, this work is done at a gentle pace, with full recognition of how difficult systemic trauma is to treat because of its pervasive and unpredictable nature. We do not pressure marginalized partners to abide by preset definitions of intimacy and healing that feel unreasonable given their context. Outcomes for these couples may look very different than they would for others. We respect their process, honor their reality, and hold space for the survival strategies that they must use under the weight of structural harm. We hold much compassion for them, giving them the room and breathing space to *pivot*, *rumble*, *imagine*, *develop*, and *evolve*. These five words best encapsulate my dream for the couples that work with me and form the acronym, which is also used as the name for this model: PRIDE.

WHAT IS THE PRIDE MODEL? WHAT IS IT NOT?

The PRIDE model is an invitation to couples and individuals to explore the present, past, and future possibilities. It is not a formula into which we slot our clients. While there is indeed a structure, as well as steps and techniques that are utilized within this model, I advise practitioners who read this to also use their own creativity, insight, and intuition. When this does not happen, we lose touch with the clients who sit in front of us, committing ourselves to models and not to people. Doing this reinforces hierarchical intervention procedures, homogenization of the work, and invisibilization of our clients. Though the model is presented in a sequential fashion, it actually does not work in this way during therapy. For example, after clients are invited to imagine their goals, they are invited to rumble a bit more. It is important to note that human beings cannot be trapped in the order of models. I have noticed in my work that some clients move among the steps in this model in various ways that feel right for them.

The PRIDE model was generated out of the distinctive ways that systemic harm exerts influence on the dynamics between intimate partners. Of note is the model's integration of collective and ancestral wisdom, an integral part of working particularly with BIPOC clients. The model aims to honor the unique epistemological assumptions of marginalized people. These assumptions have typically and disproportionately been estranged in therapy, and so the model is *social justice in practice*. It invites *both* the clients and the therapist to practice "PRIDE." In Chapters 5–8, we begin to slowly examine the *steps*, *strategies*, and *methods* of this model. For now, I provide a general overview of the *essence of* this model, and its *practice underpinnings*. Welcome to PRIDE!

Pivot

I often say that pivoting contains four components: *turning inward*, *turning outward*, *turning backward*, and *turning forward*. Let's take a brief look at each of these components:

1. *Turning inward*: This involves noticing the thoughts, feelings, sensations, and behaviors that are connected to our experiences. In this case, we

ask each partner to not only take a look at the cognitions they hold about their relationship but their individual emotional and embodied experiences of their relationship. They also are invited to witness and name their relational dynamics and patterns.
2. *Turning outward*: Clients are invited to consider the structures that they occupy and their experiences of marginalization and discrimination.
3. *Turning backward*: In this process, we support clients in articulating the stories of their ancestors—their joys, successes, pains, struggles, and traumatic experiences. If we consider what we will discuss later in this chapter about epigenetics, we can see the immense value of paying close attention to the experiences of those who have come before.
4. *Turning forward*: This entails a process called "setting relational and systemic intentions," which we learn more about in Chapter 6. This process necessitates holding room for our clients so that they can articulate their personal hopes and goals for their relationships. They are also invited to share the ways in which a shift in their relational dynamics can serve as a catalyst for wider systemic and structural change.

Here, we spend some additional time delving into the idea of turning inward.

Turning Inward

As our clients reflect on and discuss their relationship in therapy, they are consistently encouraged to develop a witnessing mindset as they pay close attention to their individual somatic, cognitive, and emotional experiences and reactions. There are many ways to attain this degree of internal witnessing. Resmaa Menakem's VIMBASI method is one of the most thorough (Menakem, 2022). By paying attention to the *v*ibrations (they experience in their bodies); *i*mages and thoughts (that they have); *m*eanings, judgments, stories, and explanations (that they deduce); *b*ehavior, movements, actions, impulses, and urges (that they wish to make); *a*ffect and emotions (that they feel); and *s*ensations and *i*maginings (that they experience), clients can attain a deeper appreciation of the ways that their entire being is making sense of their relational reality. This type of witnessing is explored to a greater extent throughout Chapters 5–8. For now, it is important to emphasize the neurobiological benefit of this type of approach. When couples come to us, they are typically experiencing emotional *dysregulation*. They are outside of their window of possibilities, sitting in variations of hyperactivity or hypoactivity due to systemic trauma. Creating a witnessing mindset, a process that is known as mindfulness, reduces stress in the body and creates an "integration of the parasympathetic and sympathetic branches of the nervous system" (Siegel, 2020, p. 67). In Chapter 1, we thoroughly examined the impact of and on these two branches for marginalized people. As such, facilitating a process that attends to these branches is a crucial part of the work. Tending to these branches is also important so that couples can begin the deeper work of rumbling.

Rumble

Of all the synonyms for the word "rumble," the word "confrontation" seems to best encapsulate what it means in this context. Clients are invited to confront all that they have discovered during their pivot. We walk with them, asking pointed and direct questions to support this encounter in a way that brings them the answers they need. For some clients, this process may feel cathartic and insightful. For others, it can feel like internal upheaval. Walking into unknown territory may force clients to rigidify and congeal. In light of this, it is of great consequence that the therapist shapes a sense of safety in the therapeutic context in order to support the rumble. The outcome of the rumble relies heavily on our practice of the BIOME.

During the rumble, clients are asked to investigate the ways that their thoughts, feelings, sensations, and relational dynamics are affected by their systemic and historical contexts. This inquiry is deliberate as well as intense, and is typically done during a stage of the work known as *relational curiosity*. Our clients are supported to see the ways in which current social, economic, and political marginalization are infiltrating their love lives.

Assisting clients in rumbling through the impact of ancestral trauma is also salient. This, however, first requires the practitioner to do some additional teaching about the mechanisms through which ancestral trauma is transferred. So much of who we are is affected by our ancestors—their traumatic experiences can shape how we experience the world. We often label this as intergenerational trauma, which refers to multigenerational trauma that is experienced by a particular ethnic or racial group of people. Some examples of this include the colonization and genocide of Indigenous people all over the world, slavery, and the Holocaust. Rakoff (1966, as cited in Yehuda & Lerner, 2018), in a highly influential paper about the effects of the Holocaust on three patients, noted:

> The parents are not broken conspicuously, yet their children, all of whom were born after the Holocaust, display severe psychiatric symptomatology. It would be easier to believe that they, rather than their parents, had suffered the corrupting, searing hell. (p. 244)

Explaining the transmission of trauma across generations has not been without disagreement among experts. Some see the explanations as primarily behavioral or psychodynamic, while others look to *epigenetics*. With regard to the behavioral explanation, it is no surprise that trauma survivors can sometimes externalize their symptoms via expressions of anger, anxiety, depression, and grief in the home. This certainly can have an adverse effect on their offspring, who, in turn, may present similar symptoms.

Conversely, the realm of epigenetics provides us with a very different insight. Epigenetics refers to the manner in which our environments and actions alter the ways that our genes are expressed. Our genes are made of deoxyribonucleic acid (DNA) and determine what we look like, how we survive, and how we act. During our lives, this DNA gathers chemical markers (also known as epigenome or epigenetic markers), which determine how much of that gene is expressed. This epigenetic regulation of gene expression can actually be passed on from generation to generation via the sperm or egg (Siegel, 2020). Of importance here is that genes and genetic expression indeed influence the function of our brain and nervous system. As you may recall in Chapter 1, our nervous systems interface with our environment. If your ancestor's environment required a genetic expression to cope with high degrees of trauma and stress, then that profile can certainly be passed on. As such, your nervous system can be influenced in a similar fashion. Knowing the above becomes paramount when we support clients. They can begin to see how their behaviors in their relationships are possibly connected to the survival mechanisms that their ancestors needed. More of this is discussed in Chapter 5, when we examine the impact of family narratives on relational privilege.

During this multifaceted rumble, it is important to ensure that clients feel a sense of compassion from the practitioner and even themselves. As practitioners, we can meet them with empathy and kindness, helping them to understand that the ways that they feel, think, and act make sense given the systems they occupy. We can also encourage them to *show themselves* compassion as well. Compassion here is synonymous with the term "kind intention" (Siegel, 2020). When we as human beings witness ourselves with kind intention, ventral vagal tone is increased. This is useful because rumbling intensely may result in a deep sense of overwhelm for clients. If they become too engulfed in the process, change may become impossible, as they will become too dysregulated during the work. Soothing and self-compassion thus become vital.

Becoming the BIOME (as mentioned in Chapter 3) supports the process of pivoting and rumbling. By being brave and doing our own personal interrogation in the presence of the client, we can model for them what it means to dig deep within to understand what drives us. By taking the relational risks necessary, we can validate all that they discover while they pivot and rumble.

The rumble is a powerful space. As the clients experience both the emotional activation of being with their lived experiences as well as the regulating presence of the practitioner, their brain enters a transformational state. More is shared on the neurobiology of this in Chapter 7. For now, we note that rumbling opens the door to unlock and shift many beliefs that clients hold about their relationships. When these beliefs are unearthed and ready to be transformed, clients are now in a place to create something new. Rumbling is the place where our clients initiate their becoming. Rumbling sets the stage for imagination.

Imagine

In her book entitled *Emergent Strategy*, adrienne maree brown (2017) notes:

> *Imagination is one of the spoils of colonization, which in many ways is claiming who gets to imagine the future for a given geography. Losing our imagination is a symptom of trauma. Reclaiming the right to dream the future, strengthening the muscle to imagine together as Black people, is a revolutionary decolonizing activity. (p. 161)*

Systemic trauma is an unrelenting and perpetual assault on the imagination of marginalized people. It is the infliction and imposition of a dominant imagination on those who have less power in the world. As such, reclaiming imagination is critical to healing and liberation. Imagination is a powerful tool.

Various traditions, theorists, and philosophers have tried to explain and explore the notion of imagination. In Buddhism, imagination is seen as a process that creates imaginal worlds. These imaginal worlds are deemed to be primary sources of healing as well as sociocultural and political transformation. The ancient Tantric master Abhinavagupta notes that imagination is a form of power of the infinite consciousness and infinite mind, which imagines worlds and brings them into reality (Ratié, 2016). According to the teachings of Muhyiddīn Ibn Arabi, in Islam, "human imagination gives substance to the inner experience, or soul (nafs), which lies in the middle of reality between spirit and body" (Albimawi et al., 2023, p. 273). The Kenyan-born philosopher Omedi Ochieng (2018) adds to the global conversation about imagination. He reveals that imagination in the African Yoruban tradition is understood as "ashe," which is the ability to command and make things happen. In this way, we can see that imagination fuels us to transform ourselves and our world.

Marginalized folks need the ability to make things happen and to experience release from the constraints of structural chains. In so many ways, this capacity is stripped from them daily, and so, practitioners can carve unique circumstances for them to think about what they wish to create or make happen in their relationships. We can create a platform for this by being mindful of our need to practice epistemic embracing and microliberatory movements as discussed in Chapter 3. We integrate their ways of knowing the world into the work and be their anchor through a process known as "building liberatory connections," which we further delve into in Chapter 8.

Develop

Building liberatory connections entails not only imagination but the creation of detailed mechanisms by which to transform one's relationships under the weight of structural harm. Development is the manifestation of imagination. It is where the partners begin to implement steps with the support of the practitioner, who reminds them of both their capacity and will. By developing clear steps, partners hold themselves accountable to the process and to each other. The practitioner here facilitates skill building during this phase in order to enhance clients' competence and confidence.

Evolve

Renowned author and Afrofuturist Octavia Butler (1993) said, "All that you touch, You Change. All that you Change Changes you. The only lasting truth is

Change" (p. 3). At the end of the process, I invite my clients to ask themselves: "Now that we have done this, who are we?" I've found this question to be a powerful invitation to be with the outcome of the healing journey in a meaningful way. It is an invitation to name and reclaim who they are.

As Somé (1997) writes, healing comes when the individual remembers his, her, or their identity. "When we are connected—to our purpose, to the community around us, and to our spiritual wisdom, we are able to live and act with authentic effectiveness" (p. 36). In a world that has undeniably labored to strip marginalized folks of their sense of self, taking time to see who we have become at the end of a process is a beautiful conclusion to (and perhaps even the beginning of) the process of building liberatory connections. It enables clients to feel into any identity shifts that have resulted from the work they have done. It permits them to occupy the role of agents in their lives and to "feel into" their own emergence as a couple. This question also allows them to figure out what new needs are becoming evident as a result of a shift in self-understanding.

The image shown in Figure 4.1 represents a recap of the PRIDE model and some insight into the essence of each step. I hope that this recap is helpful to you as we are going to begin to delve deeper.

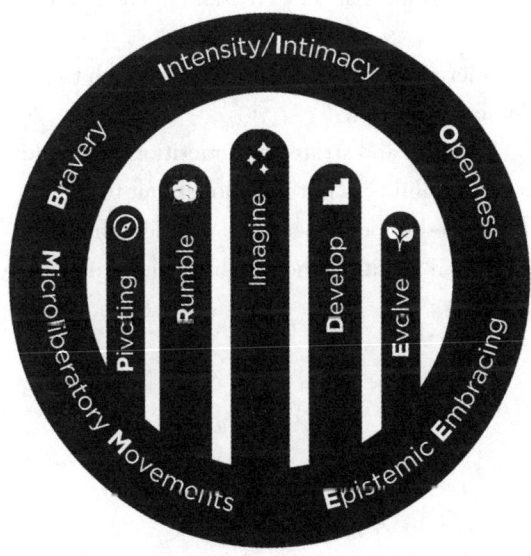

Figure 4.1: The PRIDE model for exploring systemic trauma with marginalized couples.
Illustration by Nikki Shaheed.

Practitioner's Reflection

As you read about the essence of the PRIDE model, what do you notice within you? What components feel scary? What components feel the most comfortable? How have you already been using aspects of this in your work? Is there anything within you that needs further exploration?

The PRIDE model requires the presence of the BIOME. Which elements of the BIOME feel most necessary in order to support the practice of this model?

CHAPTER RECAP

- Practitioners can facilitate a therapeutic process for clients in which they can pivot, rumble, imagine, develop, and evolve.
- Pivoting entails turning inward, outward, backward, and forward.
- Rumbling entails confronting the partner's relational dynamics and the ways in which the wider system is shaping these dynamics. In this phase, the partners also unlock and unlearn unchecked assumptions about their relationship.
- Imagination is the result of rumbling. It is the beginning of the couple's transformation, and an opportunity to visualize new possibilities.
- Development is the manifestation of the imagination. It is the space during which the partners craft steps that they envisioned during the imagination phase.
- Evolving is the practice of emergence. It is the step during which the clients ask themselves: "Who are we now?"
- Though the PRIDE model has steps and strategies, practitioners should remember that their first responsibility is not to a model, but to their clients. The model is not designed to be prescriptive. Readers should remember the value of their own intuition and insight while using or referring to this work.

PART III

Facilitating Healing: Working With Marginalized Couples

In the first four chapters, we discussed the impact of systemic trauma and what our orientation to this work can look like. Now, we deeply examine the practice steps and methodology. In the next chapters, we look at case examples in order to support your implementation of the methods proposed. It is helpful to remember that throughout the steps, we seek to remain the BIOME for our clients.

The practice steps that are explored are relational curiosity, responsible externalizing and setting intentions, continuous trauma work, and building liberatory connections. These steps are part of the PRIDE model for couples.

Finally, we explore the often-overlooked places within therapy and the journey of healing, particularly when working with marginalized couples. Here, we delve into the GLITCH framework, and unearth the ways that grief, liminality, and imagination move both clients and practitioners to a place of creativity and liberation. As we navigate through these landscapes of our practice, we learn to embrace the complexities of living in a marginalized reality and our therapeutic practice.

CHAPTER 5

Relational Curiosity

One must go slow to go fast.
—Uncle Bob Randall,
Yankunytjatjara elder

It is time for us to slow down. It is time for our clients to pivot and rumble with their realities, as we support them with both curiosity and compassion. This is the first step of the work with marginalized couples. During this step, we invite them into a process called "relational curiosity," which entails the use of several methods, and enables them to assess the impact of systemic trauma on their relationships. I consider this portion of the work a key part of learning and growth for the partners. It is a stage where they are generating knowledge about their relationship. It is de-colonial and generative in its essence.

Relational curiosity has components of an Aboriginal process known as *yarning*. This is a method of "knowledge production and transmission" (Yunkaporta, 2020, p. 151). In the yarn, everyone engages in a thoughtful, collaborative, and inclusive conversation. The practitioner does not wield power and slot the couples into diagnostic criteria or make autonomous intervention decisions. It is collaborative, and the partners are deemed to be co-experts on their realities. To be quite transparent, so much of my model has come from yarning with marginalized communities. During relational curiosity, yarning principles, such as reciprocity, responsibility, relationship, dignity, equality, integrity, and self-determination are employed. In addition to the principles mentioned, let's take a look at the ways in which we can integrate the PRIDE model and BIOME framework into relational curiosity.

THE PRIDE PROCESS

Pivoting and rumbling are central to relational curiosity. We are accompanying our clients into a deeper understanding of what factors are shaping their relational dynamics. In particular, they will be turning outward, inward, and backward as highlighted in Chapter 4. As you work through this phase with your clients, you may find yourself moving gracefully (or not so gracefully, in some cases) between pivots and rumbles. This dynamic interplay between pivoting and rumbling is extremely important. Pivoting provides the directional shifts. It supports the couple in exploring various aspects of their experience—the external pressures, internal realities, and historical influences. On the other hand, rumbling is where the real excavation happens.

Imagine it like this: Pivoting is adjusting the focus on a camera lens, bringing different elements into sharper view. Rumbling is like digging into the soil to unearth the roots of a plant. You can't effectively dig without knowing where to focus your efforts (pivoting), and you can't truly understand the plant without exploring its roots (rumbling).

Moreover, pivoting and rumbling during this phase of relational curiosity set the stage for the rest of the PRIDE process. Clients are given a powerful platform from which to proceed with agency, intention, and connection.

The process is not without challenge, though. Difficult feelings can emerge. This discomfort is understandable when wrestling with these deeper truths and discoveries. Some couples may even begin to feel a huge sense of overwhelm. Our responsibility in these cases is to enact the BIOME to provide our clients with the therapeutic presence that they require.

THE BIOME

To truly facilitate relational curiosity, we can actively embody all elements of the BIOME. As we discussed in Chapter 3, bravery requires critical consciousness, which as you will see in this chapter, is a valuable component of relational curiosity. We empower clients by supporting their examination of the systemic roots of their relational challenges. Equally vital is our own self-awareness: as practitioners, we must vigilantly identify how our practices might cause harm. Only with this humility can we ethically navigate the intensity of this transformative phase.

Navigating this phase also requires relational risks. Bringing a level of presence and vulnerability into the therapeutic space while our clients journey into these hard, emotionally turbulent spaces helps validate what emerges and cushions the voyage. Our clients may unearth heartaches and unrelenting agony when they face the beast of the wider system. It is our job to let them know that this is real and that it is okay to feel. We must make the invisible visible.

We extend this commitment to visibility by also clearly explaining to our clients the steps we use during relational curiosity. Openness is paramount: by transparently sharing the steps, we are disrupting power dynamics in the therapeutic alliance. We amplify this with microliberatory movements. By having them practice embodied awareness while pivoting, we offer marginalized clients an opportunity to undo the disconnection from self that systemic forces necessitate, thus reclaiming agency and fostering resilience.

Agency is also fostered when we recognize the inherent validity of their discoveries during relational curiosity. This is epistemic embracing, a cornerstone component of the BIOME framework. Their interpretation of reality should be respected, as this will enhance their sense of freedom to explore. This is also active decolonization in the therapeutic space.

Now that we understand the role that the PRIDE process and BIOME play in this stage of the work, let's look at the specific methods used in relational curiosity. For each of these methods, I provide examples and the ways it helps us and the clients understand their relational privilege. Though these cases have been generated for your understanding, my own experience in therapy doing this work has informed the scenarios that I present here. I am deeply grateful to the many clients whose journeys in various parts of the world have allowed me to truly comprehend how systemic harm remains a pervasive force that has shown up in their relationships.

At the time of this writing, there are six strategies used: *theater of oppression, habits of survival, coming out story, family narratives, relational terrain,* and *relational privilege score,* as shown in Figure 5.1.

THEATER OF OPPRESSION

> *They assign you a role and they expect you to play it, and when you get outta hand, they put you back in your place.*
> —Jinelle, a Black female youth in the Caribbean

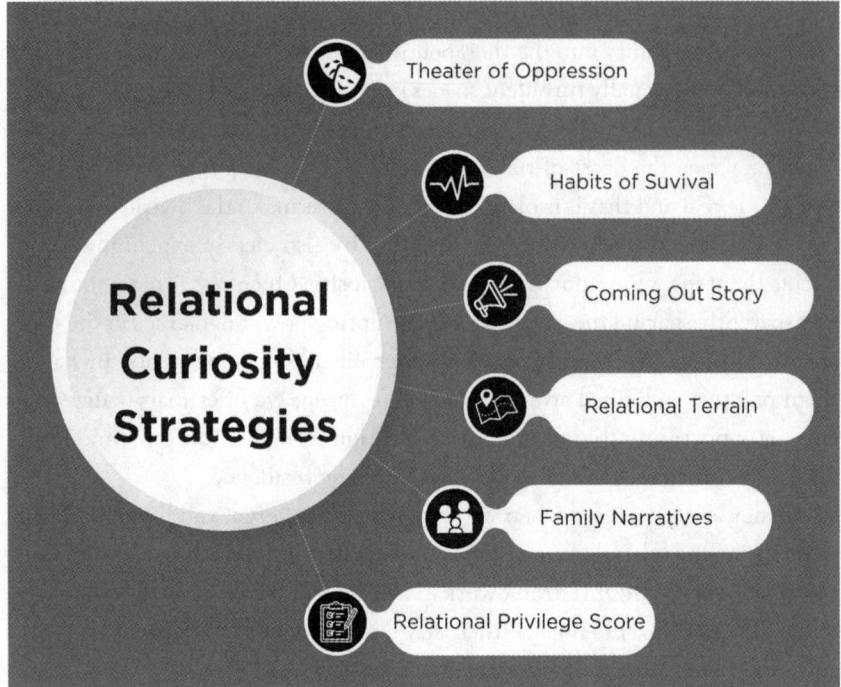

Figure 5.1: Relational curiosity strategies.
Illustration by Nikki Shaheed.

As you may recall in Chapter 2 during our discussion on relational privilege, many marginalized people are not able to live their truth. Instead, the way that they understand themselves and relate to the world is largely a product of the systems they occupy. As Jinelle shared in the above quote, marginalized people not only learn to play these roles, but they are cognizant of the cost of acting outside of the scripts for their lives. They understand what they are expected to do to survive. According to Ken Hardy (2016), the "Privileged play a central role in the lives of the Subjugated. How the Subjugated is perceived by the Privileged is a major organizing principle" (p. 142). Hardy continues by noting that the subjugated persons must concern themselves with the needs of privileged people. In other words, they often manage themselves to suit the needs of the powerful. They are directed by these needs, moment by moment, consciously or unconsciously.

With this understanding, we can conceptualize oppression as being a theater, where persons are assigned clear roles and act according to the theme of this reality. This metaphor is a useful way of engaging clients to understand the impact of oppression on their nervous system, and consequently on their relationships. It is useful to understand the potent role of their system because our environments, as well as our culture, shape our brains "and the ways we sense and conceive of who we are" (Siegel, 2020, p. 482).

You may recall our discussion in Chapter 1 about the window of tolerance, as well as the states of hyperarousal and hypoarousal. Our states change in part based on the activity of our parasympathetic and sympathetic nervous systems. A good way to help our clients assess and understand their nervous systems is to use creative methods, such as imagery, metaphors, movement work, and somatic engagement. These methods enable clients to access many parts of their internal world that they perhaps never considered or were aware of before. As such, when we use the "theater of oppression," the following questions are asked:

1. If we could understand daily experiences of oppression, prejudice, and marginalization as theater, what would be the theme of this dramatic piece?
2. Who is directing this piece?
3. How have you been cast? How have others who are just like you been cast?
4. What roles have you taken up just to survive?
5. How have these roles shown up in your relationship?
6. How has the theme of the dramatic piece shown up in your relationship?
7. As you speak about it now, what are you feeling or noticing in your body?
8. Can you ask about those sensations or movements: "What are you trying to tell me?"
9. Has speaking about it now felt liberatory, or is it more oppressive?
10. Where does this moment sit in your liberation journey?

It is extremely important here that I recognize the work of Augusto Boal as I discuss this tool. He was a Brazilian theater practitioner, who coined a form of interactive theater known as "Theatre of the Oppressed" (Boal & McBride, 1993). While the theater of oppression and the Theatre of the Oppressed are *not* the same techniques, because the names are so similar, it is only right and ethical that I pay tribute to this wonderful practitioner who has provided powerful and influential liberation work. He is one of many leaders who have opened doors for all of us who are committed to doing liberation work.

The questions listed in the theater of oppression technique encourage clients to pivot and rumble. These are two processes addressed in Chapter 4. Clients are given the space to *turn inward* and *outward*. They are paying close attention to what is emerging within them and how the external system is contributing to this reality. To further understand how this is implemented, consider the case example below.

Case 1

Roxanne and Thianna are a female middle-age same-sex couple who had been in a committed and cohabitational relationship for 20 years. They experienced considerable relationship challenges and also were open about experiences of homophobia in their lives. Thianna deemed Roxanne to be aggressive and distant. She complained that Roxanne would seldom draw close to her, and she was ready to end their relationship. The following is an excerpt from one of our sessions where we practiced the theater of oppression. Note that in this example (and all the others below), I refer to myself as "Practitioner" in the dialogue. This was done to support your understanding of the process with ease. For your benefit, within the written dialogue, I clearly identify the PRIDE skills and elements of the BIOME that are employed. I also connect the dialogue to elements of relational privilege.

> **PRACTITIONER:** Roxanne and Thianna, I want to invite us into a process. It's a process to help us understand what's happening here. I want us to think about the system that you live in and the ways it may be impacting both of you. You mentioned that you have experienced considerable homophobia and I want us to simply explore if it is playing a role here. Does this feel like a comfortable exploration? We will use a tool called the "theater of oppression." In this tool, we think about homophobia and other forms of discrimination as a play and theater. We use it to learn from you. [*This is an invitation to pivot, turn outward, and look at the system. I am also practicing epistemic embracing and openness. I am demystifying the process and explaining why the tool is being used.*]

THIANNA: Sounds good.

ROXANNE: Yeah. I can try it.

PRACTITIONER: Okay. Is it okay if we agree to start with Roxanne?

THIANNA AND ROXANNE: Sure.

PRACTITIONER: If we could understand daily experiences of oppression, prejudice, and marginalization as theater, what would be the theme of this dramatic piece? [*Here we are deepening the pivot and starting to rumble.*]

ROXANNE: The Tide of Torment.

PRACTITIONER: Ooh . . . as you say that, I can feel that. I can feel the pain and heaviness around this. It's a lot, the torment and having to live in this. Am I catching it right? [*This is the practice of intimacy. I am taking the relational risk and showing how it's impacting even me. I let them know here that the disenfranchised pain is being seen. This section also entails some bravery on the part of the practitioner. Though we may not entirely understand or agree with the client's understanding of their world, we must have the courage to interrogate our understanding.*]

ROXANNE: Yes!

PRACTITIONER: Who is directing this piece? What roles have you taken up just to survive? [*Here, we are deepening the pivot and engaging in the rumble. Helping them see this is also a microliberatory movement.*]

ROXANNE (*angrily*): Straight people! They want to tell you how to be, how to live, how to think. It's them and rules running the show!

PRACTITIONER: What you think makes sense to me. This is not okay. Being told how to live and be is not okay. I can feel heat within my body as you say it. It is maddening. What about you? How does it feel to say this? As you say it now, what do you notice in your body? Are there any images coming up for you? [*The client is invited here to witness her body using elements of VIMBASI. The practitioner here is also supporting the rumble with epistemic embracing and intimacy.*]

ROXANNE (*sighing*): I feel a tightness in my shoulders, and I'm pissed, but let's keep going. What's next? We can't stay here forever.

PRACTITIONER: What roles have you used to survive in this theater? [*Here we are rumbling again. At this point, I am also practicing an element of bravery. I want to sit with the tightness in her chest and explore it, but she wants to keep going, and I have to follow her lead. Following her lead is a microliberatory movement as there is already an assumed power differential in therapy. She needs to be given the power here in a world that strips it from her all the time.*]

ROXANNE: Hmm. Let me sit with this one a bit. I feel so cheated. I feel like two characters. I feel like the Hulk. I am just so mad all the damn time, you know? That's how you survive the tide of torment. You just can't rest. I am always barking at somebody. I can't turn that off. But then, sometimes, I feel like Quasimodo. I'm deformed. I'm like a monster in a corner and all the townspeople are afraid of me. Perhaps they think that what I am or what I have is contagious. It's crap if you ask me. [*I was able to hear the way in which relational privilege is being impacted by the wider system. Two components, social welcoming and belonging, as well as self-worth, are being adversely affected.*]

PRACTITIONER: It's more than crap. It's injustice. What do you think this role has done to your relationship? [*I am taking the relational risk and adding my voice to her experience to ensure that she feels seen. I am encouraging her to pivot and rumble again. Here we are beginning to generate an understanding of the impact. Epistemic embracing is important here.*]

ROXANNE (*sighing again*): I am Quasimodo here too. I guess that sounds pathetic to say, but I feel dirty, you know? I feel like I brought this sin to us. I brought my . . . my hunchback. I just want to stay by myself. But even though I want to stay by myself, I know I am mad a lot, and I bite, and I know Thianna feels how much I bite. I really am ashamed of this. [*Again, we can hear the impact on relational privilege and the ways in which it is showing up in the relationship.*]

PRACTITIONER: Who is directing the play, Roxanne? [*The client is redirected to pivot again and to turn outward. This becomes necessary because the* client appears to be owning the societal narrative, and a systemic lens is important. The role of the system, when present, must always be highlighted.]

ROXANNE (*tearfully*): Straight people.

PRACTITIONER: What's happening for you now as you say this? What are you feeling or noticing in your body? How are your shoulders? [*Client is invited again to practice elements of VIMBASI.*]

ROXANNE: I am sad. My shoulders feel droopy. Not sure if that makes sense, but that's how it feels.

PRACTITIONER: The droopiness is important. The droopiness lets us know that what is being done to you and Thianna is not okay! Has speaking about this felt helpful or harmful? When you think about your own freedom from these forces, does this type of conversation help you on that path? [*Again, we are normalizing the feelings with intimacy. We are openly creating a microliberatory movement and practicing bravery by asking her to situate this moment in the context of her own freedom from systemic harm and its impact on her relationship.*]

ROXANNE: It's helpful. It's just so nice to finally talk about it, to be honest.

Nurturing Your Creativity

There are various other ways that you, as a practitioner, can use the theater of oppression. Here are a few ways that you can consider:

1. *Role playing*: Clients can be asked to act out experiences of oppression they have encountered, and then reflect on their emotions and reactions. They can then process how these feelings and responses have shown up in their relationship.
2. *Dramatic tableaux*: You can ask your clients to create frozen images or tableaux that demonstrate significant moments when they have experienced marginalization or discrimination. Using this, they can explore their thoughts and feelings, and again note how these are sometimes transferred to their relationships.

3. *Creative dance and movement*: As practitioners, you can allow clients to express experiences they have in the world via dance and motion. This somatic process fosters the ability to connect deeply to their experiences and bodies. This connection permits the discovery of themes that are critical to understand.
4. *Drawing and/or Play-Doh*: You can invite clients to draw the roles and the theme of the drama on paper. In this way, they are mapping the roles they play and the impact on their relationships. Clients can also use Play-Doh or craft items to construct the roles and scenes.

You can also think of other ways that feel aligned with your practice style that can capture this material. I want you to dive fully into your ingenuity!

HABITS OF SURVIVAL

Habits of survival refer to "rigidified, automatic, habitual responses that are driven by survival anxiety and the orientation toward survival" (Hardy, 2023, p. 330). Marginalized people often navigate day-to-day life by using these. It is useful to explain this to our couples, and have them consider the habits of survival that they use daily as well as the ways that these show up in their relationships. Using the practice of bravery, we must enact critical consciousness and not pathologize or vilify our clients' habits of survival. These habits are functions of their nervous system that are trying to enhance their safety and empower them in largely unsafe environments.

These instrumental habits become necessary when our clients are outside of their window of possibilities, a concept we examined in Chapter 1. We can support them in understanding this, while facilitating their insight into the ways in which these habits can be harmful to their relationships. Here are some questions that you can consider when using this mechanism:

1. During direct experiences of racism and/or homophobia, how do you keep yourself safe?
2. When you expect to experience discrimination, marginalization, or prejudice, what are your typical responses?
3. On a daily basis, how do you feel in your nervous system? How do you typically respond to these feelings? Which of these feelings and

behaviors are connected to expectations or experiences of racism, homophobia, or transphobia?
4. Have you seen any of these feelings or behaviors surface in your relationship with your partner(s)?
5. Where do you think you typically exist on the window of possibilities? Can you recount one or two actual incidents with me? Let's track to see what was happening for you using VIMBASI. Has this impacted your relationship with your partner? If so, how?
6. Has speaking about this now felt liberatory, or is it more oppressive?

As you can see here, the client is encouraged into a deep process of pivoting and rumbling. Let's deepen our understanding by looking at the example below. As usual, I refer to myself as "Practitioner" to help you follow along easily.

Case 2

Solomon and Ayanna are a Black couple living in Seattle. They are both of Nigerian descent—their parents migrated from Nigeria to the United States. Solomon deemed Ayanna to be an "angry Black woman." He found her to be temperamental, but averred that she expressed her anger silently and never openly. He complained: "She always looks like she wants to kill me, but when I ask her what the hell is wrong, she never wants to say. What am I supposed to do with that?" He no longer wished to speak with her on many matters, as he deemed conversations to be risky. Ayanna, too, admitted that she often felt incredible rage that she struggled to manage. In this session, we looked at habits of survival.

As was done in Case 1, throughout the written dialogue, I clearly identify the PRIDE skills and elements of the BIOME that were used. Relational privilege is also addressed. In this session, both partners agreed that I would work with Ayanna.

> **PRACTITIONER:** Ayanna, I want us to start looking at how you often feel in the world and how you survive. Is that okay with you? I know you mentioned the rage that feels hard to control, and I want to explore this with you. We want to see if it's coming from something outside of you. Please let me know if this feels right. [*This is an invitation to pivot and rumble.*]
>
> **AYANNA:** Sure. All good.

PRACTITIONER: On a daily basis, how do you feel in your body? How do you typically respond to these feelings? Which of these feelings and responses are connected to expectations or experiences of racism?

AYANNA: Ha! Those are good questions. People are always saying or doing something stupid where I work.

PRACTITIONER: At work? Can you say more?

AYANNA (*grimacing*): I work at an IT (information technology) company and honestly, there are a bunch of White folks there who don't always know how to act right. Like they would slip into some crap about immigrants, blaming immigrants for problems in this country. They think I can't hear, but oh, I can hear them. I can hear them real good. I don't say anything though. I shut my mouth, you know. It's a bunch of White boys with God complexes. I shut my mouth and say nothing. I don't know what they will do to me there. [*Two elements of relational privilege are being compromised here: protection and living your truth.*]

PRACTITIONER: That's awful that they do this to you. I can see right now what this is doing to you! This is not okay! [*I am taking the relational risk to express how I feel with and for this client. This is the practice of intimacy, which helps to validate the trauma.*]

AYANNA: Tell them that!

PRACTITIONER: Indeed. Ayanna, you mentioned that you say nothing a lot. When people say those xenophobic things, do you often keep quiet?

AYANNA: What else do you want me to do? Do you want me to say something? Come on! Be real, Akilah! [*The habit of survival is becoming apparent even during this session. It is important for the therapist to practice openness and not become defensive. There is a power differential in the room, which is probably awakening this survival habit. I recognize that even my question could have been phrased differently in order to communicate better and validate the survival habit.*]

PRACTITIONER: I am sorry, Ayanna. I could have shown up differently here. Please know that I understand how that question might land for you. A bit more grace on my end should have been communicated. Is there anything that you need from me here so that I can show up in a way that feels supportive? [*This is the continued practice of openness and a willingness to have this be rejected or accepted. It is unclear if there is a rupture, but a rupture makes sense when there is a need to survive in this power dynamic.*]

AYANNA: I'm good. Do your thing! [*It is possible that she feels more comfortable or the habit of survival (self-censorship) is manifesting again. There is a need to give her room and not dictate how she should respond to my own power here.*]

PRACTITIONER: Saying nothing makes sense, to be honest. Some may call it a habit of survival. It may be your body's way of keeping you safe in an unsafe environment. Who knows what may happen to a young Black woman when she stands up to White men. That would scare the hell outta me! Does that feel right to you? [*Here we are encouraging the client to pivot, turn outward, and rumble. This is also a practice of epistemic embracing. I am being brave enough to practice critical consciousness so that I too can understand the value of this habit.*]

AYANNA (*beginning to cry*): You can't say anything. You can't say anything.

PRACTITIONER: Of course, you can't say anything. It doesn't feel safe and it isn't safe. That is living in your body. Does it also feel that way with Solomon? [*Ayanna is being invited to turn outward and inward. She is being allowed the room to rumble and look at the relationship. I am not sure if the two are connected. It is not certain that the system is impacting the relationship. There can be many issues playing a role here, including Solomon's own personality or even Ayanna's family history. As such, there is a need to go slowly and check in with her. We are yarning. We are trying to generate an understanding. There is no rush.*]

AYANNA: A lot of times.

PRACTITIONER: Does Solomon remind you of these men at work?

AYANNA (*sobbing*): He isn't like them. He is kind. He doesn't say that crap. We both know what it feels like to be second-generation immigrants in this place, but . . . but . . . but everything just feels so hard since I started working at that godforsaken company. I wasn't around that many White men before, to be honest. [*The link to the system is now apparent so it is safer to explore this as a habit of survival that is impacting the relationship.*]

PRACTITIONER: How do you feel now as you have said that? What thoughts, feelings, or sensations come up for you in your body? Are there any images you see? Is there anything you want to do? [*This is the practice of VIMBASI.*]

AYANNA: Confused, but that's okay. I want to stand and stretch. I know that may sound weird.

PRACTITIONER: Let's do it together then. Is that okay? (*Ayanna nods affirmingly.*) How has this conversation felt? Does it feel more like a burden or is it freeing?

AYANNA: I feel lighter and sad, to be honest. It's not like I can make all those White men disappear. [*The contradiction here is important to note. There is a shift, and she is also seeing the reality. We share more about how to deal with these types of moments in Chapter 9.*]

PRACTITIONER: That makes sense to me. When you think about this moment, does it support or stifle your liberation?

AYANNA: Well, I am stretching, so that's your answer there, but I know we have more work to do.

Nurturing Your Creativity

Remember that even with this technique, you can be creative. Let's browse some ways that you can make this happen:

1. *Life mapping*: You can have your clients develop a visual map of their life journeys, highlighting moments of oppression and the survival tools they used. This map can help them notice patterns in their responses.
2. *Writing metaphors*: Clients can be asked to create metaphors that symbolize their survival habits and observe how they show up in their relationships.

3. *Use of art*: You can encourage your clients to use paintings, drawings, and collages to express their survival habits.
4. *Two-chair work or two-chair enactment*: These practices are aligned with both psychodrama and Les Greenberg's (2010) emotion-focused therapy. You can invite clients to create a dialogue with the parts of them that exist as habits of survival. Being in conversation with these parts helps them understand if or how these parts are connected to systemic trauma.

While delving further into the above techniques is beyond the scope of this book, awareness of these approaches and your own existing toolbox can help you see other ways that you can assess habits of survival.

COMING-OUT STORY

I didn't come out. I was outed!
   —Sanaa, a gay client living in the Caribbean

Coming out is often a pivotal experience for persons in the LGBTQIA+ community. In many cases, it can be a very difficult experience and can have a damaging impact on one's future and existing intimate relationships. Furthermore, coming out is often not experienced as a singular moment. LGBTQIA+ folks continue to have many experiences in their lives when they are coming out. Some of these experiences are harmless, while others are extremely traumatic.

The weight of coming out to others around them can have a lasting impact on a person's nervous system. Furthermore, the lessons learned from the experience can influence how they engage with others. A person's coming-out experience can hamper all elements of relational privilege, especially their sense of feeling accepted in the world and the ability to live their authentic truth. When working with clients to appreciate the effect of their coming-out story on their relationships, the following questions are helpful:

- When did you first become aware of your orientation or identity?
- Who did you tell?
- How was it received?

- Did you feel safe to share?
- Were you allowed to speak your truth?
- How did you respond to their reaction?
- Has this impacted your relationship with your partner? How so?

As you saw in the techniques above, at the end of this inquiry clients are invited to situate the questions within their own liberation journey. In order to explore this in greater detail, let's look at the case below.

Case 3

Sylvia and Jan are two women who had been in a romantic partnership for approximately 20 years. Sylvia reported wanting "invisibility" in her relationship with Jan. She did not wish for Jan to be open with her work colleagues about their relationship. As a result, she and Jan would constantly argue about this. Jan felt hidden and thought that Sylvia was ashamed of her. There were little to no displays of affection between them even when they were at home. Though they were obviously in a relationship, Sylvia never officially declared so to her family. Sylvia shared that Jan was reckless and too open about their relationship. Jan resented Sylvia for the secrecy of their involvement.

> PRACTITIONER: Hey, Jan and Sylvia. I want to take this opportunity for us to talk about your experiences of coming out. Is that okay with you? This is an exploration for us to see if there has been any impact of this on who you are and your relationship. [*This is an invitation to pivot and rumble.*]
>
> JAN: Okay. It's cool.
>
> SYLVIA: Fine with me.
>
> PRACTITIONER: Would either of you like to start?
>
> SYLVIA: I guess I can.
>
> PRACTITIONER: Sure. Sylvia, please start in a way that feels comfortable for you.
>
> SYLVIA: Well, to be honest. I didn't come out. I was outed. I remember the experience vividly to this day. I was about 15 years old at the time.

My mother allowed me to have a diary at the time. It was really cool to have that. It was a safe space for me, especially when I realized that I was different. I found a place to say it all, right? I could say what I was feeling. At the time, I knew I had a crush on this girl. Her name was Adanna. So I would draw Adanna in my diary. Every single day, I would draw her. Then, one day, I couldn't find my diary. She took it. My mother took it. I don't even remember all the details, but I remember her face. She was holding a rosary in her hand, and looking at me, and telling me that we needed to go quickly to see my priest to get forgiveness, and that I could never tell my father. I could never tell my father. The truth is I think Dad knew. He knew, but I couldn't tell him. It was the secret we all knew. It was the secret we all knew and we knew I had to be forgiven.

PRACTITIONER: I understand. As you share this story now, what do you feel? See if you can pay close attention to the sensations in your body, or even any images or thoughts that may come up. Is there anything that is happening? Are you feeling any vibrations? [*Here, we are pivoting and rumbling. We are also delving into elements of VIMBASI.*]

SYLVIA: I feel tightness in my throat. I can see a hand around my throat. That's it.

PRACTITIONER: I want to ask you a question. If this doesn't feel like an okay question to ask, please resist. Also feel free to let me know if you don't understand the question. If the tightness in your throat could speak, what would it say? [*Here, we are deepening VIMBASI. Encouraging resistance is also very important. Encouraging resistance is a microliberatory movement.*]

SYLVIA: Hide. Hide and seek repentance.

PRACTITIONER: Sylvia, as I hear this, I feel sadness. I too am beginning to feel the tightness, though it's in my chest. [*Here, I am taking the relational risk to express how I feel.*]

SYLVIA: I just need to hide.

PRACTITIONER: Sylvia, I'd like to ask another question. Please feel free to say that you don't want to answer if it feels uncomfortable for you.

Does the feeling in your throat have any thoughts on your relationship with Jan? [*We are continuing to rumble. This is also a practice of epistemic embracing.*]

SYLVIA: What in the world does that mean?

PRACTITIONER: Thanks for asking this. I may have been unclear. If the tightness in your throat could think, if it had the capacity to think at all, what would it think about the relationship with Jan?

SYLVIA: Same thing . . . hide. [*It is apparent here that different elements of relational privilege are being affected. The client does not feel that she can live her truth or that she will feel a sense of welcoming and belonging in the world.*]

PRACTITIONER: This makes sense to me. It makes sense that it would say this to you.

SYLVIA: It does?

PRACTITIONER: Yes. I can hear that the same part that woke up when you learned that you had to hide years ago is also waking up now. It makes sense to me.

SYLVIA: I'm glad it makes sense to someone.

At the end of this process, Sylvia explored the role of this process in her growth and liberation. She reported being a bit confused and scared, but felt ready to delve deeper, as she wanted a happier relationship for her and Jan.

Nurturing Your Creativity

Just as with the other techniques, you can also use multiple modes to explore the coming-out story. Below are a few for you to consider:

1. *Visual storytelling*: Your clients can design a comic strip or graphic novel to illustrate their coming-out story.
2. *Art or Play-Doh*: You can use these means to demonstrate the story and its impact on the client.
3. *Poetry*: This can be used to recap the details of clients' experiences when coming out.

4. *Playback theater*: Practitioners who may wish to explore the coming-out story in a group setting with drama and trained actors can also use techniques such as playback theater. Using drama in this way can create the distance needed to explore the story and note its impact on current reality.

Clients can use all the aforementioned modalities to not only examine the coming-out experiences they had with their families but also in various settings, such as the workplace and with friends. This is important to process as well.

RELATIONAL TERRAIN

> It feels like a dangerous swamp. On the surface, it can look like it is still. But under there, there are creatures just waiting to destroy you.
> —Jamal, a Black man in the United Kingdom

As mentioned earlier, we can really get a clear sense of how our clients feel in the world using metaphors and analogies. With their permission, these can be safe entry points into their nervous systems and relational worlds.

As discussed in Chapter 2, creator of the STAIR (self-trust and integrated resilience) method, Juliane Taylor Shore says that our sense of the world can be understood as a "psychological floor" (Shore, 2025). We walk on this floor daily, and it is shaping our lived experiences. I have leaned on her insight here to construct the idea of the relational terrain, which I describe as our felt sense of how relationships work. Using this technique, we can get a deep sense of how marginalized people feel in their interactions and relationships with the world. In this method, clients are asked to compare their relationship with the wider system to a type of terrain, and they are given examples to support them. These examples include mountains, deserts, hills, seas, plateaus, and many more. Typically, when this question is posed, clients pause and allow themselves the opportunity to really "feel into" the moment to determine which best describes these interactions with the macrosystem. They then rumble and explore how it affects their intimate partner relationship(s).

Recalling our discussion about the nervous system in Chapter 1, we can see the value of this to many of our clients. The state of our nervous system affects how we show up in our interactions. Also, our earlier discussion on "stress spillover" in Chapter 1 can provide some perspective here. Just like the Theatre of the Oppressed, this technique can furnish us with an appreciation of what is "spilling into" the partner's relationships from the outer world. Here are some questions that can be supportive:

- How would you describe your relationship with the wider system? Think of the religious, educational, financial, and criminal justice systems. What terrain would best describe your relationship with these systems?
- Why would you say it is this terrain? What is happening?
- As you speak about this terrain, what do you notice in your body? What images, thoughts, or memories come up?
- How would you describe the terrain that exists in your relationship with your partner? Is it similar or different to the terrain you feel in the world? Is one molding or affecting the other? How so?
- Has speaking about this now felt liberatory, or is it more oppressive?

Case 4

Adrian and Lenora are an interracial couple living in Portugal. Adrian hated living there and complained constantly about experiences of racism. He was originally from the United States and moved there to live with Lenore when they got married. She was originally from the United Kingdom but moved to Portugal for work. They had four young daughters, and Adrian desperately wanted to move. He felt that he could not find happiness or peace there. Though they didn't fight often, when they did, the arguments were explosive. In this session, we decided to focus on Adrian's experience, using the relational terrain.

> **PRACTITIONER:** Adrian, I want to take this time for us to just be with the way you feel in the world. Does that feel like an okay thing to do? I want to use an exercise called the relational terrain to support this. This helps us get an idea of how it feels for you. Metaphors usually help us to get a fairly accurate picture. [*This is an invitation to pivot and rumble. Acknowledging the client's agency is also a microliberatory movement. Explaining to Adrian the purpose and nature of the process is a practice of openness.*]
>
> **ADRIAN:** I can do this.

PRACTITIONER: If you were to think of your experiences and your relationships in the wider system as a type of terrain, what would it be? I invite you to think about your experiences and relationships, particularly as a Black man in Portugal. Would you be willing to think about how you feel interacting with various systems just as the school system that your children are in, or even the health care system and other spaces? If it were a type of terrain, what would it be? For example, is it a mountain, a swamp, the sea, a forest, or anything like that? [*This is an invitation to pivot and rumble. Client is being invited and asked to turn outward.*]

ADRIAN: It's quicksand.

PRACTITIONER: Hmm. Are you willing to share more?

ADRIAN: I keep feeling like I am sinking, you know? But I am not sinking on my own. Someone is pushing me. It's quite deliberate. There isn't anything accidental about it.

PRACTITIONER: Oof. I am feeling into that—the deliberate nature of it. [*I am beginning to take a relational risk, demonstrating my emotional connection to what he has shared.*]

ADRIAN: It is!

PRACTITIONER: As you speak about it, what do you notice? What images do you see? What sensations do you feel? [*This is the practice of VIMBASI.*]

ADRIAN: I see the quicksand, to be honest. I feel my feet sinking in it.

PRACTITIONER: Sinking in it. [*I am repeating for emphasis and to deepen the rumble.*] Do you get that same feeling in your relationship? Are you sinking in it? [*Client is being invited to turn inward.*]

ADRIAN: Sometimes it is. Sometimes it isn't. Something else is happening there.

PRACTITIONER: Are you willing to share more?

ADRIAN: I'm already sinking, you know? I'm already below whatever there is that exists, and when we get into these arguments . . .

PRACTITIONER: And when you get into these arguments . . .

ADRIAN: I feel like I have a lot to do just to be able to catch myself, just to be able to stand.

PRACTITIONER: Hmm, thinking of your relationship with Lenora, how would you describe that relational terrain? [*Client is being invited to pivot.*]

ADRIAN: That's a mountain for sure. A steep one.

PRACTITIONER: Adrian, is one terrain molding the other? [*This is an invitation to examine if the cause is systemic. It may be systemic or may not be. It is best to go slow.*]

ADRIAN (*pauses to think for some time*): I think so. Now I really think so.

PRACTITIONER: Are you willing to say more?

ADRIAN (*visibly melancholic*): When you are sinking, everything around you feels like something you have to climb!

PRACTITIONER: This is a difficult thing to experience and very unfair to you. I see you. I see how this can feel. As I see it, I can feel the strain of trying to climb out of something that is drowning you. It is hard! [*I am taking a relational risk here.*]

ADRIAN: It is. It is affecting my relationship.

Adrian and I were able to talk further about how this exploration supported his own emancipation. We also discussed how we could all work together to set goals for his partnership with Lenora. I share much more about this in Chapter 6.

Nurturing Your Creativity

You can become really imaginative when using this tool. Here are two ways:

1. *Arts and crafts*: You can ask your clients to draw or paint what their relational terrain looks like. They can also use Play-Doh, paper, sand, blocks, slime, or any other medium to represent their terrain.
2. *Use of movement*: Clients can use dance or movement to represent their relational terrain.

FAMILY NARRATIVES

Feelings. What are feelings? We couldn't have feelings. My parents were immigrants to this country. We didn't have time to feel. My husband wants me to feel, but I don't have time to feel.
—Liana, a Mexican American woman, living in the United States

We learn so much about how to navigate the world based on our families. Both overtly and covertly, they taught us how to emote, how to connect, how to deal with conflict, and how to understand ourselves in relationships. Many of these lessons were their survival strategies. They were learning how to cope with their systemic realities, and as Liana noted in the quote above, sometimes these realities required them to shut down their connection to their emotions just to ensure their survival. In other situations, they were forced to find other mechanisms to navigate difficult systems.

As we mentioned in Chapter 4, families that hold marginalized identities, such as immigrant or BIPOC families, have deeply embedded survival strategies that, in many cases, have been passed on to their children. This is why it is salient for us to examine the impact of historical or intergenerational trauma on relational privilege and couple dynamics.

In order to support couples in this examination, the following questions can be considered:

- What was your family's narrative or story about their experiences of discrimination and prejudice?
- How did your family address these experiences?
- How did these experiences affect the family dynamics and the relationships within the family?
- What role did everyone play in the family to deal with the impact of oppression and marginalization?
- What stereotypes did members of the family own or play in order to deal with oppression and marginalization?
- What habits of survival did the family adopt?
- Do any of these stories and stereotypes affect how you interact with your partner(s) now?

The above questions can be asked generally or in reference to a specific challenge that the partners may be experiencing. The case below gives deeper insight into this.

Case 5

Let's reflect on the story of Wajid and Malaika. They are a Black couple living in the United States, who were on the brink of divorce. Wajid found Malaika to be incredibly controlling and domineering. She found him to be unavailable and irresponsible. In this session, we spent time examining the impact of their family narratives. The dialogue below took place after the couple was educated about historical trauma.

> PRACTITIONER: I would like to invite you to a process where we can process the impact that your family's experiences had on you. You can tell me if this feels right for you, and please know that you can stop at any time. [*Invitation to pivot and rumble. The clients' agency is honored as well, even in this context. This is a microliberatory movement.*]
>
> WAJID: Cool.
>
> MALAIKA: Sounds good. I am willing to go first!
>
> PRACTITIONER: Oh, great. If you could work on one thing in your relationship, what would it be?
>
> MALAIKA: Well, he says I am controlling. I'd wanna look at that because in some ways, I get it.
>
> PRACTITIONER: Let's sit with this and be with this together. Sometimes, the behaviors we see can be connected to our experiences in the wider system. Sometimes, living in a system in which discrimination and other forms of harm are present can drive this. This isn't always the case but sometimes it is so. Did you ever see anyone else in your family be controlling? [*This is an invitation to pivot and rumble. Here, bravery and the willingness to practice critical consciousness are also present.*]
>
> MALAIKA: Ha!
>
> PRACTITIONER: Can you help me to understand more?

MALAIKA: It's a similar complaint Pop-Pop, my grandfather, would make about Nana. Nana was my grandmother and she ran the show. He'd always tell my mother that she was too much, and that she believed it was her way or the highway. My mother also felt the same. She found Nana rigid, overbearing, and overprotective.

PRACTITIONER: Hmm. Can we be with that a bit more? Do we know what was happening for her and outside her family that may have been feeding that behavior? [*Here I am deepening the rumble. I am inviting the client to turn backward and outward.*]

MALAIKA: It is what was happening to all of them . . . all the women.

PRACTITIONER: Are you willing to share more?

MALAIKA: Pop-Pop was in jail once, you know? He doesn't share that often. Not his fault but he was! I think it was for 5 years, or maybe it was more. But I heard about that from Nana. It wasn't so much that he went to jail. She could deal with that. If you were wrong, you get what you deserve. The truth is that he didn't deserve that, but nobody wanted to hear that. My mom said she would cry a lot, saying that it wasn't fair and that they weren't listening. When I was younger, I wasn't always sure who "they" were. I figured it out in my teens when I would hear my older brothers talk. "They" were the police. "They" were the judges in the courthouse. "They" didn't like Black men. He shouldn't have gotten locked up in the first place. He wasn't in the wrong place at the wrong time. He was in the wrong skin at the wrong time. Would have been very different if he was White. It messed with Nana, watching the world be unfair to him like that. It changed her, and she had three dark-skinned boys and my mom to raise, and she saw how in other ways, White people would mess with them, so she'd manage them like a hawk. Wouldn't let them take a breath.

PRACTITIONER: It makes sense to me that this would be tough on her. My own body feels like it's tight just hearing that. Did your mom ever feel what she felt? Did she feel this way about the system? [*This is an example of a relational risk that is being taken. The client is again beginning to turn backward and outward.*]

MALAIKA: Oh yeah, for sure! My brothers were hardheaded, and they got that from her. She was tough. My dad never got locked up though, but he might as well have been. Sad to say, but she managed him. We all knew she was like Nana, fierce and domineering, but what else could a Black woman be in America?

PRACTITIONER: I can understand that. This was how she felt she could survive. Has their story become yours? [*Here, I am practicing critical consciousness again and epistemic embracing.*]

MALAIKA (*tearing up and looking at her husband*): Yes. Their story has become mine.

PRACTITIONER: As you say this, do you notice anything happening in your body? [*Client is being invited to turn inward. This too is a microliberatory movement.*]

MALAIKA: It's tight, you know. Strangely enough, I can see Nana. She always looked so . . . tight. She had to protect what's hers. I gotta protect what is mine. It's tight.

PRACTITIONER: What do you mean?

MALAIKA: My family. Wajid and Naima. [*Naima is their daughter.*]

PRACTITIONER: Hmm.

MALAIKA: I don't know how else to do this. In my family, the women had to take charge. If you don't take charge, you will lose your family!

During the rest of the session, we normalized this sense of the world that Malaika possessed. Given the reality of her family's experience, this was totally understandable. We also examined where this exploration stood in her liberation journey. She noted that seeing the tightness helped her be aware of her reality.

Nurturing Your Creativity

There are many ways that you, too, can capture the family narratives connected to systemic trauma. Let's process the following:

1. *Family tree art*: You can encourage clients to develop a visual family tree that highlights significant events that have shaped the family's story. With this, they can also demonstrate reactions to these events.
2. *Role play*: You can request that your clients employ role-playing techniques to act out family dynamics and narratives.
3. *Mapping metaphors*: Clients can be invited to present metaphors that signify the dynamics within their families. For instance, they may say that their family is a "rough ocean." This can stimulate conversation about how these also affect their relationships with their partner(s).
4. *Psychodrama*: If you are using group work for this exploration, you may also find Tian Dayton's (2015) psychodrama processes with safety valves useful here.

Of course, remember that you should not feel limited to these strategies. Your own skill set also has much to offer.

RELATIONAL PRIVILEGE SCORE

The final strategy we examine now is the relational privilege score. This is a direct and simple tool where our partners are asked to rate themselves on each of the dimensions of relational privilege and determine how their scores are affecting their intimacy stories. As you may recall in Chapter 2, the dimensions of relational privilege are *living your truth*, *protection*, *social welcoming and belonging*, and *self-worth*. To get an idea of how the questions can be presented, consider the list below:

1. For each of the dimensions listed on the relational privilege wheel (Chapter 2, Figure 2.1), can you rate your experience of this in the wider system on a scale of 0–5, with 0 being the lowest? For example, if you do not believe that you are able to live your truth in the wider society, then your score may be 1 or 2. If you do not feel a sense of being protected in the world at all, your score may be 0. If you feel a strong sense of self-worth in the world, you may have a score of 5 in that domain. Feeling a deep sense of belonging and welcoming in the world may earn a score of 4 or 5. For a clearer understanding, see Table 5.1.

Table 5.1: Relational Privilege Score Assessment

Rate your experience in each domain on a scale of 0–5, with 0 being the lowest (*no experience with this privilege*) and 5 being the highest (*full experience with this privilege*). Consider your experiences both in your personal life and within your intimate relationships.

Dimension of relational privilege	0 (no privilege)	1	2	3	4	5 (full privilege)
Living your truth	Unable to be authentic self in any context	Rarely able to be authentic self	Sometimes able to be authentic self	Often able to be authentic self	Usually able to be authentic self	Freely able to be authentic self in all contexts
Protection	No sense of safety or protection	Infrequent feelings of safety or protection	Occasional feelings of safety or protection	Frequent feelings of safety or protection	Mostly feel safe and protected	Consistently feel safe and protected
Social welcoming	Feel unwelcome or excluded in most social settings	Rarely feel welcomed or included	Sometimes feel welcomed or included	Often feel welcomed or included	Usually feel welcomed or included	Feel completely welcomed and included in all settings
Belonging	No sense of belonging	Rarely experience a sense of belonging	Occasional sense of belonging	Frequent sense of belonging	Mostly feel a sense of belonging	Feel a deep and consistent sense of belonging
Self-worth	Low sense of self-worth; self-criticism is dominant	Occasionally experience feelings of self-worth	Sometimes feel a sense of self-worth	Often feel a sense of self-worth	Mostly feel a sense of self-worth	High and consistent sense of self-worth

2. Do any of these affect how you interact with your partner?
3. Do any of these affect your intimacy story? To understand your intimacy story, consider the additional questions below:
   a. How do you define intimacy?
   b. How do you seek intimacy?
   c. What allows you to be emotionally and physically intimate?
   d. How do you communicate intimacy?

e. How do you communicate vulnerability, empathy, safety, and accountability?
   f. How do you address moments when you harm your partner?
   g. How do you address moments when you are harmed in your relationship?
4. Has speaking about this now felt liberatory, or is it more oppressive?
5. Where does this moment sit in your liberation journey?

Let's now see how this technique can be used in an actual case.

Case 6

Millie, Amanda, and Kes are a trans throuple that had been in a relationship for 5 years. They practiced ethical non-monogamy. Both Kes and Amanda described the relationship with Millie as frigid and boring. Amanda said that they felt more like "roommates than lovers." This often angered Millie, who felt that Amanda's description of their relationship was harsh and unkind. She (Millie) felt that she was doing the best that she could, and thought that her partners simply wanted too much. I decided to utilize the relational privilege scoring system with this partnership. Below, we examine Millie's responses:

> **PRACTITIONER:** Hi, Millie. I'd like to invite you to an exploration of the possible impact of transphobia on your relationships. The process for this includes using the components of relational privilege and scoring them on a scale of 0–5. Does this feel comfortable for you? [*Invitation to pivot and rumble. Openness is also being practiced as the client is being informed about the process.*]
>
> **MILLIE:** I can try.
>
> **PRACTITIONER:** Awesome. Can we look at the following components: living your truth, protection, social welcoming and belonging, and self-worth? On a scale of 0–5, with 0 being the lowest, can you rate your experience of each of these domains in the wider system? I invite you to think of your experience in the medical system, educational system, criminal justice system, and any other system you have had to interact with.
>
> **MILLIE:** Do you really wanna know? I've never been able to live my truth so that's a 0. No one cares for trannies so that's a 0. Social welcoming,

I'd give that a 2 because they like to see us at drag shows, and for self-worth, I'd give that a 3, but that's because I fight hard to have it.

PRACTITIONER: Those figures are quite low. This must be an awful emotional space to be in. [*Relational risk is being taken here.*]

MILLIE: I get by, but it's crap for real.

PRACTITIONER: Do any of these affect how you interact with your partners? I want to invite you to focus on just one for now, and we will take them one by one if you wish. [*This is an additional invitation to turn inward and rumble.*]

MILLIE: I can do the one on living my truth. That's a no-brainer for me. Nobody really wants a tranny around. Well, they want you around to gaze at and make fun of, and to entertain them. But nobody really wants to be chatting with a tranny, or listening to us, or being with us in any kinda real way. I am an entertainment piece. I don't wanna feel like that. So I often have to be someone who I am not; it's exhausting. I'm just exhausted. That's what they are getting from me: exhaustion. And the thing is, when I am around anyone, not just Kes and Amanda, I feel like I have to perform. Not sure I can even be the real me.

PRACTITIONER: How does feeling like you have to perform affect your understanding of intimacy? How does it affect your ability to be emotionally and sexually intimate with Kes and Amanda? [*Here I am deepening the experience of turning inward.*]

MILLIE: Like I said, I'm exhausted. I just don't have energy for them. I also can't figure out which part of me they want to see. I don't know who they want to be intimate with.

PRACTITIONER: Oh Millie. I understand.

MILLIE: Nobody wants to see me, so I can't figure out which part of me they want to see.

Millie's struggle to share herself with her partners was a result of her general inability to share herself with the world. As we discussed more of this, Millie admitted that this exploration created a sense of ease within her.

Practitioner's Reflection

As you reflect on the various tools for assessing the impact of systemic trauma on relationships, which ones harmonize most with your practice style? Which ones feel the most challenging? What do you think that you may need to explore to help you feel more competent and at ease with the challenging ones? What other questions do you believe may be useful in helping you to assess the role of systemic trauma in partnerships? If you would like a quick overview of the tools you have learned in this chapter, see Table 5.2. This will serve as our recap of this chapter.

CHAPTER RECAP

Table 5.2: Overview of Relational Curiosity

This table is for illustrative purposes. The actual implementation varies depending on the specific context and the client's needs. Always adapt the techniques to fit the unique situation.

Technique	Description	Purpose	Key questions (examples)	BIOME aspects emphasized	PRIDE stages
Theater of oppression	Uses dramatic metaphors to explore the impact of systemic oppression on relationships.	To highlight the role of systemic forces in relational challenges, facilitating a deeper understanding of the client's experience of oppression within a larger system.	What would the theme of your experience be in dramatic terms? Who is directing this play? How are you cast?	Bravery, openness, microliberatory movement	Pivot, rumble
Habits of survival	Examines habitual responses used by marginalized individuals to cope with systemic trauma.	To identify and understand adaptive mechanisms used to cope with ongoing threats, facilitating a shift from pathologizing these habits to recognizing them as a response to unsafe environments.	What do you do to keep yourself safe? What are your typical responses in situations of marginalization?	Bravery, openness, epistemic embracing	Pivot, rumble
Coming-out story	Explores the client's experiences of coming out and its impact on their relationships.	To recognize the significance of coming out and its lasting impact on relational themes, supporting clients to acknowledge and process their unique experiences.	When did you first come out? Who did you tell? How was it received? How did this impact your relationships?	Bravery, intimacy/intensity, openness	Pivot, rumble

Table 5.2: Overview of Relational Curiosity (continued)

Technique	Description	Purpose	Key questions (examples)	BIOME aspects emphasized	PRIDE stages
Family narratives	Examines how family stories and experiences have shaped the client's current relational dynamics.	To uncover intergenerational trauma and its impact on relational patterns, fostering a shift from blaming individuals to seeing how trauma is passed down through generations.	What is your family's narrative about discrimination? How did your family address those experiences?	Bravery, openness, epistemic embracing	Pivot, rumble, turn backward
Relational terrain	Uses metaphorical landscapes to represent the client's experience of relationships within wider systemic contexts.	To understand the client's experience of the wider systems within their relationships, creating space for processing emotional experiences.	How would you describe your relationship with various systems (education, criminal justice, etc.) as a terrain?	Openness, epistemic embracing	Pivot, rumble
Relational privilege score	Measures the extent to which clients experience various forms of relational privilege.	To assess the impact of systemic oppression on clients' relational experiences, guiding development of targeted interventions.	Rate your experience in various areas (living your truth, protection, social welcoming and belonging, self-worth) on a scale of 0–5.	Openness, intensity/intimacy, epistemic embracing	Assessment, not directly linked to PRIDE stages

CHAPTER 6

Responsible Externalizing and Setting Intentions

The Dagara people believe that when two people share a spirited and balanced intimate life, they have the power to raise a healing energy for everything around them. For this reason a couple might dedicate their sacred intimacy to some higher purpose, in addition to the well-being of their own relationship.
— SOMÉ (1997, P. 85)

In Chapter 5, we examined many ways to practice relational curiosity. Now, we delve into two phases after this: *responsible externalizing* and *setting intentions*.

WHAT IS RESPONSIBLE EXTERNALIZING?

Though responsible externalizing is identified as the second and immediate step after relational curiosity, the truth is that there are elements of responsible externalizing even during relational curiosity.

Responsible externalizing is the process of definitively attributing the challenging dynamics in the partners' relationships to the external system and domains of oppression. It is important that this process be practiced *responsibly* since not all difficulties in a relationship are caused by systemic harm. Some problems originate solely from the couple's relational dynamics. As such, we must be careful not to unwittingly implicate the system when this may not be appropriate.

Responsible externalizing is a practice that involves turning outward and turning backward. Clients are given the space to explore how both systemic and ancestral trauma are crafting their interpersonal interactions. However, it is still a step further than relational curiosity because it includes the following three components:

1. Practitioner externalizing (deliberate and clear externalizing by the practitioner)
2. Co-contacting and naming the harm
3. Grieving

We now take a closer look at each segment.

Practitioner Externalizing

As we noted in Chapter 5 during the process of relational curiosity, clients are encouraged to use creative means to investigate the ways in which systemic trauma manifests itself into relational conflict. While we gently escort couples to these realizations, we are also required to seal their understanding with our own bold declaration of what they have discovered. In many ways, this bold declaration requires the use of both bravery and intimacy by the practitioner. We must help our clients unearth the role of the system with immense clarity. We are the ones who must name the system's impact with no equivocation. The strength in our conviction is the cushion they need to move forward to the next step.

When I have clearly said to clients, "The system is the problem. It is not you," I have seen different reactions. For some clients, there is a deep sense of relief. One client reported to me an ease in her chest as she no longer blamed her partner but attributed their challenges to the real culprit. Her ire and overwhelm shifted to joy. I have also seen some people draw closer to each other, as if the wall between them began to collapse. Naming the ways in which marginalization shows up seems to create an aperture in the darkness for many partners. Our courage to say this boldly here helps make the invisible visible, and clients become more confident.

The extant literature also supports this notion. Where appropriate, attributing couples' relational discord to external dynamics truly supports them in moving forward. Ogolsky et al. (2017) reported that this form of attribution is an important strategy in helping partners maintain their relationships while mitigating environmental stressors. According to Ogolsky et al., attribution assists with threat mitigation, which refers to the couple's ability to manage forces that hamper relationship stability and satisfaction.

After partners engage in this process, we can support them in making safe contact with the harm that has been inflicted on their relationship by the system. This is where we direct our attention next.

Co-Contacting and Naming the Harm
I wonder what it would feel like for the both of you to hate it together.

This is a line I have used during the phase of "co-contacting and naming the harm." I have extended the invitation to partners to look at the harm together, jointly "feel into it," and together express their thoughts and emotions toward it. This is different from relational curiosity because it is a co-created encounter and a joint exercise.

First, the partners work together to depict the harm. There are different ways that a practitioner can inspire clients to do this. Sometimes, we can encourage them to draw the harm together. While they are drawing, they are working together to construct what the harm looks like in their relationship. At other times, we can request that they imagine the harm to be a creature sitting in an empty chair, and then make contact with it. This is the empty-chair technique that is quite popular in psychodrama. Again, we ask them here to co-imagine, and to build an image together.

No matter the approach you provide to support clients, having them name what they sense and feel as they look at the harm is significant. While doing so, they must feel the supportive presence of the practitioner. Our presence provides some breathing room for them to tap into much of what they are experiencing within.

After this is done, the parties are asked to give the harm a name. The name can be a word or a phrase that they will use in moments when they believe that the harm is showing up in their relationship. For example, during a tense moment such as an argument, if one person realizes the incident to be an effect of the system, they can say the word aloud. This can alert the partners to what is truly building the chasm between them. In these moments, their partner no longer is the enemy. The system is!

Jointly agreeing on a word shines some light into the relationship and gives couples more room to figure out how to move ahead. They also need this room to be able to grieve.

Grieving

The final step is to issue a tender invitation to our clients to grieve the impact of systemic trauma on their relationship. It is often impossible to confront the reality of this type of harm without lamenting its presence and effects. The forces that affect marginalized people are extremely potent. While there are so many ways that BIPOC and LGBTQIA+ persons organize themselves to reclaim power in an unfair world, the reality is that feelings of helplessness and defenselessness are quite justified as well. This is why grief is essential.

Grieving is a deeper experience of externalizing. I often tell my clients that what they are feeling is theirs to feel, but not theirs to hold. They need to deeply feel the grief over what is taken from them because of continuous systemic harm. However, they cannot hold responsibility for the system. Space is needed.

As our clients grieve in the space that we offer, it is perfectly okay for us to take the relational risk and grieve with them. This assists them in knowing that they are not alone, and that what they are experiencing is quite real. This is also how we help make what is often ignored, seen. While they experience this from us, we can considerately urge them to provide themselves with compassion as well. Their grief needs validation and tending.

From the earlier parts of this discussion on responsible externalizing, you may have noticed that I mentioned some elements of the PRIDE process and BIOME framework that are central to this part of the work. However, I still wish to further elucidate how the PRIDE model and the BIOME feature in this phase.

THE PRIDE PROCESS

PRIDE certainly comes to bear in this process of responsible externalizing. Primarily, the act of *rumbling* is most apparent as clients confront, with intentionality, the systemic forces that have insidiously infiltrated their relational dynamics. This process compels a deep dive into their shared history, ancestral wounds, and societal contexts, propelling them to unearth the hidden connections between relational struggles and the wider landscape of harm and oppression.

THE BIOME

The BIOME framework also informs this phase. Specifically, the practitioner's *bravery* is a vital vessel for articulating the insidious nature of systemic injustices that often remains unspoken. This bravery must be coupled with *intensity and intimacy*, creating a resonant connection that validates the clients' experiences and disrupts feelings of isolation. At the heart of this lies epistemic embracing, a commitment to validating and honoring the clients' unique understanding of their experiences and the systemic forces that shape their realities. We actively resist the urge to impose external frames or downplay their perspectives.

Now that we have spent time examining the contextual features of this work, let's focus on a short example of responsible externalizing. In Chapter 5, we explored the narrative of Roxanne and Thianna. Do you recall how relational curiosity was used with them? They are a same-sex couple with whom the theater of oppression was employed. Roxanne compared her experience in the world and in her relationship to that of Quasimodo. She believed that she was dirty and needed to hide away, even in her own relationship. Below, we look at the course of externalizing with this couple:

> **PRACTITIONER:** Roxanne and Thianna, I know that you are really struggling and that Roxanne often feels dirty and needs to hide. Thianna, I know how this affects you as well. Neither of you are the problem. The system is the problem. The system is the unfair way that it treats LGBTQIA+ persons. Homophobia is the problem. This is what is shaping how you are experiencing your relationship. How does that feel to hear? [*This is practitioner externalizing. I am using bravery here and critical consciousness. Assessing what this feels like for them is a microliberatory movement.*]
>
> **THIANNA:** That feels really good to hear, actually.
>
> **ROXANNE:** It does. I think I started to realize that a bit when you asked me what character I am, but it's still good to hear it again.
>
> **PRACTITIONER:** I am so glad to hear that. I want to invite you to explore something. Let's look at it together. I want to invite both of you to watch the damage to the relationship together, but I want you to witness the damage as something outside of you. For example, you can draw together what it looks like in your relationship, or you can imagine

it in a chair in front of you. Do either of these feels right for you? [*This is an invitation to co-contact the harm. Ensuring that this is a request and not a demand is a microliberatory movement.*]

ROXANNE: I want to do the drawing.

THIANNA: That can work. (*Roxanne and Thianna draw an image of a black insect with huge eyes.*)

PRACTITIONER: Would you be willing to share with me how you are feeling as you look at this image?

THIANNA: Disappointed to be honest. I never thought we would have to be combatting something like this, you know? It's a pretty ugly insect, and its ugliness is real.

ROXANNE: Sad, pretty sad. But somehow I feel like when I put it on paper like this, I can put it away sometimes, you know?

PRACTITIONER: I get that. I want to invite both of you to consider something. If we were to give this harm a name, what would we name it? Would you be willing to come up with a name together? This may be helpful to both of you. You see, in moments when both of you may be feeling distant from each other, if one person notices this and uses the word, it may help alert you both to what is really happening, and help you move out of the moment.

ROXANNE: Ah, I get it. What word would you like, Thianna?

THIANNA: Hunchback!

ROXANNE: That works. So we can use that word then!

PRACTITIONER: Ah, yes. That can be helpful. I want to circle back a bit. Roxanne, I recall you speaking about sadness when noticing the harm. What would it be like to grieve? I don't view grief as a defeatist stance but as an opportunity to sit with the reality of what is being taken from you while giving tenderness to yourself. If we were to be with this grief, what would it be like?

THIANNA: It's taking away our freedom to be ourselves. That's what I am grieving.

ROXANNE: To be ourselves, even with each other.

PRACTITIONER: Where do you feel that grief in your bodies? [*This is an invitation to turn inward, and to practice VIMBASI.*]

ROXANNE: I feel the grief in my hips. I feel tight there.

THIANNA: For me, it's in my tummy. It's a hollow feeling.

PRACTITIONER: Ah, okay. Can you each imagine yourself sitting next to those feelings and being with them? Can we offer something compassionate to say to these feelings? Is there a way that we can let them know that this is normal?

THIANNA: I think that I can give it a big hug.

ROXANNE: A hug is a stretch for me.

PRACTITIONER: I get that. Maybe we can just let them know "I see you."

ROXANNE: That works. I see you!

As you can see above, we worked on all three elements of responsible externalizing. It should be mentioned that it is perfectly okay if our clients do not wish to engage in all these components. For example, a couple may decide to listen to the practitioner as they externalize, but the couple may have no desire to contact the harm or to grieve.

SETTING INTENTIONS

After we accompany our partners in the process of responsible externalizing, it is helpful to support them in setting their intentions for the work. This is the process of turning forward that we discussed in Chapter 4. We do not set the intentions for them. We allow them to do this given the conclusions they have drawn from the previous processes. As we explore the undertaking of setting intentions, we consider the following questions:

1. What are intentions?
2. What are the two types of intentions?
3. What components of the PRIDE process are activated during the setting of intentions?
4. What aspects of the BIOME are needed to facilitate the setting of intentions?
5. What happens if clients do not wish to set intentions and want us to do so for them?
6. What happens when we as practitioners want to set the intentions?

What Are Intentions?

Intentions are your clients' dreams and goals for the work. It refers to what shifts clients would like to see as a result of what they have learned about themselves, their systemic realities, and their relationships. For some clients, these may be shifts in behaviors toward each other. For others, it may be a shift in perspectives or how they feel about their partner. Additionally, intentions also include their dreams for the world and systems they occupy. It includes the ways in which they would like to see their environment transform.

Types of Intentions

There are two types of intentions that I have considered useful in the work: *relational intentions* and *systemic intentions*. Relational intentions refer to clients' hopes for their relationships, while systemic intentions are the changes they would like to see in the world. It is important for partners to consider both if they are willing to do so. Given that systemic intentions are sometimes a bit unclear, I will spend some time here explaining more about what these look like and how they are connected to couple therapy.

As you would have noted in Chapters 3 and 4, critical consciousness is a huge part of this work with marginalized people. As practitioners, we must consider the role of the system in all things. This reflection on the system extends beyond the impact that it has on couples. Clients are also invited to consider how their own work in therapy and the shifts in their relationships can influence the systems around them. This is a relatively simple process, and we can easily ask questions, such as the following:

1. If you and your partner were to achieve your relational intentions, what impact do you think this may or would have on the systems around you?
2. Do you think that the goals you have set here in therapy with me have any connection to what changes you would like to see in the wider system?
3. We have discussed the system's impact on your relationship. Have you considered your relationship's impact on the system? What might this be or look like?

These questions are largely exploratory, and it is perfectly okay if clients do not have answers for them. We remain open to where our people are. Some clients have clarity though, and for them, their relationships shift the wider system in the following ways:

1. Strong and sturdy relationships give partners the courage to challenge systemic harm. In other words, having a secure base in their relationships gives individuals the ability to do advocacy work and activism.
2. Healthy relationships are examples for other marginalized couples to follow. Changes in their relationships can inspire other members of their community.
3. Solid intimate relationships are more likely to provide solid economic footing to the partners, undoing systemically induced financial harm that we discussed in Chapter 1.

We have listed just a few of the shifts that can happen. There is so much more. Feel free to consider and add your thoughts.

The PRIDE Process

Let's discover which elements of the PRIDE process are activated when generating intentions with our clients. Intention setting is closely aligned with *imagination*. It is the natural step after rumbling that is facilitated during both relational curiosity and responsible externalizing.

I often say that rumbling is the place where clients usher in their own emergence. During rumbling there is grief and heartache, but there is value to this process of mourning. The realization of the loss opens the path to creativity and visioning. When we can face what we have lost or are losing, we can deepen our insight into what we must generate. With the support of the practitioner, our clients' nervous systems can experience the regulation needed to envision new ways of being in their world. Generating this new vision is also a part of the *pivoting* process. Here, the clients are *turning forward*—forging new paths ahead.

The BIOME

What components of the BIOME are most needed during imagination? Though all of the elements indeed have some utility during this phase, I would argue that epistemic embracing is the most impactful. Being with our clients and allowing them to define intimacy and their relationship in ways that feel best for them and their systemic contexts provides a beautiful environment for imagination. I can imagine that it is tempting to instruct couples and partners on what we think their relationships should look like, but the reality is that *our* definitions of relationality are tied to *our* own relational privilege. The degree to which we can live our truth, as well as feel protected, worthy, and accepted, governs how we define connection. Our definitions have a political and cultural context. It is important therefore to give couples the space to imagine and create what they desire and need.

When we are tempted to impose our own understanding, we need to be brave enough to confront ourselves. As we discussed in Chapter 3, we must pivot and interrogate our intimacy stories and their origins. Are these origins situated in the realities of marginalized people? Often, they are not.

Let's examine how we can support clients in setting intentions, both relational and systemic. When engaging in this process, the following are useful questions to pose to our clients:

1. Given what you have learned about yourselves, your relationship, and the role of the system thus far, what are your thoughts about the way forward?
2. Given the realities of who you are, your relationship, and the impact of the system, how would you define what healthy intimacy looks like for your relationship? What are you dreaming about for this relationship?
3. What support do you need from me and this process to help you achieve your own definition of intimacy?
4. Do you have any fears connected to setting your intentions? How can I be of support with these fears?

5. How would you know when you have arrived at the place that you wish to be in your relationship?
6. Are there any other goals for your relationship that we should consider in this work?
7. Would you like to see any shifts in the wider system? Do shifts in your relationship contribute to wider shifts? How so? How do they not?

As you may recall in Chapter 5, your creativity is important here. You can use imagery, craft, somatic work, or even direct questions to support your clients in answering the above questions. Now let's be with an actual case.

Case 1

Do you remember the scenario of Sylvia and Jan in Chapter 5? They are two women who experienced immense challenges in their relationship. Sylvia did not wish for others to know about her relationship with Jan. Jan resented Sylvia for this, and was upset by the limited displays of intimacy in the household. Sylvia found Jan to be impetuous and too candid. We now explore how the process of setting intentions can become a reality for this pair. Again, throughout the dialogue, I demonstrate how elements of the BIOME and the PRIDE model are apparent.

> **PRACTITIONER:** We have spent a lot of time looking at the impact of coming out on your relationship. I know we also had to sit with the externalizing process and all the feelings that came with that. I am wondering if you feel ready to look ahead. If this doesn't feel right, we can pause here. [*This is an invitation to pivot and turn forward, which the client has the right to refuse. This invitation is also a microliberatory movement.*]
>
> **SYLVIA:** I am okay to move forward.
>
> **JAN:** It was tough, but we can go ahead.
>
> **PRACTITIONER:** Okay, and please know at any time, you can ask me to stop. Given what you have learned about yourselves, your relationship, and the role of the system thus far, what are your thoughts about the way forward for your relationship? [*This is an invitation to imagine.*]

SYLVIA: That's a good question. I'd like to start, and to be honest, what I am about to say may make Jan very happy. I think us attending events together and sitting together at events would be the way forward. We have gone to some queer events together, but maybe some straight spaces can be up for discussion as well.

JAN: I'd for sure love that! Dinner next week?

SYLVIA: Let's not get ahead of ourselves. I am thinking of a movie. It's dark and I feel okay there.

JAN: Okay. I can do that.

PRACTITIONER: You have shared a lot about how Sylvia's coming-out experience is currently affecting both of you. Do we want to tackle that together? Given what your experience has been like, what is your dream for this relationship? I'd like to invite you into a process. Can you close your eyes for me? I want you to think of your current reality, the reality of the system, and the reality of your relationship. Pay attention to your heart and belly. Then, see if you can come up with an image, a word, or even a metaphor to answer the following question: What does intimacy mean for us? [*Asking them to determine their own definition of intimacy is epistemic embracing and a microliberatory movement.*]

SYLVIA: I see a turtle. Hmm. Healthy intimacy is slowness in a shell.

PRACTITIONER: Do you want to say more?

SYLVIA: I just can't move at the pace of other people. It needs to be slow for me. Everything needs to be slow and safe, even when we are alone. That's my dream. Slowness, and when it feels fast, I need Jan to be okay with my shell. I'm not trying to be distant but I can't live without a shell. I will crash.

PRACTITIONER: I am hearing this, Sylvia. I am hearing how much this means to you. [*Validating the definition is epistemic embracing and a microliberatory movement.*]

JAN: For the first time, I think I am hearing it, too. I saw a cloud. I'm not exactly sure what that means but I do know that I want to be slow with you, and let you have your shell when you need it. I want to focus on the shell and we can handle the cloud later.

PRACTITIONER: I am hearing this. So, we are focusing on the shell and slowness. This slowness that you both want? Do you think it can have a wider impact on the world? Do you think that in any tiny way it can help shift the reality for other queer folks? [*This is an invitation to create a systemic intention.*]

SYLVIA: I am not sure. But maybe it can help other queer folks to see that they can be slow, too, if they want. It can show them that they can take their time and figure things out.

JAN: I think being slow in our own relationship can help us be slow with other queer folks too, you know? All the stuff we have learned here we can share, but in a way that is slow, in a way that can really help. Like I said before, we go to queer events. We are around the community. Maybe as we do our own work in the community, the slowness in our relationship can help us do better and slower work in the community so that we can help others more.

Sylvia and Jan used their own journey to begin to create their systemic intentions, and that is perfectly okay. During this, we practitioners remain as the BIOME, creating a safe space for persons to be as they are. We practice containment so that their definitions of intimacy predominate. This containment is not performative though. It is important that we fundamentally believe in our clients' right to define what feels coherent for them.

Now let's examine a case that is a bit different.

Case 2

In Chapter 5, we met Adrian and Lenora. They are an interracial couple that reside in Portugal. Adrian loathed living there due to his experiences of racism, and when asked about his relational terrain, he said that he felt that he was in quicksand and that his relationship felt like a mountain. We now follow their sojourn to their intentions.

PRACTITIONER: Adrian and Lenora, I'd like you to think about what you would like to see shift in your relationship. Does that feel okay? [*This is an invitation to pivot and turn forward.*]

ADRIAN: It does. What do you think, Lenora?

LENORA: It's fine!

PRACTITIONER: I want to invite you to deeply consider what you have learned about yourselves, your relationship, and the role of the system thus far. What are your thoughts about the way forward for your relationship? Adrian, I recall you saying that your relationship with the world felt like quicksand and with Lenora, it felt like a mountain. Lenora, you said that you can relate to that. I wonder if you want to consider something that is opposite to a mountain or are there any other considerations? [*This is an invitation to imagine. Here, I am also practicing epistemic embracing and a microliberatory movement.*]

LENORA: Hmm. Steady ground!

ADRIAN: Steady, unshakable ground! A plain.

PRACTITIONER: Would you mind sharing what that would look like for your relationship? [*This is an invitation to deepen the imagination. This is also epistemic embracing and a microliberatory movement.*]

LENORA: That's a good question. For me, it feels like keeping our knowledge of who we are here always at the front of our mind.

ADRIAN: What do you mean?

LENORA: What is it about us that makes us special? I think that's what we need to remember. We need to rest our feet on that. That's what makes us steady.

ADRIAN: I get you. The odds were against us when we got together because we were really different.

LENORA: Thinking of the things that make our union strong and resilient, and deciding how we can improve those things will keep us on steady ground.

PRACTITIONER: That makes sense to me. How can I be of support? [*This is epistemic embracing. I am validating and supporting their imagination.*]

ADRIAN: You gotta help us to remember, Akilah. We forget. Help us to remember.

PRACTITIONER: I can do that, and let me ask one more thing. How would you both define healthy intimacy? [*Again, this is epistemic embracing.*]

ADRIAN: Acting out of our strengths. Being deliberate and every day, we gotta remind ourselves what our strengths are. That's what it is for me, I think. This place . . . this system makes me forget.

LENORA: This system makes *us* forget.

ADRIAN: Yup! So figuring out what those strengths are and being real deliberate about how we are gonna show up just like that. That's it there! We don't need anything else.

PRACTITIONER: I want to invite you to think of how this change that you want to make may affect the wider system. The system affects you. I am wondering if you would like to explore how you and your relationship can affect the system. [*I am inviting them to turn forward and set the systemic intention.*]

LENORA: That's a good question. Never thought of that before.

ADRIAN: Hmm. Dignity.

LENORA: How do you mean?

ADRIAN: Well, by making our relationship work, we are showing the world that we each have dignity, you know. White folks don't always treat me with dignity out there, but I feel like if we can have that between us, and represent that to the world, we are putting a different vibration out there—an example for folks to see.

PRACTITIONER: I totally support that.

LENORA: I do too.

As you can see in the two cases above, we can work with our clients in different ways to develop both relational and systemic intentions. It is perfectly okay if our clients do not wish to do any of this, though. We must employ a practice that is liberatory both in content and process. Clients should take their time. For some clients, the process ends at responsible externalizing. I have experienced that, and I have learned that though I may wish to go further, my own self-management and authentic respect for their journey is important.

When clients are willing or ready to move forward, we take them into the next phase: continuous trauma work. We explore this next in Chapter 7.

Practitioner's Reflection

As you think about the experience of responsible externalizing, what are your feelings? Does explicitly naming the system as a cause of relationship challenges give you any angst or concern? How would you facilitate the grieving process in a way that is different from what I have proposed? How would you bring your own ingenuity to that? What are your thoughts on couple therapy also being blended with systemic change? Do you think that partners should be invited to consider systemic intentions? How is this helpful? What may be the challenges here?

CHAPTER RECAP

- Responsible externalizing is the process of clearly attributing relational challenges to the system. It is only done in cases where dynamics can be clearly connected to systemic harm.
- There are three components to responsible externalizing: practitioner externalizing, co-contacting the harm, and grieving.
- While all components of the BIOME are important during this phase, epistemic embracing and microliberatory movements are of extreme importance.
- Practitioners can develop creative ways of executing these components. We should be mindful that clients do not need to do all these components if they do not wish to.

CHAPTER 7

Continuous Trauma Work

In Chapter 1, we noted that two of the signature characteristics of systemic trauma are its chronic and unpredictable nature. This can make it very difficult to treat in therapy. In fact, the word "treat" in the context of systemic trauma may even be an inappropriate and unfair way to label our work with this type of trauma. Our clients are dealing with a form of harm that will continue despite their best efforts. We must be careful not to turn the therapeutic experience into an encounter where clients believe they have to bear the sole burden of fixing themselves to thrive under awful forms of marginalization. It is the system that needs to be fixed. Nonetheless, the impact of the system must be processed through various measures. We look at these measures in this chapter, and seek to answer the following questions:

1. Which components of the BIOME are most useful during this part of the work?
2. Which aspect(s) of the PRIDE model is(are) being employed during trauma work?
3. Is the work one-off or continuous?
4. What is the aim of trauma work when addressing the impact of systemic harm on intimate partner relationships?
5. What are the neurobiological underpinnings of this work?
6. How do we use ourselves in this work?

THE BIOME

While I actually believe that *all* components of the BIOME are helpful during trauma work, I feel safe saying that the trauma interventions listed in this chapter are microliberatory movements that require deep epistemic embracing and intimacy. The interventions present an opportunity for clients to move through the effects of marginalization on their relationships and reclaim their power. Their power is apparent when they define what healing means to *them*. Additionally, some of the techniques used in this chapter directly tap into the client's own sociocultural background. This deepens the client's sense of authenticity and self-worth, two parts of relational privilege that are stripped from them because of constant harm.

THE PRIDE MODEL

As you may recall in Chapter 4, I shared that the PRIDE model is not a sequential process, and perhaps, it is this aspect of the work that best reveals this. Trauma work can be considered rumbling. The clients' relational and systemic intentions (imagination) direct the trauma work. However, this isn't always the case. Some clients may be unable to set intentions or may even be unwilling. In those cases, the trauma work may come much earlier. We are guided by their needs and wants as usual.

Is the Work One-Off or Continuous?

In many cases, this trauma work will be continuous. Because of the enduring nature of systemic trauma, we may do a deep dive into the trauma during one period of time with our clients, and then be required to do a similar dive quite some time after. It can never be fully resolved because the context of systemic trauma will always be alive and present. It is important that we let our clients know that this is normal. Sometimes, our clients can blame themselves when they have not attained contemporary definitions of "healing" or "resolution." In those moments, we can take the relational risks and also practice bravery. We can gently remind them that the system is and remains a problem. Moreover, we can grieve with them around the way that healing looks very different in this type of work.

How Do We Use Ourselves in This Work?

Though we may not be able to fully identify with our clients and their experiences, our challenges and interactions with various systems of power can also be valuable. I distinctly remember one Saturday morning at 8 o'clock when

I contacted my dear cousin, Hayden. I spoke with him while in agony over the ways in which I was being harmed in an institution for which I worked. I felt dismissed, trapped, paralyzed, and powerless. Though I desperately longed for a way out, I knew that none was available to me at the time. I saw no opportunity for fairness and was gripped by pain. It was in the midst of this that Hayden reminded me of the work that I do, and the value of this anguish to my journey with marginalized people. He reinforced the need to metabolize the pain into a sense of self that walks with deeper conviction for the work that I do. He distinctly highlighted the parallels between my own experience and the pain of my clients, positioning me to imagine various ways that I could continue to expand my trauma work with marginalized people. This bolstered my creativity, resolve, and courage.

As usual, I continue to encourage you to tap into your own experiences and unearth your innovative voice in this work. Notice the ways in which systems of oppression feature in your own life. Though they may not be experienced with the same intensity as your clients, they are an indispensable glimpse into the disheartening reality of those who are minoritized.

THE AIM OF TRAUMA WORK

In this work, it is our clients (not us) who define the aim of their trauma intervention using their relational and systemic intentions, if these have been provided. Typically, the work is steered toward undoing the damage done by structural harm. The following questions are a useful guide for you as a practitioner:

- What have the clients learned about themselves from their wider environment that is not true or no longer true in this relationship?
- What have the clients inherited or learned from their ancestors that is not true or no longer true in this relationship?

These are questions that we can also pose to our clients in various imaginative ways to obtain the goals of the work. Remember that the word "goals" should be interpreted with a great deal of flexibility as systemic trauma is long-lasting.

What Are the Neurobiological Underpinnings of This Trauma Work?

Do you recall our discussion about one's "felt sense" of the world in Chapter 2? This felt sense can be referred to as emotional memories or emotional learnings. Emotional memories or learnings include, but are not limited to, our feelings about the world, our relationships, and ourselves. For many of us, it is actually unconscious. These emotional learnings are operating in the implicit memory system of the brain. This system supports us without conscious awareness. We are not consciously thinking about them. Furthermore, no one consciously decides what emotional learnings they have. This is why we can't quite articulate them. We just sense them in our bodies as fundamental truths. According to Ecker et al. (2024), "emotional learnings are learned models" about how the world works (p. 6). These models underlie and drive many behaviors, thoughts, feelings, and sensations that people experience.

When persons consistently endure systemic trauma, they may develop painful emotional learnings about the world and others. They may have a felt sense that all their relationships are unsafe, aggressive, and turbulent. Experiencing systemic trauma can also erect emotional learnings about the self as inadequate and unlovable. These learnings are anchored in the brain through a process called consolidation. Simply put, *consolidation* refers to the process of changing new learnings and memories into long-term learnings and memories that guide one's life.

Can these learnings change? Neuroscience suggests that this may be the case through a process called memory reconsolidation. Memory reconsolidation underlies many of our popular therapeutic models even when the concept itself is not explicitly identified. In many cases, we are doing it without even knowing that we are. How is this so? Well, here we can take a closer look. Memory reconsolidation is not a therapeutic approach or a therapy technique. It is a natural process that allows the implicit memory system to update learning. Many of the knowings we hold are important to hold so we wouldn't want this system to update too easily. For example, this system knows about gravity as well as what is and isn't food. These are the types of learnings we want to keep. Other emotional learnings aren't so great and often were never true, such as learning that you do not deserve love. Sadly, these kinds of learnings are held in the same way, and they update only when certain events coincide. Consider the following steps that must occur for an update to happen:

1. An emotional learning or knowing must be alive in the brain. In other words, the neural network in the brain that holds the emotional learning must be active.
2. A separate and subjectively disconfirming emotional learning must also be active. In other words, *another neural network* that holds information that makes the first knowing practically untrue must also be active.
3. The brain must be regulated enough so that a mismatch between the first emotional learning and the disconfirming bit of knowledge is actually noticed or perceived.
4. When this happens, the first network (as well as the second) enters a state called "network lability." This is a flexible state that makes it possible for the first knowing to change.
5. If during a 4- to 5-hour window new learning is offered to the original emotional knowing, new emotional content is incorporated and the old emotional knowing is replaced by the new emotionally learned information.

Your compassionate presence may contribute to the regulation needed for the mismatch detection to occur. If the client is too activated, memory reconsolidation will not happen. The client must be experiencing *both* activation and regulation. It is important to remember that we do not force mismatches on our clients. We do not compel them to unlearn anything. Some emotional learnings are still helpful for them and we must be extremely mindful and careful. We should not force a healing agenda on them. If a mismatch does not happen, then it is perfectly okay. Additionally, because the mismatch is subjective, it is unlikely that the practitioner would know what would truly disconfirm the knowing.

As we explore the trauma interventions used in this PRIDE model, I show you how these steps are employed. Some of the emotional learnings that our clients have acquired from the system or from their ancestors may not be useful or may even be deleterious to their relationships. We want to support them in unlocking these where possible.

At the time of this writing, there are three techniques that are employed:

1. Intergenerational compassionate network
2. Finding exceptions
3. Relational healing circles

THE INTERGENERATIONAL COMPASSIONATE NETWORK (ICN)

The ICN is an opportunity for the client to turn backward and rumble. During this process, clients are supported through the following steps:

1. Activate the inherited emotional learning.
   – The practitioner supports the client in activating an emotional learning that they have adopted from the ancestor and historical trauma.
2. Adopt a witnessing stance toward the learning using VIMBASI.
   – While activated, the practitioner encourages a witnessing stance from the client. The therapist also shows empathy for the client and the inherited emotional learning during this component.
3. Send compassion toward the ancestor and imagine the ancestor's response.
   – The client is invited to send compassion toward the ancestor and also imagine the response. We can also ask the client if the ancestor has any compassionate offering to make toward them.
4. Capture the mismatch (either highlighted, created, or spontaneous).
   – If possible, the practitioner supports the client to be with a disconfirming emotional learning that may occur during this experience. Usually, we can detect if a mismatch has occurred by the client's facial expression or things that they may say. We may see elements of confusion or surprise. However, these are not the only ways—your own intuition is paramount here. If the practitioner believes they have heard something that could be potentially disconfirming, they could support the mismatch by saying something like "Since the emotional learning you have been carrying is _____ and now the ancestor and you are saying _____, what happens inside your body as you process both of these together?"

- Once the mismatch is captured, the practitioner then juxtaposes this against the initial learning. Continuous toggling between the two learnings is important. At least four repetitions are done.
5. Assess for initial inherited emotional learning.
    - The practitioner should check to see if the initial learning is still perceived to be true at this time or in their relationships with their partner(s).

Now, I will share an example of what this can look like. Do you remember the story of Wajid and Malaika in Chapter 5? They are a Black partnership that resides in America. Malaika was deemed by her husband to be controlling. Through the family narratives exercise, we were able to attribute her behavior to that of her grandmother, who had to do the same to protect her children after her husband's (Malaika's grandfather's) incarceration. Here, we examine how we can use the ICN. Again, I demonstrate how the BIOME is being applied to this process. I also display how the memory reconsolidation steps are being made alive.

The conversation here begins with me highlighting the couple's relational and systemic intentions and presenting the ICN as a trauma modality that can support their intentions.

> **PRACTITIONER:** Malaika and Wajid, you have noted that your relational intention is to have a more egalitarian space where both of you feel heard and have equal power. You also said that you think this will be a great example to other Black relationships. Am I tracking right? [*Here, I am naming the relational and systemic intentions.*]
>
> **MALAIKA:** Yup. I want this for us.
>
> **WAJID:** Me too!
>
> **PRACTITIONER:** Okay. For this intention, I would like to offer you a few techniques to address the traumas you have experienced. Would that be okay? Would it also be okay if we started with Malaika?
>
> **WAJID:** No problem.
>
> **MALAIKA:** I am good with that.

PRACTITIONER: Malaika, if your intentions were to become a reality for you, what would need to shift within you? [*Here, we are connecting the intentions to the trauma work, and obtaining a clear goal for the work.*]

MALAIKA: Well, I'd like to feel that I don't have to run things all the time. I need a break, and from what I am hearing, so does Wajid.

PRACTITIONER: Okay, Malaika, I would like to invite you into a process called the intergenerational compassionate network where we can gently take a look at the learning that is possibly driving your behavior. As we look at it, we will see what emerges and build a network of compassion around what materializes. Sometimes, a mismatch may occur. A mismatch happens when another or second learning emerges. For it to be a mismatch, we must see that the two learnings cannot be true at the same time. If this happens, we can pause and be with that. Is that okay with you? [*Here we are practicing openness and demystifying the process. We are helping the client to understand what we are about to do, which is also a microliberatory movement.*]

MALAIKA: It is. Once I can stop, I'm good.

PRACTITIONER: Yes, you can. Malaika, I have heard you say, "If you don't take charge, you will lose your family!" I want you to feel into that. Visualize what that looks like. See yourself not taking charge and the consequences of that. Let the truth of those consequences fill you up. [*Here I am restating what she said in order to activate the emotional learning.*]

MALAIKA: Yes, you will!

PRACTITIONER: As you say that, I'd like you to be with or say the statement again and notice how you feel or what images come up. You can also consider what other thoughts or memories come up. The statement is "If you don't take charge, you will lose your family!" [*Here, I am trying to increase the activation a bit. I am also using VIMBASI.*]

MALAIKA: I see my grandmother, but . . .

PRACTITIONER: But?

MALAIKA: I also see a scared mother slave.

PRACTITIONER: Can you say more about this? [*Here, I am encouraging the client to deepen the witnessing stance.*]

MALAIKA: I see a scared mother slave, pulling her children and grabbing them close to her because she feels this is the only way she can protect them. I feel heat in my body as I see her.

PRACTITIONER: Thank you for sharing this with me. This makes sense. I can understand why she is scared and I can also see how you can feel just having to hold all this. You are holding her fear, too. Which part of these do you want to be with? Do you want to be with the scared mother slave or the heat? [*Here, I am showing empathy for her and for the image that has been activated. An attempt is also being made to focus on one of the elements of VIMBASI.*]

MALAIKA: I feel the need to be with the scared mother slave. She is the source of the heat.

PRACTITIONER: I get it. Can we offer compassion toward her? If that feels comfortable for you, what would compassion look like here? [*Here, I am inviting the client to send compassion as noted in Step 3 of the ICN.*]

MALAIKA: Honestly, I feel like I just want to give her a big hug and let her know that I get it, you know? I just get it. She looks terrified out of her mind, and I want her to know that I get it.

PRACTITIONER: I understand. Let's give that to her then. I'm going to pause and give you a moment to do this and you can let me know when you have finished. You can say it aloud or quietly if you wish.

MALAIKA: I have done it.

PRACTITIONER: Let's be with her. Is there anything she wants you to know? I wonder if there is anything that she has to offer that may be compassionate as well. Let's ask her if there is. [*This is a continuation of Step 3, where we are examining for a response.*]

MALAIKA: I just feel kindness from her. I can't find words for it but I feel kindness.

PRACTITIONER: Ah. Take that in. Take in the kindness.

MALAIKA: I am.

PRACTITIONER: As she is looking on, what is she seeing? What are her thoughts on your relationship with Wajid? Does she think that you need to do what she did? [*This is an implementation of Step 4, where I am checking for a potential mismatch. We are assessing to see if a different emotional learning may emerge. This is not a forced process, and it is perfectly okay if there is none.*]

MALAIKA: She is seeing the ways in which we are still being hurt, you know? It is hard to not want to protect.

PRACTITIONER: Yes. She is right. As she looks on, is there anything different between her time and now? [*Again, I am slowly assessing for a mismatch.*]

MALAIKA: Well, to be honest, she thinks that I still need to take charge, but not as much.

PRACTITIONER: Hmm. How would she say that if she were to put that in words? What does she think about you being in charge and losing your family? [*I am trying to have her articulate the words attached to this other emotional learning, which may or may not be different from the initial learning. I am still taking my time to determine whether there is a true mismatch.*]

MALAIKA: She says, "If you let go sometimes, you won't lose your family."

PRACTITIONER: How does it feel to hear? How does it feel in your body? [*I am checking to see if it feels different in the body. This helps me to ascertain if it is indeed a mismatch.*]

MALAIKA: It feels strange, you know? It feels very different. I am surprised that she would say that. [*This sense of surprise suggests that a mismatch has probably occurred. If this is so, the initial learning is labile and open to change. With this assumption, I now invite the client to move back and forth between the two statements with a minimum of four repetitions.*]

PRACTITIONER: Hmm. I'd like to invite you to move between these two statements with me. You can say, "If you let go sometimes, you won't lose your family" and then pause for 5 seconds and say, "If you don't take charge, you will lose your family!" [*Malaika moves through this process with me. She moves back and forth between the two statements seven times. The minimum is four, and I followed my gut to use seven repetitions. At the end of this, I check in to assess her relationship with the two learnings.*]

PRACTITIONER: I'd like to check in with you now just to see how you feel. Can you say, "If you don't take charge, you will lose your family!" and let me know how it feels to say it?

MALAIKA: Ha! I feel pretty cool saying it, but that's a good thing. It seems so far away now. Like something that someone else believes and not me.

As you can see above, the sense that she needed to be in charge seemed less believable to Malaika than it did before the process. Is this always the case? No. There are a few reasons why it may be difficult in some cases to achieve this outcome. Consider the following reasons below:

1. When supporting the client through the process, the client may either become too overwhelmed by their emotions and sensations, or they may be too calm. In order for this process to be fruitful, there must be an adequate amount of activation and regulation.
2. We may not have truly found a mismatch. Though two emotional learnings may appear to the practitioner as a mismatch, the reality is that it must be experienced as a mismatch by the client's system. This is a subjective process.
3. Sometimes, the client is not able to find a disconfirming learning because the initial learning continues to feel true, or is in fact, true. When this happens, we trust the client's system and continue to work on supporting the mutual flow of compassion.

Nurturing Your Creativity

As you use the ICN in your work, you can consider incorporating different creative techniques to aid your exploration. Let's look at some examples:

1. *Ancestral art creation*: You can ask your clients to develop a piece of art that signifies their ancestors and the stories they hold. This can help

your clients visualize the emotional learnings that have been passed down from generation to generation. Painting, drawing, or collaging can be used here.
2. *Generational story mapping*: Clients can create a visual map of their family's history. On these maps, they can highlight significant events, traumatic incidents, and moments of resilience. This can assist them in noticing or detecting specific emotional learnings.
3. *Compassionate letters*: You can prompt clients to write letters to their ancestors in which they express compassion for the traumas they endured. In these letters, clients can also acknowledge how these experiences have shaped their own lives.
4. *Embodied movement*: Clients can engage in movement exercises where they physically express the feelings tied to the experiences of their ancestors.

FINDING EXCEPTIONS

In clinical work, exceptions often refer to the moments where the challenges that have brought our clients to therapy in the first place are either not present or less intense. In the PRIDE model, we can assist clients in determining the emotional learnings they have gained from the system and finding exceptions within their relationships when these same learnings are not true. We help them to reflect on experiences with their partners that are in direct contrast to these learnings. Sometimes, these moments of exception are even alive in the therapy room, and when they are, we emphasize them to our clients. The steps utilized in this process are quite similar to what is employed in the ICN. See the steps that follow:

1. *Activate the inherited emotional learning*: The practitioner supports the client in activating an emotional learning that they believe has been inherited or learned from the wider system.
2. *Adopt a witnessing stance toward the learning using VIMBASI*: While activated, the practitioner encourages a witnessing stance from the client. The therapist also shows empathy for the client and the inherited emotional learning during this component.

3. *Send compassion toward the learning*: The client is invited to send compassion toward the emotional learning and the ways it has manifested into the elements of VIMBASI.
4. *Capture the mismatch (either highlighted, created, or spontaneous)*: If possible, the practitioner supports the client in being with a disconfirming emotional learning that has come from moments of exception within the relationship. Sometimes, the moment of exception is apparent even within the session. The practitioner then juxtaposes this against the initial learning. Continuous toggling between the two learnings is important. At least four repetitions are done.
5. *Assess for initial emotional learning*: The practitioner should check to see if the initial learning is still perceived to be true.

We now reflect on an example in order to reinforce your understanding of this technique. We refer to the case of Millie, Amanda, and Kes. They are a throuple that was discussed in Chapter 5. While engaging in relational curiosity, Millie stated, "Nobody really wants a tranny around." As we explored further, we realized that this was a deep emotional learning that she held due to the rejection she felt from the wider system. As we proceeded into trauma work, the partners set relational and systemic intentions. They then agreed that we would address Millie's concerns first. When asked about the goals of the trauma work, Mille divulged: "I just want to feel like I am welcomed here with Amanda and Kes." In the excerpt below, we located exceptions and supported a process of memory reconsolidation.

> **PRACTITIONER:** Mille, it is so unfair that you live in a world that tells you "Nobody wants a tranny around." Every part of my being knows that this is not right. [*Here, I am leaning into the BIOME and taking a relational risk.*]
>
> **MILLIE:** It does feel very unfair. I can't stand it.
>
> **PRACTITIONER:** I'd like to invite you to say the statement, "Nobody wants a tranny around," and when you do so, I want to ask you if you can tell me any vibrations, thoughts, feelings, memories, impulses, or images that come up for you. [*I am inviting her into the rumbling process*

and using VIMBASI. Here I am also supporting the client in activating the emotional learning.]

MILLIE: Hmm, I have a memory of literally being in a moment where I walked into a gathering of folks. It was at a function and I was fully dressed just as I am now, and someone literally said that to me: "Nobody wants a tranny around." I felt so gutted. I can hear the guy who said it as plain as day.

PRACTITIONER: Oh. That is painful. As you say it, I too feel gutted. There is also a heaviness in my chest. [*Again, I am taking a relational risk and sharing empathy, which helps to regulate the client while she is activated. If she is too activated, memory reconsolidation will not occur. There is a need for balance.*]

MILLIE: Thank you!

PRACTITIONER: I'd like to invite you to notice this moment right here. You are here with Amanda and Kes. They have come with you to therapy, and when you all set your relational intentions, they said that they want to build a closer bond with you. [*Here, I am slowly assessing to see if the present moment is a moment of exception. It is important to note here that it is Millie, not me, who needs to perceive it as an exception.*]

MILLIE (*smiling*): Yes, they did.

PRACTITIONER: Do you believe that in this moment right here they want you around? Before you answer, I want you to take your time. Feel into the moment and all that they said and see if it feels that way for you. [*Again, I am assessing for a moment of exception and a possible mismatch. The process is deliberately slow.*]

MILLIE (*thinking deeply and looking at them*): They do want me around. They want a tranny around. [*Millie begins to smile here, and it is possible that we have captured a mismatch.*]

PRACTITIONER: Hmm. I'd like to invite you to move between two images for me. The image of the moment when you were told that nobody wants a tranny around, and this moment when you know that these two people want you around. Is that okay?

MILLIE: Yes, it is. [*Millie enters the process with me, and she moves back and forth between the two images six times. My intuition told me to use six repetitions. At the end of this, I check in to assess her relationship with the two learnings.*]

PRACTITIONER: Millie, I'd like to check in. When I say, "Nobody wants a tranny around," how does it land for you?

MILLIE (*thinking*): Hmm. Well, some people don't want a tranny around and some people do. Some people do.

PRACTITIONER: These people do. [*I am stating this gently to assess if she agrees.*]

MILLIE: Yes, they do.

Millie's ability to note that her partners wished for her to be around suggests that a new learning had emerged. She realized that the system may not want her, but her partners certainly do. As I shared previously, there are other ways that a mismatch could have been acquired. We could have requested that Millie reflect on past moments when she felt that she was wanted, and then assess for any of the elements of VIMBASI during her reflection. After this, we would have then toggled between the VIMBASI element connected to the past moment of feeling wanted and the VIMBASI element connected to her horrible experience at the function. For example, if Millie noted that she felt a light flutter in her chest when thinking about feeling wanted, and a heaviness in her stomach when thinking about feeling unwanted, we would move between these two sensations. Going slowly to establish that we have gotten a mismatch is critical. Remember that it is the client (not the practitioner) who must sense something different. If it is not experienced as a mismatch by the client within a context of activation and regulation, reconsolidation will not occur.

Nurturing Your Creativity

Remember that your ingenuity is a potent force in the therapeutic environment. You have so much to offer. From your own insight and past training, you can offer clients other ways to find exceptions. Let's view some suggestions here:

1. *Exception journals*: You can encourage your clients to keep a dedicated journal where they write moments that their emotional learnings are not true.
2. *Visual representations*: Clients can be invited to develop a visual representation, such as a drawing or collage, that demonstrates moments of exception.
3. *Mind mapping*: This is a personal favorite of mine. Clients can create a mind map that connects their emotional learnings to specific exceptions that they have encountered in their relationships. This tool can assist them in seeing the relationship between their own understanding and their current realities (exceptions). Viewing these contrasts can be quite powerful.
4. *Role-playing scenarios*: As a practitioner, you can ask clients to role-play moments of exception. This can permit them to embody the emotions connected to these moments. By immersing themselves in these scenes, they can deepen their connection to these experiences.

RELATIONAL HEALING CIRCLES

Relational healing circles are therapy treatment groups for couples that hold marginalized statuses. We can facilitate these groups with a maximum of four partnerships to ensure that persons are given the attention and consideration they need. These groups are designed to help couples move through the impact of systemic trauma using mutual aid dynamics (Shulman, 2009) as well as the memory reconsolidation principles. Below is a list of some mutual aid dynamics that are effective in this setting. Later in this section, via a step-by-step guide, we examine how to utilize these dynamics.

1. Sharing Data

Though these groups are facilitated by a practitioner, much of the wisdom that is used emerges from the group members themselves. Marginalized couples are pools of insight, and we need to harness their strengths. In order to set this in motion, during the group's orientation, the practitioner should encourage members to contribute their thoughts with one another on ways in which they can work through systemic trauma. During the sessions, the practitioner should actively solicit perspectives from members of the group. Participants can share their knowledge and even past experiences.

We can also encourage participants to share useful cultural wisdom and central cultural beliefs. Various cultural sayings and lessons can assist couples in overcoming the impact of systemic trauma on their relationships. In the Latinx community, these profound cultural nuggets are known as "dichos." *Dichos* impart life lessons via brief stories, concepts, and reflections (Flores-Torres & Ramirez, 2006; Zuniga, 1991). They also provide "subversive strategies" in the form of "adaptive responses to oppression, colonization, and internalized oppression" (Comas-Díaz, 2006, p. 444). I recall working with a Trinidadian woman who employed one of these strategies when dealing with systemic trauma. She noted:

> *In my mother's Trinidadian culture, there's something called picong, a unique style of humor filled with wit and sarcasm. My mother would talk about the struggles of growing up Black in Trinidad right before independence. She spoke about racism and the Black Power Revolution. As she and her friends moved through the struggles of the time, their picong kept them going. That picong is often heard in Trinidadian calypso music. It's a form of resistance and survival. I've used it when I felt overwhelmed. It's kept me sane.* (Riley-Richardson, 2023, p. 57)

Within the LGBTQIA+ community, there are also powerful cultural sayings that have been found to be helpful in this work. For example, "We're here. We're queer" is a common pride quote that subverts the widely held belief that LGBTQIA+ should not occupy space in the world.

Allowing our participants to tap into and share these strategies is a microliberatory movement. We are shifting some much-needed power to them. The group should never feel compelled to defer to our viewpoints, but instead see one another and their culture as a hub of rich understanding.

2. Discussing a Taboo Area

Generally, therapeutic groups give their members the opportunity to deliberate over issues that are rarely discussed. In Chapter 1, emphasis was placed on the disenfranchised and invisibilized nature of systemic trauma. It is often dismissed by those who hold systemic power and privilege. As such, it can be considered a taboo issue, and relational healing circles accord marginalized couples a moment to process this type of trauma in a safe space. This is significant as the world, and quite frankly, the field of psychotherapy, does not always create adequate room for discussions of this nature. Discussing taboo issues helps persons know that they are not alone, and this is truly comforting for structurally minoritized communities.

3. All-in-the-Same-Boat Phenomenon

> *Discovering that feelings are shared by other members of the group can often help release a group member from their power. Guilt over "evil" thoughts and feelings can be lessened and self-destructive cycles broken when one discovers they are normal and shared by others.*
> —SHULMAN (2009, P. 289)

Do you recall our discussion on social baseline theory in Chapter 3? We noted that human beings can be one another's biome. When we are in safe relationships, there is less activation in the parts of the brain associated with threat. Relational healing circles can serve as a biome for its members. When persons feel seen by other members of the group, their sense of aloneness eases and there is a deep experience of safety.

4. The Dialectical Process

It is valuable to be in an environment where experiences and viewpoints can also be challenged when necessary. This is the essence of the dialectical process. As practitioners, we can foster this dynamic by letting our group participants know that healthy debate of different perspectives is encouraged. During these debates, which are facilitated in an atmosphere of mutual respect and compassion, participants may experience a mismatch between deeply held emotional learnings and newly internalized perspectives from the group. As you recall from our earlier discussion on memory reconsolidation, these mismatches can allow painful emotional learnings from the wider system to be transformed.

It is very important for us as practitioners to pay close attention to the moments when these emotional learnings are challenged by other group members. When this occurs, we should pause the moment, assess to see if the member experiences the new information as a mismatch, and highlight it. We can even have people toggle between their original learnings and the new perspectives that are being offered.

Now that we have considered the mutual aid dynamics, let's explore some more in-depth guidance on how to move through a relational healing circle. If you decide to host a relational healing circle, consider the following steps that may be helpful to the process:

1. Before establishing your group, it is productive to determine the number of sessions and their lengths. I would advise approximately eight 2-hour sessions. However, you are free to consider other durations and frequencies.
2. Orient persons to the purpose of the group. Educate about systemic trauma and its impact on couples by teaching about the concept of relational privilege.
3. Educate the group about the BIOME and have the group discuss ways in which they can foster the spirit of the BIOME for one another.
4. Share about the notions of pivoting, rumbling, and imagining. Explain to the group how you will be facilitating those three components.
5. Employ some of the strategies within relational curiosity (Chapter 5) to assist members in assessing the impact of systemic trauma on their relationships. You can use innovative methods to enact these.
6. Support members in creating relational intentions and systemic intentions (Chapter 6).
7. Have the group revisit the impact on their relationships. Guide them in exploring emotional learnings from this impact.
8. Use the mutual aid dynamics listed above to build a balanced context where the learnings can be activated via the use of VIMBASI as clients experience regulation from other group members. Regulation can be achieved by the group's support, compassion, and normalization. The all-in-the-same-boat phenomenon and the ability to discuss a taboo area foster these components. Be sure to amplify the compassion and care that the group provides while helping clients activate the learning.
9. Pay close attention to the offerings that other members give while discussing the emotional learning under consideration. Amplify different perspectives, especially those that come from the culture of the

marginalized couple. Sometimes, these diverse perspectives may be mismatches to the learnings they hold in their bodies. Even if they are not, helpful cultural wisdom should always be emphasized.
10. Assess to determine whether any of the perspectives are truly a mismatch.
11. Where possible, have persons toggle between their own initial learnings and offerings from the group.
12. Highlight any new learnings that evolve and have the group reflect collectively.

Nurturing Your Creativity

Though I have listed distinct steps, you can certainly structure your group in a way that is in alignment with your personal style. Getting to know your group and tapping into their pace, interest, and personalities can help you determine what methodologies are most useful. Remember that the group holds a lot of experience, wisdom, and insight.

Practitioner's Reflection

What are your feelings and thoughts about doing this type of trauma work? As you sit with the techniques proposed, I welcome you to use VIMBASI to notice what is stirring within you. Is there disquiet within you? Is there calmness? At what points of the work do you feel shifts in your nervous system? Notice the tough and seamless points. They hold handy data for you as you journey through this work.

CHAPTER RECAP

- ICN, finding exceptions, and relational healing circles are three approaches that can be used to facilitate trauma work.
- The goals of the trauma work are tied to the clients' relational and systemic intentions.
- For each of these approaches, we apply the tenets of memory reconsolidation.
- For memory reconsolidation to take place, we must enable a context of both activation of emotional learning and regulation.
- We may need to do trauma work at different stages of the work as systemic trauma is continuous.

CHAPTER 8

Building Liberatory Connections

Committed partnerships are ecosystems that are designed to force both people up against themselves and each other, over and over, day after day. Both partners get ground together in the same way that a rock gets polished into a jewel. Over and over, you and your partner have a choice: you can polish each other into jewels or you can grind each other to dust.
                    —Menakem (2023, p. 4)

Relationships are profoundly meaningful and potent crucibles for personal and social change. The connections formed here can transform the individuals, but also enact broader societal shifts. After supporting our clients through the process of responsible externalizing and continuous trauma work, it is imperative that we help them connect to their relational and systemic intentions and begin the process of building liberatory connections. This helps clients thrive amid adversities and reclaim the narratives they hold about their relationships.

I define *liberatory connections* as sites where both relational and social change converge. These are connections that directly address the impact of systemic trauma by cultivating a context where the couple can still survive, or possibly even grow, despite the weight of systemic trauma. Liberatory connections are hubs of joy and reimagination. It is the opportunity for partners to create something new for their relationships. As we delve further into liberatory connections, consider the following questions:

1. Which components of the BIOME are most useful during this part of the work?
2. Which aspects of the PRIDE model are being employed during this part of the process?
3. What are the neurobiological underpinnings of this work?
4. How do we connect this part of the work to the partners' relational and systemic intentions?

THE BIOME

When you don't have community, you are not listened to; you don't have a place you can go to and feel that you really belong. You don't have people to affirm who you are and to support you in bringing forward your gifts. This disempowers the psyche. . . . Also, it leaves many people who have wonderful contributions to make holding back their gifts, not knowing where to put them. And without the unloading of our gifts we experience a blockage inside, which affects us spiritually, mentally, and physically in many different ways. We are left without a home to go to when we need to be seen. (Somé, 1997, pp. 22–23)

During this phase, partners are supported to erect connections that feel enriching and emancipatory. As a result, the practitioner's presence is a pivotal force. It is the essence of who we are and our firm belief in their right to liberation and agency that become important. Their relationships evolve through their connections with us, and the way we engage them is a potent catalyst for change. Once again, metabolizing microliberatory movements and epistemic embracing is fundamental here. The techniques in this phase are designed to restore agency, wellness, and creativity. Clients must experience their power, assets, and strengths.

THE PRIDE MODEL

Building liberatory connections requires imagination, development, and evolution. Clients are invited to ponder what they would like to create for their relationships and to carve explicit steps for these to come to fruition. After they complete this process, they are asked the question "Now that you have done this, who are you now?" This question is important for two reasons. Marginalized persons require, and quite frankly deserve, the space to decidedly reclaim their identities in the world. In a world that brutally strips them of the ability to live in their own truth, having a clinician who supports the reclamation of selfhood in this way can be a profound encounter. As we noted in Chapter 2, it is also a requirement for building and preserving healthy interpersonal relationships. Second, having a strong sense of identity is a protective factor against discrimination (Trail et al., 2012). Later in this chapter we probe this idea even more.

What Are the Neurobiological Underpinnings of This Component?

Do you recall our discussion on the window of tolerance, the parasympathetic nervous system (PNS), and the sympathetic nervous system (SNS) in Chapter 1? As we discussed before, the PNS manages the body's rest and relaxation mechanisms. A hyperactive SNS signifies that the body is in survival mode, a common reality for marginalized persons. Well, after undergoing trauma work, our clients' neurobiological potential to develop new possibilities for their partnerships increases. This is because trauma work permits greater access to the PNS state, which promotes emotional regulation and an expanded capacity for creativity. We can use the concept of the window of tolerance for deeper insight. Being in one's window of tolerance permits reflective thinking and problem solving. There is greater space for higher-order thinking and decision making.

RELATIONAL AND SYSTEMIC INTENTIONS

Continuity in therapeutic work is paramount when supporting marginalized couples in creating liberatory connections. Before implementing techniques, we must remind clients of their relational and systemic intentions, as these intentions serve as foundational anchors throughout their journey. By ensuring that there is alignment, practitioners can ensure that the strategies reinforce the client's dreams for themselves. Moreover, concluding the process with a reflection on these intentions is critical. This helps them develop a sense of accountability to themselves and deep purpose. This cyclical approach of reaffirmation and reflection is instrumental to their path.

Now, let's explore the various techniques that we can use to help our clients build these liberatory connections. They are as follows:

1. Identity and relational cherishing
2. Individual and relational resilience
3. Relational declarations
4. Decolonizing the relationship
5. Boundary work

Let's take a look at each of these. I am eager to explore this using our usual format. We discuss the technique and then delve into a case example, highlighting the elements of the BIOME and PRIDE model that are being discussed.

IDENTITY AND RELATIONAL CHERISHING

> *through my tears i found god in myself*
> *and i loved her fiercely*
> —Ntozake Shange

Sitting in the depths of who we are, and cherishing every crevice and contour of our multifaceted identity is an immense gift. Being intimately aware of the value of one's racial, gender, and sexual identity is valuable to one's personal well-being and the well-being of one's relationships (Dennis, 2022; Hughes et al., 2015; Osmetti & Allen, 2024; Trail et al., 2012). As practitioners, we have a phenomenal opportunity to support our clients with the discovery of this gift. We can create a space for them to experience themselves in beautiful, yet previously unimagined ways. During the process of identity and relational cherishing, clients are permitted to cultivate a space where they can deeply witness the beauty of their identities and their unique relationships. This exploration is centered on an understanding that their identities and partnerships are like no other. As such, they are worthy of pause and celebration. They deserve to be cherished, especially under the relentless assault of the system. During the process of identity and relational cherishing, our clients can enlarge their narratives about who they are in the world and even see new relational possibilities.

We can support clients through this with the following questions:

1. When you reflect on your racial identity, gender identity, or sexual orientation, what is there to be cherished in this identity?
2. Reflect on the unique elements of your relationship that exist because of the identities you just mentioned. What is there to be cherished in your relationship?
3. What is the unexplored privilege that sits in your identity and this relationship?
4. What boundaries are needed to protect what is cherished?
5. From this exploration, what are you liberating yourselves from?
6. Now that we have had this conversation, who are you now? What do you believe you have the potential to become?
7. How is this connected to your relational and systemic intentions?

Case 1

Together, we explore these questions in the upcoming case. In Chapters 5 and 7, we followed the narrative of Millie, Amanda, and Kes, who are a trans throuple. Millie struggled with a sense of worth in the relationship and she felt that nobody in the world truly wanted to be in the presence of trans women. Nonetheless, after being encouraged to find exceptions for this narrative, she successfully noted that this is not the truth in all cases. Her partners desired and valued her. Let us explore how identity and relational cherishing are used in this context.

> **PRACTITIONER:** Millie, Amanda, and Kes, I remember that you noted for your relational and systemic intentions that you wanted joy. You wanted joy for yourself and joy for the community. I would love you to think about your unique identities as persons of trans experience and the ways in which it shapes your world. What do you cherish about these identities? [*Here, we are encouraging epistemic embracing. This is also a microliberatory movement. A discussion of their own power reinforces the experience of it.*]
>
> **MILLIE:** Well, I do like the perspective it gives me in life. I think I have the value of perspective. I would not be happy if I were cisgender. That experience is so 2D [two-dimensional]. I am in the 3D experience. There is no box for me. It is freeing. I like being not masculine. I like that I am not. I like my ways of being feminine in my own way. Yes, it has its drawbacks, but I like that I get to be creative about how I want

to show up. Interestingly, I think I also embraced my marginalization. It has given me empathy. This is empathy that I would never have had if I didn't have the experience of being ostracized.

PRACTITIONER: Ah, yes. I can see that, and I can agree. You have learned so much from being in and occupying your body. [*Here, I am reinforcing epistemic embracing.*]

AMANDA: You know what I have also realized? I experience that my transness is never static. I feel very much nonbinary. I won't be stuck in binaries. Because of this, I am open to other things in relationships and in life that other people won't be open to. I am so accommodating of changes in life because I am accommodating of myself, my body, and the way it changes.

PRACTITIONER: I see this. I can feel into this.

KES: I agree with them.

PRACTITIONER: This is powerful. Would each of you like to consider what you most cherish about your relationships? What are the unique features of your love as a trans partnership that you hold dear?

AMANDA: Well, I would say supporting your partner when they are transitioning. It was tough but that's a very special experience.

MILLIE: For sure, those were some rough times. The side effects of the hormone therapy weren't easy but having them with me led to some very special moments. We would also talk a whole lot and that really connected us. You never forget having a person with you during that time.

KES: You also never forget how special it is to have a space where persons affirm you all the time. Here is my safe space, and it's my affirming space. It also feels good to know I can change here, and it will still be home.

PRACTITIONER: Ah! Thanks so much for sharing. It is so important for you to note the very special characteristics of your love! It is unique in its own way and unlike other relationships. Remembering that is so valuable. What do you think you need to do to nurture the characteristics that you cherish? [*Here, I am practicing epistemic embracing and we are also in the development component of the PRIDE model.*]

MILLIE: Those conversations. Those conversations.

PRACTITIONER: Do you want to say more?

MILLIE: The gender-affirming convos we would have were so powerful. This space was my cheerleading club throughout my transition. In fact, we have always been one another's cheerleaders. We made each other feel so sexy and fluid. We need more of those.

KES (*jokingly*): We talk a lot already.

MILLIE (*smiling*): We do.

AMANDA: Maybe we can do weekly letters to one another, just reminding ourselves why we are so special, you know? We can give it to each other every week.

KES (*smiling*): Maybe every other week.

MILLIE (*laughing*): I can do it every other week.

PRACTITIONER: Now, as you consider these cherished aspects, what boundaries do you think are needed to protect what is valuable to you in your relationship?

MILLIE: I think one boundary we need is to ensure that we always have time for those affirming conversations. Life shouldn't get in the way of us creating that safe space to talk.

AMANDA: Absolutely, Millie. Also, I believe we should set boundaries around how we deal with this outside negativity. If someone makes a disgusting comment about who we are, we need to agree on how we will protect each other from that. We can't let that stuff in.

KES: I agree with both of you. I think we also need to establish boundaries with each other. It may sound weird, but we need it. Sometimes when one of us is feeling low, the other person gets too emotional and takes in the heavy feeling. That ain't good. We need to be there for each other, but not in that destructive way.

MILLIE: Yes! It's important that we recognize when to step back and not feel guilty about that.

AMANDA: That way, we can remain strong as a group.

PRACTITIONER: That sounds really nourishing. It sounds beautiful. By having this conversation, what do you believe you are liberating yourselves from?

MILLIE: Hmm. For me, it's not just this conversation. It's the whole thing. I don't feel like I am the problem anymore. I am liberating myself from that.

AMANDA: I feel really good witnessing us feeling worthy, you know? It hurt my heart to know that Millie didn't feel loved, or well, as you are saying now, cherished. I think it's freeing for all of us to witness her feel like she could be cherished.

KES: That I can definitely agree to.

PRACTITIONER: This is quite powerful to witness. Thanks for being so brave and bold to say this. Now that you have had this conversation, who do you believe you are now? What do you believe you have the potential to become? [*Here we are practicing the evolve piece.*]

AMANDA: Well, I don't quite know who we are but I believe we are becoming fierce.

PRACTITIONER: I'd love to hear more.

AMANDA: Well, my body feels stronger after this conversation for some reason.

KES: I think we are now grounded, grounded in who we are. My feet feel more anchored. I think our relationship is more anchored.

MILLIE: I need to think some more, but I can definitely feel a shift.

PRACTITIONER: How does this connect to your relational and systemic intentions?

MILLIE: It so does. The shift is taking me to joy and I can see us sending that into the world.

AMANDA: Fierce joy!

KES: Yes, Amanda! Fierce joy!

Feeling cherished can significantly enhance one's emotional well-being and foster deeper connections with others. It cultivates a sense of worth and belonging, which are fundamental human needs. Making a firm decision to foster this for marginalized people can be considered our professional obligation. We are stepping in to support their journey to deeper self-acceptance, a feature of relational privilege in the world.

Nurturing Your Creativity

Countless opportunities for your imagination abound in this space. Here are some options that you can consider:

1. *Identity collages*: Couples can build a collage that represents the richness of their identities.
2. *Cherishing letters*: You can request that partners write wholehearted letters to each other. These letters indicate what they cherish about each other and their relationship.
3. *Affirmation jar*: Practitioners can support clients in creating an affirmation jar where each person can write compliments about the other and place them in the jar. Partners can read these affirmations together at specific times of their choosing.
4. *Celebration rituals*: Partners can be encouraged to develop rituals that celebrate their unique identities and milestones in their relationship. For instance, they can dedicate time to practice these rituals.
5. *Storytelling sessions*: As a practitioner, you can organize storytelling sessions, where each partner shares an individual journey that is connected to their identities.
6. *Conversations under the stars*: Partners can be encouraged to have regular outdoor conversations under the stars. During these conversations, they can reflect on their identities and what they value most about their relationship.
7. *Identity hearts*: You can ask your clients to create tiny hearts and detail the things they cherish about themselves there.

INDIVIDUAL AND RELATIONAL RESILIENCE

This body is resilient. It can endure all kinds of things. My body offers me the power of presence. My body is powerful.

—Roxane Gay,
Hunger: A Memoir of (My) Body

Resilience has been long understood as a necessary and crucial contributor to the well-being of both LGBTQIA+ and BIPOC individuals and couples. It can be defined as the ability to recover from hardship. This capacity is bolstered by protective factors, such as one's mindset, external support, and coping methods.

There are so many ways in which marginalized people utilize protective factors that exist within themselves and their environments to maintain their well-being under extremely burdensome circumstances. However, they often overlook how powerfully they are showing up against the odds to care for themselves. We need to slow them down so they can witness these factors. As practitioners, we must support them in exploring both their individual and relational resilience. For marginalized people, I define *individual and relational resilience* as the unique protective factors that are *specific* to their realities and their relationship forms. The following questions that I typically pose on this topic may support your understanding of this in greater detail:

1. What are the unique protective factors that your relationship form provides to you?
2. What are the building blocks you must implement to foster individual and relational resilience?
3. What are you liberating yourself from by reflecting on your resilience?
4. Now that you have had this conversation, who are you now? What or who are you becoming?
5. How is this connected to your relational and systemic intentions?

By reflecting on these questions, marginalized couples can cultivate a stronger sense of resilience, empowering them to navigate their unique challenges and build stronger connections. Let's explore what this can look like by revisiting the case of Roxanne and Thianna. They are the same-sex couple we met in Chapter

5. They had been in a cohabitational relationship for 20 years and Roxanne struggled to connect with her partner due to rampant homophobia. She defined her reality as the "tide of torment," and felt that she was deformed and should be hidden away. They were able to successfully externalize the harm as the source of challenges in their partnership. In the dialogue below, you will see the ways in which individual and relational resilience is discussed and encouraged.

Case 2

> PRACTITIONER: I remember that you said you wanted a deeper sense of safety. That was your relational intention. You said that you had not thought much about systemic intentions, which is perfectly fine. What would you say are the unique protective factors of each of you and your relationship form that help you deal with all that is coming at you? Please take your time. [*Here, we are encouraging epistemic embracing. This is also a microliberatory movement. A discussion of their own power reinforces the experience of it.*]
>
> ROXANNE: Certain things that just naturally accrue to cishet [cisgender heterosexual] couples don't accrue to us. There is no real recognition of our love. The system doesn't recognize it so there is no financial safety or real physical safety. Because of that, we have to put a lot of effort into maintaining our relationship. We gotta do the work to keep each other connected because the system is against us.
>
> PRACTITIONER: Ah, can you say more about this? Thianna, do you want to weigh in?
>
> THIANNA: That's fine. I have realized that we have to be more deliberate and intentional than other couples to connect. We can't miss a moment because it doesn't come easily to us. We always have to find moments to validate our relationship and that builds us up.
>
> PRACTITIONER: I get this. This makes sense to me. [*As I validate their feelings, I am practicing epistemic embracing.*]
>
> THIANNA: I want to say that having to validate so often makes you stronger, and in some ways, it can make our relationship stronger. Because I had to fight for us to be seen, it has made me stronger.

ROXANNE: Yup!

PRACTITIONER: Ah. I see you. So it seems that there is both relational and individual resilience. I wonder how we can be intentional about continuing to build this here. What needs to be done here? [*In addition to practicing epistemic embracing, I am also using the development step in the PRIDE model.*]

ROXANNE: That's a good question. I'm stumped, though.

THIANNA: I am not. I know we validate our relationship, but we kinda do it naturally. Maybe we can make agreements, you know?

ROXANNE: Agreements?

PRACTITIONER: I think I understand. Go on.

THIANNA: Like we can discuss this resilience thing some more, and think about what makes us be resilient, and actively plan to do those things. In that way, when we do it, we know that we are doing it.

PRACTITIONER: Ah yes. You are paying attention to actively constructing what supports your relationship. [*Here, we are deepening the epistemic embracing and supporting their development of what works for them.*]

THIANNA: Indeed!

PRACTITIONER: I want to ask you something. As you have processed this, what are you liberating yourself from now?

THIANNA: I need to think about that some more. This isn't a cure-all. It's still crap that we live in, but I feel like it won't grip as tightly if we pay attention more to this resilience stuff.

PRACTITIONER: I understand. Now that you have focused on this stuff and discussed your resilience, what does this mean about you now as a couple? What are the two of you evolving into as a couple? Who are you now?

ROXANNE: What a question! I do feel a little different. I can't name it, but I do feel a bit different. I need more spaciousness though.

THIANNA: Me too. I do feel safer in my body though.

PRACTITIONER: Ah yes. Is this connected to your relational intentions?

THIANNA: Indeed it is.

ROXANNE: I have to think some more, but I can see that too.

I have had the pleasure of utilizing this technique with BIPOC clients. I distinctly remember working with an African American couple that candidly shared that, due to systemic racism in the United States, they felt compelled to draw closer to each other, forging a bond that transcended mere partnership. This closeness and their protective nature toward each other enhanced their sense of safety in the world. They created a sanctuary of safety amid external adversities. Given that one of the components of relational privilege is protection, it's important to note that through individual and relational resilience, couples can increase their relational privilege to some extent. Furthermore, developing resilience may foster authenticity and a deep sense of self-acceptance, which are also critical components of relational privilege. Couples can act in ways that truly honor their individuality and partnership. Ultimately, their connection is reinforced when they can experience this.

Nurturing Your Creativity

How can you explore individual and relational resilience in other innovative ways? Though I primarily rely on in-depth discussion, I certainly believe that there is room for creative techniques. Consider the following:

1. *Resilience mapping*: We can encourage partners to create a visual map of their resilience. They can use visual elements or even draw images that signify the protective factors in their lives.
2. *Affirmation stones*: Couples can create affirmation stones by writing short phrases or words that signify their resilience on small stones. They can place these in parts of their living space to serve as daily reminders.
3. *Collaborative resilience poetry*: Partners can be asked to create a poem together that captures their resilience. One approach is a technique by Ross and Adams (2016) known as "alphapoems," where themes are delineated and expressed via acrostics. Each line of the poem can

correspond to a letter in a chosen theme word, such as "resilience." This process prompts clients to explore and articulate their understanding of the theme through associated themes and personal experiences.

4. *Resilience rituals*: Couples can be asked to establish rituals that acknowledge and honor their individual and relational resilience. This could incorporate weekly check-ins where they share their achievements and express appreciation for each other's support and presence.
5. *Building blocks*: You can consider integrating toy building blocks into your work. Each block can be labeled to represent a protective factor for clients. These blocks are a tangible way to visualize and discuss their unique strengths. This is a hands-on approach that can be extremely effective.

RELATIONAL DECLARATIONS

I think a poet should be able to recreate the world
as an act of imaginative memory.
—Derek Walcott

How do we create the relational worlds that we want to have in the midst of daunting realities? How do we carve these amid uncertainty, grief, and pain inflicted from powerful and dangerous forces? How do we envision and build a future for ourselves that feels nourishing and authentic? I've looked to the beautiful and insightful work of Staci Haines (2019) and her text *The Politics of Trauma* to answer some of these questions. In her work, she eloquently speaks about the transformative power of "declarations" and asserts "When we declare, we are intending and calling forth a future. We are mobilizing ourselves, and often others, into action to build it" (p. 165). This notion of declaration summons us into a powerful space of possibility and our clients deserve it. They deserve to actively shape their worlds and relationships.

Inspired by Haines's insights, I have collaborated with clients to create "relational declarations": bold, co-created statements that articulate their intentions for their relationships. These declarations are not static; they are organic and can evolve over time as our clients grow and their realities change. Moreover, these declarations can also encompass clients' desires for and commitments to social change, thus reinforcing the interconnectedness of personal and collective healing. This aspect of the declaration aligns with the systemic intentions we discussed in Chapter 6, highlighting the broader implications of relational choices. Let's review the kinds of questions we can ask our clients to help them craft their declarations. As mentioned before, I have fused some ideas from Haines's contribution to conceptualize these questions:

1. What are your deepest longings and yearnings for your relationship?
2. If you had permission to long for something, what would you long for?
3. What within you or within your relationship wants to heal?
4. What would become possible if you heal?
5. What do you want that is requiring you to heal?
6. Why should you heal?
7. Who do you need to be to embody your declaration?
8. What were your ancestors' greatest wishes for you?
9. How can a shift in this relationship help change our world?
10. How does this connect to your relational and systemic intentions?

By engaging in this reflective process, the partners are invited to develop a statement using the following sentence stem: "We are a commitment to . . ." This statement is both future and process oriented. The following are examples of future- and process-oriented statements:

1. We are a commitment to building a love where we each feel cherished and held.
2. We are a commitment to supporting each other in living our fullest truth.
3. We are a commitment to creating a space where we both feel physically and psychologically safe.

As you can see, the partners are embodying their declaration statements by labeling themselves as the "commitment." This commitment is not merely something that they have. It is who they actually are, and their day-to-day interactions with each other will resonate with and radiate this decision. The verbs in the declaration are deliberately presented in the continuous tense (building, supporting, creating), emphasizing that this is an ongoing process that will unfold throughout their lives together. This approach acknowledges the reality that we never fully attain certain goals. The essential undertaking is to keep these desires vibrant and evolving in their daily consciousness. By framing their intentions in this way, partners are reminded that commitment is a dynamic force—one that requires continuous nurturing and adaptation.

As their declarations evolve, it is important for partners to reflect on how they themselves are shifting as individuals and as a partnership in response to these evolving commitments. This reflective practice fosters not only growth but also a deeper connection between partners as they navigate their shared journey. Now we delve into what this looks like by examining the case of Wajid and Malaika. As you may recall from Chapter 5, Wajid perceived Malaika as highly controlling and assertive in their relationship. We realized that some of this was directly tied to historical trauma and the experience of her own ancestors during slavery. While working with her, Malaika was able to find relief while doing the ICN that we explored in Chapter 7. Below, you will see how the clients create and engage with the relational declarations.

Case 3

> **PRACTITIONER:** Wajid, Malaika, for your relational and systemic intentions, you mentioned that you wanted more "delicate courage" in your relationship with each other. That is such a beautiful expression. You said that you wanted to use that courage to undo the oppression of Black folks in the world. I'd like to deepen that. I'd like to explore your relational declarations with you. Can you think about your deepest longings and yearnings for your relationship? What comes up for you as I say this? [*Here, we are practicing epistemic embracing. This is also a microliberatory movement.*]
>
> **WAJID:** I don't want to be controlled. What I really want is a space where we can openly express ourselves. I want to feel heard and understood, not just controlled.
>
> **MALAIKA:** I hear that. I am truly sorry. I really long for us to have mutual trust. I know I can be overwhelming, but I just want us to be okay. It's not easy to let go of that control sometimes.
>
> **PRACTITIONER:** Reflecting on that is important. If you had permission to long for something without hesitation, what would that be? [*Here, we are again practicing epistemic embracing and a microliberatory movement.*]

WAJID: I'd long for a relationship where it is okay to be vulnerable. I want a relationship where it is okay to mess up.

MALAIKA: And I'd long for a love that helps us each to grow, where we actively work on healing our pasts together instead of letting them interfere with our actions.

PRACTITIONER: Beautiful insights. Now, let's consider what within you or your relationship wants to heal. What thoughts arise?

MALAIKA: Well, based on what we did in the ancestral work, I am seeing that we have to heal how we communicate. If we don't address our historical baggage, we will be stuck in those cycles.

WAJID: Yes, and I think healing means acknowledging our past but not allowing it to control the future we are gonna have together.

PRACTITIONER: Absolutely. What would become possible if you both healed these components of your relationship? [*We are practicing imagination.*]

WAJID: I can see us becoming more connected. I can also see us feeling into each other's needs more. I don't do that often.

MALAIKA: And we could create a loving home that feels safe for both of us. That's a huge goal for me.

PRACTITIONER: Fantastic. Now, how about creating a statement using the sentence stem "We are a commitment to . . . " Think of a statement that embodies your desires for the relationship. I want you to think of it as something you will be doing continuously in the future. We will use the continuous tense. For example, you can say, "We are a commitment to building a love where we each feel cherished and held." [*Here, we are in the development step and also practicing epistemic embracing.*]

WAJID: I'd say, "We are a commitment to building a partnership where vulnerability is embraced and where our voices can be heard."

MALAIKA: I love that, Waj. I'd want to add "We are a commitment to healing together and building a space of trust and support."

PRACTITIONER: Beautifully stated! Let's combine these two into one cohesive declaration.

WAJID: That sounds great. How about "We are a commitment to building a partnership grounded in vulnerability, trust, and healing, allowing us to navigate our shared journey with openness and love."

MALAIKA: Yes, that is it! I feel a sense of hope from this.

PRACTITIONER: This is wonderfully powerful. As you think on this declaration, how do you believe it will impact your actions moving forward? [*This again is development and epistemic embracing.*]

MALAIKA: I am seeing that it will help us remember what we are creating so that we can remember it every day. It is like a compass that will hold us accountable.

WAJID: Agreed. Indeed.

PRACTITIONER: Exactly. And remember, this process is ongoing. What actual steps can you see yourselves taking? [*Here, I am supporting the process of development.*]

WAJID: I think we need to think on that some more.

MALAIKA: Me too.

PRACTITIONER: I respect that. You do not have to know it all now in this session. These things can take time. Being intentional about your commitment evolves with your journey together. What are you liberating yourselves from with this conversation and new understanding?

MALAIKA: I feel like I'm liberating myself from the fear of being seen as controlling. I really feel good now. I feel like Waj and I are working this thing together. I also feel like I can step back a bit.

WAJID: And I'm freeing myself from the belief that I have to hold back my feelings to keep peace between us.

PRACTITIONER: I get you. This makes sense. Who do you believe you are both becoming as a couple with this declaration? [*Here I am practicing the evolve step.*]

WAJID: Malaika and I are becoming friends, you know? I know that may sound weird, but now we are becoming friends, just as we are lovers, and that means a lot to me. We are in this struggle together. I know she felt she has to go it alone, but I am with her.

MALAIKA: Yes! We are evolving into a loving couple that navigates this hard stuff together.

PRACTITIONER: Yes, that is beautiful. Does this connect to your relational and systemic intentions?

WAJID: Yup. This is the delicate courage we can take out into the world to change it.

MALAIKA: Yup. This makes us braver.

Being with couples as they write their relational declarations often brings me such joy, as I notice that they feel a new sense of direction and an internalized pathfinder. Truthfully, as you have seen in the case above, it isn't always a seamless process. Sometimes, they are not very clear on the next steps but even beginning the conversation is helpful. We do not pressure our clients to know their next steps. This is not the essence of liberatory practice. Their healing is seeking them, just as much as they are longing for it. We hold space for the pace of their journey.

For some clients, I have found that using a visual reminder can help. They can create signs or pictures in their home with their declarations, written explicitly or expressed through art. This helps them remember their declarations in their daily lives.

Can Declarations Change?

I assume you may be wondering if declarations can change—of course they can. Our clients are free to add other declarations or change them along the way if they don't feel right. The most important thing is that they experience it as their own, and that it feels infused in their system as an authentic expression of their desires.

Nurturing Your Creativity

While working with your clients, consider inviting them to express their relational declarations in other ways as well. Here are just a few:

1. *Painting*: This artistic exploration permits clients to visualize and interpret their intentions in a personal and meaningful way. They can then interpret their paintings and build a statement that feels right for them.
2. *Sculptural representations*: Partners can create a sculpture or a physical representation of their declarations using clay, natural materials, or found objects. In this way, they can certainly embody their declaration in a lasting form that they can display in their home environment.
3. *Artistic vision boards*: Partners can be encouraged to create a vision board that visually represents their relational declaration. They can use images and symbols that resonate with their intentions for their relationship. This tangible representation can serve as a daily reminder of their commitments.
4. *Declaration collages*: Partners can work together on a collage that combines their individual contributions, creatively depicting their shared desires. They can use materials such as textiles, recycled items, or magazines to build this.
5. *Poetry or letters*: We can ask partners to write a poem or a letter to their relationship. In these letters, they can detail their feelings, desires, and importance of their relational declarations.
6. *Movement and dance*: Partners can choreograph a short piece that reflects their commitment and perform this during session or afterward.
7. *Audio declarations*: We can ask our clients to record themselves reading their declarations aloud. Additionally, we can also invite them to create a short audio piece that highlights their vision for their partnership. Listening to these accessible daily reminders can support their connection.

No matter what they decide, it is important to gently remind clients that the declarations and even the path to creating these declarations are theirs to hone and claim. It is a deeply personal process and a celebration of their unique narratives and self-discovery.

DECOLONIZING THE RELATIONSHIP

> *I often feel I am trapped inside someone else's capability.*
> *I often feel I am trapped inside someone else's imagination, and I must engage my own imagination in order to break free.*
> —ADRIENNE MAREE BROWN

The above quote from adrienne maree brown has guided me personally in my life for many years. This is part of the reason that the PRIDE model was created. I wanted to create a space for marginalized persons to move through a process where they can sit in the essence and wonder of their own imagination. I didn't want them to feel stifled or trapped. I also don't want you as a practitioner to feel that way.

The truth is, in so many ways, marginalized people are trapped within the confines of others' imagination. I think of LGBTQIA+ folks whose relationships are often seen as vile and desecrated. I remember sitting in the presence of two women, one of whom felt that she was dirty because she was gay. She also opined that because of this, she made her partner and their love dirty. These heart-wrenching understandings come from a society that has denied the validity of various types of relationships. Practitioners can support partners in helping their relationships flourish. "Decolonizing the relationship" refers to the facilitation of a process where persons confront the ways their beings and their relationships are perceived by dominant society. They then begin to reclaim their narratives, dismantling the oppressive frameworks and stereotypes that have dictated what their love should look like. When we support clients in this practice, we foster a space where they feel seen for who they really are. They can then redefine love on their own terms. It allows their connections to be more authentic, and provides them room to thrive in their unique relationships.

What types of questions support this process? Here are a few:

1. In what ways is this relationship affected by heteronormative norms or norms centered in Whiteness or White body supremacy?
2. How can you grieve the impact of these norms on our relationship?

3. How can you normalize and compassionately tend to all feelings surrounding the impact of these norms?
4. In what ways can you remove these norms from the relationship?
5. What would the removal of these norms look like?
6. What would it be like to reclaim the relationship?
7. What are you liberating yourselves from now?
8. Now that you have had this conversation, who are you now?
9. How does this connect to your relational and systemic intentions?

Now we continue the story of Sylvia and Jan so that you can have a deeper appreciation of decolonizing the relationship. We learned of them earlier in Chapter 5. They are two women who had been in a romantic partnership for 20 years. Sylvia longed for invisibility and felt that Jan was too open about their partnership. Her discomfort stemmed from her horrible "coming-out" experience in her family. Jan was very unhappy about Sylvia's desire to remain private. Though their intentions, as articulated in Chapter 6, were to be more visible, they still abided by oppressive, heteronormative understandings of their relationship. The dialogue below demonstrates the use of "decolonizing the relationship" with this couple.

Case 4

> **PRACTITIONER:** Sylvia, Jan, I remember that you talked about going slow and that you wanted to show that slowness to your community. I want you now to both think about how your relationship has been shaped by societal norms, particularly those centered around heteronormativity, and the expectations placed upon you. How do you think that these norms have affected your partnership? [*Here I am practicing epistemic embracing.*]
>
> **SYLVIA:** For me, it's been so tough! It's hard to expose the relationship without thinking you're gonna be judged. People think this is dirty and unclean. I know that's what my mother thought for sure. That it's nasty! My mother surely thought this wasn't of God, and that there was only one way to be, so she wanted me to hide.
>
> **JAN:** I feel that too. People think our love is wrong.

PRACTITIONER: That's great insight. How do you process the impact of feeling like your love is deemed "nasty" and not in alignment with God?

SYLVIA: Invalidated and ashamed. I feel like I am betraying some sort of spiritual essence. I find myself constantly wondering if our love is not worthy of being celebrated. I know for Jan that it is infuriating, especially when she sees me wanting to hide because of that.

PRACTITIONER: It is super important to acknowledge that pain and frustration. How can you grieve the impact that these harmful norms have had on your relationship? [*Here, we are practicing epistemic embracing again.*]

SYLVIA: We gotta let ourselves feel angry about it.

JAN: Agreed, because I am damn angry.

PRACTITIONER: That sounds like a productive step. Now, how can you actively start to dismantle these oppressive norms within your relationship? [*Here, this is a microliberatory movement and epistemic embracing.*]

SYLVIA: We could make a super conscious effort to talk about our love in ways that affirm its beauty—reminding ourselves that our love can be sacred, despite what other folks think.

JAN: Yes! Yes! I love it!

PRACTITIONER: Excellent plan. I love it as well! Let's explore what it would mean for you to actually do that and to reclaim your relationship from these narratives that oppress you. What does that look like for you? [*Here, we are practicing development.*]

JAN: Well, we have to reclaim our relationship by redefining what love means for us. Our love is valid in its own right, you know? Nobody else has to like it!

SYLVIA: Exactly! It's about finding our spirituality within our love. We create our own sacredness, Jan!

PRACTITIONER: How do you think you would then define your love?

JAN: Our love, queer love, is a sacred revolution. Our love is a spacious love. It was created out of the need and bravery to have more space to show up as we are. It continues by giving space to each of us to figure out who we are. Space. Space. Space.

SYLVIA: Wow. I'd say our love embraces loneliness as a gift. We know that by having this love, the two of us have to be lonely together. But loneliness in a crappy world is not a problem. It's an art.

PRACTITIONER: That's so, so empowering and moving! Truly powerful! Reflecting on this conversation, how do your relational and systemic intentions fit into all of this?

SYLVIA: Ah. Good question. I really do think that reclaiming our relationship is aligned with slowness. We are taking our time with who we are and being very deliberate about it. People need to see us take our time as we take our relationship back. So I see it as being aligned.

JAN: Yeah. I see it as aligned, too, because we are finding and creating the sacredness in our relationship. That requires slowness; slowness that we are ready for.

PRACTITIONER: That is beautiful. What do you feel you are liberating yourselves from as you speak about this?

SYLVIA: I am liberating myself from the belief that our love is unclean. This thing is sacred!

JAN: Sacred is the truth! We are liberating ourselves from the stupid fear that we don't deserve a loving relationship because it doesn't fit into someone else's idea of what sacred love should look like.

PRACTITIONER: That's a powerful realization. Now, who do you believe you are becoming as a couple after this conversation? [*Here, we are going to evolve.*]

SYLVIA: Jan, I think we are becoming stronger together, hon. This was something else. I feel the power though to stand up against people who say we are nasty. We are redefining the thing. We are redefining the thing!

JAN: Yes! We are evolving into a couple that values our connection as beautiful and divine. We are redefining the thing.

The tool "decolonizing the relationship" is also invaluable for BIPOC couples as it empowers them to challenge the oppressive beliefs and stereotypes about their relationships that sometimes shape their love and intimacy. BIPOC individuals may carry the weight of cultural stigmas that impact their self-worth and relationships. Engaging in the decolonization process helps them grapple with the ways that their love has been influenced by hegemonic narratives centered around Whiteness and dominant cultural expectations. We can hold space for undoing these narratives by asking BIPOC partners critical questions about the impact of societal norms on their relationship and helping them take back their narratives in a way that honors their unique heritage and experiences. This practice creates a context where they can redefine love on their own terms, thereby creating thriving relationships that are aligned with their true selves, untethered from external judgment.

When either BIPOC or LGBTQIA+ couples find themselves enacting or abiding by dominating narratives or stereotypes, they must alert themselves to these stories so that they can stop them immediately. This is how we decolonize the relationship in real time. For example, it is not uncommon for Black men in relationships to view their female partners as "angry Black women," or for Black women to deem their partners as "lazy no-good Black men." Often, when these emerge during our attempts to decolonize their relationships, we can ask clients to "halt the dance of the stereotypes." This metaphorical halt invites them to pause and reflect on the dynamics at play, permitting them to realize how these imposed narratives affect their perceptions of each other and behavior. By interrupting this cycle, they can experience a shared commitment to challenging societal influences, ultimately leading to healthier, more authentic partnerships. This type of halt can also be used for LGBTQIA+ couples where stereotypes about each other may come to the fore as well. For instance, during an argument between two gay male partners, one may dismiss the other by labeling him as an "overly dramatic gay man," a stereotype often imposed on men in the community who may express themselves openly. Recognizing and addressing these stereotypes is crucial, as they can distort perceptions and undermine healthy communication. It is important that these stereotypes be noted and that we encourage our clients to consider their most generous interpretation of the other. I first learned of this concept from Becky Kennedy (2022), author of *Good Inside*. By leaning on this lens, we can invite partners to reflect on their interactions by asking themselves "How can I interpret my partner's behavior through the most generous lens?" This shift in perspective allows individuals to see their partners in a more compassionate light, which fosters empathy and understanding. By reframing their thoughts, partners can see beyond stereotypes and begin constructive dialogue, ultimately helping them break free from destructive dynamics.

Nurturing Your Creativity

As we embark on the journey of decolonizing relationships, it is essential to be creative while doing this work. Here are some exercises that may be helpful:

1. *Reflection prompts*: You can have partners embark on journal reflection prompts. By using guiding questions that deepen their understanding of how societal narratives affect their relationship, they can note the answers through the journaling process and construct the way ahead. They can even write letters to each other about the ways societal norms have harmed their relationship, and articulate their hopes for the future.
2. *Embodied movements exercises*: Partners can do a short dance together that conveys their journey of decolonizing their relationship. This routine can also assist with emotional release and foster deeper connection.
3. *Role-playing*: This can be an amazing tool to explore how societal stereotypes manifest in the relationship. We can help clients act out scenarios that challenge dominant narratives, allowing them to rehearse healthier responses and build empathy for each other.
4. *Vision boards*: We can encourage partners to create vision boards that depict their ideal relationship, free from societal constraints. A tool of this nature can help them communicate their shared aspirations with each other.
5. *Soundscapes of connections*: Partners can create a playlist of soundscapes that signifies their relationship and the journey toward decolonizing it. Music is a potent avenue and is quite inspirational.

BOUNDARY WORK

> *Boundaries are the distance where I can love both you and me simultaneously.*
> —Prentis Hemphill

Because the weight of systemic oppression can seep into relationships, marginalized couples have to be very intentional and deliberate about the care that they give to their unions. This care often necessitates the establishment of healthy boundaries which are essential for preserving their emotional well-being. This is paramount given the intricate landscape of harm in which these relationships exist. Boundaries protect the couples and permit a space where they can focus on nurturing their connections. As we have seen throughout this book, when there are no boundaries, couples may inadvertently internalize societal messages and harm each other. How do partners do this though? How do they create a space to protect their relationships from harm? Additionally, how do couples protect each other even *within* their relationships? How do they each ensure that they do not say or do things that can do irreparable damage to the other person? To answer these questions, I turn to the work of Juliane Taylor Shore, and her phenomenal work on psychological and containing boundaries. The need for boundaries for marginalized couples cannot be overstated, as their connections can genuinely struggle in the absence of these clear limits. We now explore each of the two types of boundaries.

Containing Boundaries

According to Shore (2024):

> *The containing boundary helps you say what you need to say while also being kind and staying in your integrity, not acting in ways you don't want to. The containing boundary is about saying only what you need to say and no more, and being respectful with how you say what you say and do what you do. The primary practice of the containing boundary is putting a pause between what you think and feel and what you say and do. (p. 97)*

The essence of a containing boundary lies in its ability to create a pause between thoughts and actions. This is critical for marginalized people whose emotional states and consequently, actions may be unfairly affected by the ravages of systemic trauma. As you may recall in Chapter 1, we discussed how systemic trauma can result in persons being and operating outside of their window of tolerance and their window of possibilities. Being outside of these windows can result in various behaviors such as aggression, retreating, and even fawning. This, for many marginalized persons, is understandable as we previously discussed in Chapter 1. The containing boundary creates the opportunity to pause and reflect before speaking and acting. It creates more space to act in harmony with their desires for their relationships (relational intentions). In this way, they engage their partners with intentionality instead of impulsivity.

Moreover, in a world that is rife with so much injustice and negativity, containing boundaries help partners to maintain kindness in their relationship. It also prevents misunderstanding and reduces strife. I have found that when partners employ these boundaries, they are able to assert their individual needs in healthy ways. They remain cognizant and compassionate while advocating for themselves with their partners. Experiencing this dynamic in a world where the needs of marginalized people are often ignored is quite therapeutic. Furthermore, this practice supports the resilience of marginalized relationships.

In order to develop containing boundaries, it is helpful to consider the following equation from Shore (2024):

$$pause + compassionate\ gesture + values\ words = containing\ boundaries$$

What does each component really mean? Let's slowly explore:

- *Pause*: When they feel upset or overwhelmed, partners should halt and not allow themselves to say or do anything that may be harmful.
- *Compassionate gesture*: While in the pause, it is helpful to use a physical movement that communicates to oneself "Though I feel distressed, I am/will be okay."
- *Values words*: These include personal integrity and relational intention words. Personal integrity words refer to the ideals that one wishes to live by. Relational intention words are how one wishes to show up in relationships. I have added a third value, which is systemic intention. In Chapter 6, we defined these as the hopes that persons have for the wider system. These are to be considered here as well.

I am hopeful that this will become clearer to you with a case example—the story of Solomon and Ayanna. They are a Black couple living in Seattle who were each of Nigerian descent. Ayanna was seen to be the "angry Black woman." As a practitioner, when working with a couple such as this, here are the questions you can consider:

1. What containing boundaries are needed here?
2. What are the values words, systemic intentions, and relational intentions that help you here?
3. What compassionate gesture would support you here?
4. What are you liberating yourselves from via this discussion?
5. Now that you have had this moment, who are you evolving into?

> **PRACTITIONER:** Solomon and Ayanna, it's great to have you both here today. We discussed a bit about containing boundaries on the last occasion and I would like to start there. What do you think are the containing boundaries that may be helpful here? [*Here I am practicing epistemic embracing and the step of development.*]
>
> **AYANNA:** I think we need to be careful with how we communicate during disagreements. Sometimes, I feel dismissed because he sees me like that "angry Black woman." I do know I need to hold back a bit more though.
>
> **SOLOMON:** We both can hold back at times, to be honest.
>
> **PRACTITIONER:** Absolutely. It's important to establish a safe space for both of you. Now, let's take a deeper look at the values words and intentions that resonate with you. Let's find one word that represents the ideal version of you. That's your personal integrity word. What personal integrity words do you want to abide by in this life? [*Again, this is epistemic embracing and development.*]
>
> **AYANNA:** I want to embody sensitivity.
>
> **SOLOMON:** Openness is it for me.
>
> **PRACTITIONER:** Great insights! And what about relational intentions?

What hopes do you have for how you show up in this relationship? [*Again, this is epistemic embracing and furthering development.*]

SOLOMON: Respect. I need to respect her more.

AYANNA: Wow. I feel the same.

PRACTITIONER: Now let's think about your systemic intentions. How do you believe that a shift in your relationship can make a shift in the world? What do you want to see?

AYANNA: I want us to break the cycle and redefine what it means to be a strong Black couple. I want to show that we can be passionate without it looking like we are angry all the time.

SOLOMON: Yes. I want the same in a way. I want to see more people being emotionally real in our community. We shouldn't have to hold back our emotions because of fear of judgment.

PRACTITIONER: Those are powerful systemic intentions. Now, let's think about a compassionate gesture that can support you. This is a physical move that you will do to help you know that you are okay when you feel distressed in your communication with each other. It is a gesture that will help you know the following: "I am okay." [*Here, we are continuing our process of development.*]

AYANNA: Maybe I could touch and rub my chest. That helps.

SOLOMON: I like that idea. For me, I will give myself a hug.

PRACTITIONER: Excellent. Now let's practice a bit. I am inviting each of you to think of a disagreement during which you would typically have a response that is unkind .You can close your eyes if you wish. *(Solomon and Ayanna close their eyes).* Let me know when you can see it.

SOLOMON: I can.

AYANNA: Yup

PRACTITIONER: Now imagine right before you are about to be unkind, you say your systemic intention, relational intention, and personal integrity words softly to yourself or in your head, while pausing and doing your compassionate gesture at the same time. What happens now?

AYANNA: I feel less inclined to say it. I feel calmer.

SOLOMON: This is interesting. I find myself wanting to say something different, but nothing mean.

PRACTITIONER: Wonderful. I am so happy for you. Lastly, by having this discussion with me, what are you liberating yourselves from?

AYANNA: Hmm. I have to think on that some more.

SOLOMON: I think that we are freeing ourselves from the societal pressures that dictate how we express frustration.

PRACTITIONER: That's powerful. Now, thinking on this moment and the steps you are making, who do you believe you are evolving into as a couple? [*Here, we are working on the step of evolve.*]

AYANNA: We are becoming people who define our love on our own terms.

SOLOMON: Exactly! That's it.

PRACTITIONER: Beautifully said!

PSYCHOLOGICAL BOUNDARIES

The psychological boundary is an inner boundary that refers to the space and the difference between your mind and other people's minds.
—S HORE (2024, P. 65)

When we have healthy psychological boundaries, we are able to manage the degree we are affected by other people's thoughts, words, and actions. In a world where marginalized identities are often invalidated, partners can benefit from clearly erecting these boundaries to protect their emotional space. They also need these boundaries to be established within the relationship so that they are not affected by each other's understandable reactivity at times. Shore (2024) proposes that a healthy psychological boundary has two central components: discernment and acceptance. Discernment is about knowing when to take in other people's feedback and when we should not. Acceptance is the process of allowing others to have their emotions without trying to influence or change them. In her work, Shore advises that persons create an image, word, metaphor, or phrase that communicates those two aspects when they are in need of a psychological boundary.

We return to Solomon and Ayanna, demonstrating their short discussion of psychological boundaries:

> **PRACTITIONER:** Solomon and Ayanna, let's talk about psychological boundaries. As we know, these boundaries help you manage how you are impacted by others. How do you both feel about the idea of building psychological boundaries within your relationship, especially considering the systemic trauma you experience?
>
> **AYANNA:** It is vital. Outside stuff really gets to me.
>
> **SOLOMON:** I agree. We need to protect our emotional space and know not to take in everything.
>
> **PRACTITIONER:** Exactly! That discernment is key. So is acceptance. Discernment is about knowing when to take in other people's feedback and when we should not. Acceptance is allowing others to have their feelings without trying to influence them. The truth is that it is important to have these within the relationship and between the two of you. Protection preserves connection. How would you both like to create a psychological boundary in your relationship with these two features? It is useful to have it within the relationship as well so that the two of you do not hurt each other. You can use an image or metaphor—something that you can imagine around you that protects you from the other person's feelings when they may be upset or saying or doing something that may distress you.
>
> **AYANNA:** I can see that already. I think of a shield made of glass. It is transparent so I can still see what's going on outside.

> **SOLOMON:** I like that idea. But mine will be a yellow fence.
>
> **PRACTITIONER:** That sounds great! So, let's test it out. Imagine a time when your partner is doing something that you would typically feel distressed by and imagine the boundary around you. [*Both Solomon and Ayanna are given time to reflect so that they can remember a moment.*]
>
> **SOLOMON** (*eyes closed*): I can definitely remember a morning when Ayanna was moving around being pretty snappy. Just angry and bossy. Hmm, but with the yellow fence up, I still feel a bit disturbed by it, but it's much less than it was at the time.
>
> **AYANNA** (*chuckling*): I don't remember that morning! What I do remember though is you being a bit passive aggressive with me one night last week, and that glass is now doing the work!
>
> **PRACTITIONER:** Beautiful! By using these images, you can remind yourselves of your boundaries whenever you feel distressed.

As usual, following this exploration, we allow our couples to discuss how they are freeing themselves as well as evolving and shifting. It is of utmost importance that we allow them the space to always connect these exercises to the bigger picture of their liberation journey. This work is political work. There is no apolitical therapy. We are either upholding, transforming, or challenging the worlds that our clients occupy.

Nurturing Your Creativity

Here are just a few other ways that you can support your clients in their work with boundaries:

1. *Boundary visualization*: You can have your clients draw or collage images that signify boundaries. They can place them in their homes.
2. *Role-playing*: You can support a role-playing process where each person practices erecting their boundaries in different scenarios.
3. *Boundary check-ins*: Clients can be guided to set aside time every week or biweekly to discuss how their boundaries are working.

4. *Sensory reminders*: You can request that clients select sensory items, such as stones, fabrics, or scents, that remind them of their boundaries. They can keep these nearby in their living space to remind them of their boundaries.
5. *Affirmation cards*: Practitioners can ask clients to create affirmation cards with their values words so that they can have daily reminders of these boundaries.

Practitioner's Reflection

We have come to the end of this chapter, and what a journey it has been. I am ecstatic that you are able now to have clear tools for building liberatory connections with marginalized partnerships. Pay attention to the personalities of your clients and your comfort level. This helps you choose techniques that feel aligned. Also note that you can blend in work from other models within this work. I don't want you to feel imprisoned by my model for this work. Your voice in this work is so essential. Listen to it as well.

As you think about building liberatory connections, are there any other tools that you think you could use? What would feel comfortable for you? What else do you see as being valuable here? Remember that liberatory connections are supposed to help our clients develop new ways of being in their relationships to confront and manage systemic trauma, and honor their relational and systemic intentions.

The sad reality is that even with the best of techniques, it still may be difficult for partners to truly develop healthier connections. When this happens, we have to pivot, grieve, and rethink our approach to the work that we do. For me, that has not been easy, but it has been so worthwhile. I share about this process in Chapter 9.

CHAPTER RECAP

- Liberatory connections are sites where both relational and social change converge. These are connections that directly address the impact of systemic trauma by cultivating a context where the couple can still survive, or possibly even grow, despite the weight of systemic trauma.
- Liberatory connections assist couples in thinking differently about their relationships. It expands possibilities.

- There are five techniques that can be used to build liberatory connections: identity and relational cherishing, individual and relational resilience, relational declarations, decolonizing the relationship, and boundary work.
- Throughout these techniques, we must remain mindful that we are supporting the partners in developing new steps for themselves. They are also invited to think about who or what they are evolving into.

CHAPTER 9

Reclaiming Lost Spaces

We are always lost, because we are too expansive to be found, too promiscuous to be faithful, too transdimensional to be fully owned. We are spread out beyond the maps, transgressing territories, perplexing our own coordinates, entangled with the wilds in ways we are always yet to realize.

—Bayo Akomolafe

With a background in both psychology and social work, I have devoted many years to the roles of social work educator, therapist, and trainer. During my journey, I embodied a belief that became my guide: "Implement the techniques, and you will witness success; apply these methods, and change will unfold." This belief was my lifeline, providing me with a deep sense of reassurance and control. It anchored me firmly in my profession, infusing my work with meaning and passion.

Over time though, I realized that I was living in a fantasy, upheld by a field that is not always honest with itself. As helping professionals, we sometimes do not have the courage nor desire to face the unrealistic expectations that we sometimes place on our clients, opting instead to blame our lack of "successful interventions" on "client failings," such as resistance, or a lack of commitment. Perhaps we cultivate these failings to soothe our wounded egos when the best of treatment plans do not work. Perhaps we cultivate these failings because it is harder to sit in the harrowing reality that what we do will not always work. Sometimes, if not many times, we are lost. Sometimes, it is our field that has failed.

I see these moments as intense turning points. They are the moments when the unexpected happens, when the decades of tertiary education and continuous education must lie prostrate before the human story. In those moments, we are sitting in what I call the GLITCH. This stands for:

G: grief
L: liminality
I: imagination
T: trying it out
C: creating
H: honoring the process

Take a look at the image in Figure 9.1 to support your understanding of this concept.

Figure 9.1: The GLITCH model helps us to move through the inevitable moments of standing in the unknown.
Illustration by Nikki Shaheed.

The GLITCH is the chasm in your work. It is the fissure that does not abide by your desires or even the tenets of this text. It is where our work falls flat and our clients do not have the transformation we hope for. The GLITCH is not uncommon when working with marginalized folks. I have had to face it at times. The intensity of systemic trauma can sometimes limit the benefit of the work that we do in session. In addition, some wounds just won't shift, and we have to accept this. Let's explore the acronym further so that we can peer into ways to be with these many moments.

GRIEF

Anyone who truly knows me is aware that I firmly believe that grief is an integral part of living. The truth of grief is etched in my heart. Grief is an ineluctable shadow that looms over every aspect of our existence. As practitioners, we cannot escape it. We must steel ourselves to acknowledge the ache of witnessing distress that stubbornly refuses to ease. We must prepare ourselves to witness when our clients' heartache grows instead of recedes. At the time of this writing, I am witnessing the world transform in ways that I never envisioned. I see persons like myself, who strive for liberation and equality, grappling with considerable fear of doing this work. I am watching as the profound work against racism, homophobia, transphobia, and discrimination is ruthlessly trampled on by those who wield more power. I am in sorrow. I do not comprehend these appalling violations. Within this tumult, I also know that so many colleagues in the field are also enduring this pain. They sometimes do not know what to say to their clients who inhabit marginalized identities. Their clients' fear is as palpable as their inability to soothe it. There is often a visceral tension due to shared helplessness. In these moments, there is a need to mourn. We must recognize what is lost and not run away from the agony. Sometimes, the system is too weighty, and our sense of helplessness is painfully apparent.

As we explore this notion of grief, I share some reflective questions that may be helpful:

1. What does it feel like to be confronted with the limitations of your therapeutic interventions? How do you navigate, validate, and tend to these feelings?
2. How do you become aware of and validate the grief your clients may feel when their progress stagnates despite your and their best efforts?
3. What elements of the BIOME do you think may be helpful to you here?

LIMINALITY

Liminality is the experience of being in between two places or states. Typically, when we are in this place, we are on the cusp of discovering something that is very new. I often say that grief is the birthplace of imagination. Grief leaves us homeless and wandering in the neighborhood of possibilities. However, we must be ready to embrace the liminal place and allow our agenda for the work to fade away. It is essential to share about this with our clients, highlighting the power of being in that space and its value to the therapeutic journey. As we normalize this space, we remind them that systemic trauma is different from other types of trauma: It is chronic and unpredictable. Thus, it is not the client's fault if they are not progressing at the pace that they would like. It is not a reflection of their shortcomings.

It is helpful in the liminal space to enhance our relationship with uncertainty. We have to temper our need for mastery in the work. Confusion is not our foe but our closest ally. We do not try to chase it away. It holds wisdom. It is here that we can be escorted into the realm of imagination. We will now look at some questions that may be helpful to you in the liminal space:

1. What feelings emerge for you when you are in the liminal space—both personally and in your therapeutic work?
2. What means do you employ to foster a sense of safety for yourself and your clients when you are in this experience of the unknown?
3. In these moments, how can you let go of the need for control? What does this look like?
4. What does it look like to welcome ambiguity and ambivalence?
5. What insights can you obtain in these phases?
6. How do cultural norms and beliefs in your wider system affect your relationship with liminality?
7. What practices or rituals may be helpful to your clients so that they can cope with the liminal period?
8. How can you support clients in reframing liminality and uncertainty as opportunities for growth?
9. How can you support clients as they endure the discomfort that is typical during liminality?
10. What creative exercises can be helpful during liminality?
11. Reflect on your own personal and past experiences of liminality. What insights did you attain?

IMAGINATION

> *And yet what we cannot imagine cannot come into being. We need imagination to illuminate those spaces not covered by data, facts, and proven information.*
> —BELL HOOKS

To imagine is to answer the invitation to transcend constraints and enlarge the realm of possibilities. As mentioned before, grief and liminality are often the portals into this realm. Imagination is not a place of refuge. It is a place of fugitivity, where we embrace the unknown and often denied or ignored parts of us.

An imaginative lens is important in this work. Here, we set aside methods that may limit us, and explore our chaotic brilliance that soars from being a bit lost in the work at times. Healing work is seldom straightforward or linear when working with systemic trauma. As we delve into the expansiveness of this experience along with our clients, we may need to redefine healing. We may even have to redefine therapy and the role of the practitioner. I have had to make awkward changes when I begin to imagine, but it has been immensely fulfilling. As I have co-created new directions with my clients in the messiness of the work, I have learned (and unlearned) many new things.

To support practitioners in this imaginative voyage, I have guided them in a somatic process called "grounded learnings," which allows them to reimagine their practice. While "grounded learnings" is beyond the scope of this text, there are elements of it that are certainly accessible to you now. Let's gently be with some questions below that may be helpful:

1. What unexpressed thoughts or emotions are deeply longing to be given a voice in your work? What do they need to hear from you so that they can be safely expressed?
2. Reflect on the metaphor of an artist's canvas. What strokes of color signify the unexplored components of your client's journey? How can you create room for more strokes?
3. If your emotions were a landscape, what would this landscape look like? How would you move through this landscape to locate new footpaths?

4. If you could request the presence of a mythical creature to move you through your therapeutic practice, what would this creature be? What advice would this creature give to you?
5. In what ways can you physically symbolize flexibility, imagination, and openness in your work? What would the gestures and movements look like?

TRYING IT OUT

In this phase, the fruits of our imagination are brought to life! We are experimenting with what has emerged during the imagination process. This requires a great deal of courage, as it is an extremely dynamic process marked by both trial and exploration. Rigidity must be discarded as both you and your clients will test new insights, ideas, approaches, and perspectives. As such, you both must remain adaptable and open. Here, clients engage with us as active participants and are given space to foster a deep sense of ownership over their journey. They are not simply passive recipients in the process. We deconstruct traditional power dynamics within therapy and work toward truly liberatory healing.

Playfulness is a vital element of this phase, as it allows us to be creative and innovative. You and your client will experiment with different ways of doing the work that feels right for them. The act of "trying it out" is steeped in a liberatory ethos that emphasizes that failure is not the end. Failure is a stepping stone toward progress. Failure provides us with insights. It is necessary.

As you aim to carve an environment that is essential for "trying it out," reflect on the following questions:

1. How can you intentionally support a spirit of experimentation within yourself and clients?
2. What personal and systemic barriers may hinder your use of nontraditional approaches? How will you address these barriers?
3. How will you actively foster a space where clients can brainstorm and co-create therapeutic interventions that feel right for them?
4. What creative activities do you think will help build an atmosphere of experimentation and honor diverse cultural expressions?

5. How do you plan to process moments when a technique does not yield the desired result? What support do you need to seek or offer in these moments?
6. How can you help clients see the value in the aforementioned setbacks?
7. How do you plan to integrate client feedback into your phase of "trying it out"?

CREATING

It is here in the creating phase that the energy of experimentation and imagination culminates in the birth of novelty. The insights obtained from "trying it out" manifest into actual tools and so, there is a deep sense of empowerment for both practitioner and client. Having a concrete artifact—be it a new perspective or a new range of strategies that are aligned authentically with their stories—is enriching. This creation serves as a bridge between the therapeutic context and the world outside.

These generated tools are meant to be shared with other communities and networks because healing is a collective endeavor. Liberation work is not individual work only. This phase is also a stage of inspiration and a commitment to exploration in the future. It is a testament to the possibilities that lie ahead.

Now we review the important questions that you can examine during this phase:

1. What new techniques, strategies, or perspectives have emerged that you can now use in future sessions?
2. How can you celebrate the creativity that has emerged?
3. How can you encourage clients to share their new techniques and insights with their communities?
4. How will you continue to build upon the successes of the creating phase in other realms of your work?
5. What systemic supports do you need or have for creativity?
6. How can you document what has emerged? How can you encourage clients to do the same?

HONORING THE PROCESS

During the phase of honoring the process, the focus is on noting the immense value of each of the preceding phases. It is a time for reflection and gratitude for what has been achieved and gained. Every step—whether marked by success, struggle, setbacks, or breakthroughs—played an integral role. In fact, these steps contribute to the broader narrative of healing for the client and the community.

In this phase, we honor that growth is not linear. We celebrate that bidirectional influence as well as mutual respect between practitioners and clients enhances the therapeutic alliance. Moreover, we as practitioners can find empowerment in our evolving identities and practices. This reciprocal honoring prioritizes a shared commitment to social justice, affirming the values of liberation and decolonization that permeate this work.

Here is the final list of reflective questions for this phase:

1. How can you help clients embrace the nonlinear nature of healing?
2. What strategies might you use to appreciate the lessons learned from both successes and failings during the process?
3. What types of closing rituals can you build to honor the process?
4. How can you invite clients to create their own closing rituals?
5. In what ways can you express gratitude for the vulnerability and trust they shared during the process?
6. How has your perception of therapy shifted during this process? What insights have you gained about yourself as a practitioner? How can you integrate these in the future?
7. How can you ensure that social justice and decolonization remain an integral part of your future work?

CHAPTER RECAP

- The GLITCH framework offers a transformative approach to therapy. The elements of the GLITCH—grief, liminality, imagination, trying it out, creating, and honoring the process—illustrate a dynamic process that emphasizes collaboration, creativity, and reflection.

- During the phase of grief, practitioners and clients are encouraged to confront their shared experiences of loss and lostness within the therapeutic space.
- In liminality, both clients and practitioners embrace the uncertainties and transitions that are unfolding.
- During the imagination phase, clients build on the insights gained from both grief and liminality.
- When they are in the "trying it out" phase, the emphasis shifts to experimenting with the ideas generated during the imagination phase.
- During creating, the outcomes of experimentation take form.
- When clients participate in "honoring the process," they reflect on the entire framework with mutual respect and gratitude.

CHAPTER 10

Conclusion
Reflecting on the Path Toward Liberation

What a journey this has been! As I type these words, I feel both immense joy to have completed this process with you and sadness over the reality of our world. It is the reality of the world that has made this book a personal mandate of mine.

In the future, I long to hear of the ways you have sat with marginalized couples and helped them witness their power, pain, defeat, despair, joy, and sorrow within a context of intense compassion. They need you! In fact, you need them, too. You need them to teach you about this work and what it requires. This is how I learned. I gained wisdom from them. They were my greatest teachers. I had to sit with them, and I firmly believe that so many of you are going to take this work and discover things I never dreamed of. You are going to meet more folks and amazing insights will emerge. That is my deepest longing. I yearn for you to support others in their liberation, but also to experience your own. I want you to find the guru within you, and the many gurus that exist in the people who allow you to work with them daily.

The narratives and insights shared in this book were not theoretical. They represent the lived experiences of marginalized couples that navigate the complexities of love and connection within oppressive systems. Being with these stories is a clarion call to action. We need to fill the gap. We need to advocate for liberation in therapeutic practice.

As we journeyed together in this book, we have dissected the horrifying impact of systemic trauma on BIPOC and LGBTQIA+ relationships. This is not the past. We are staring into the present and from the looks of things, the future as well. Many marginalized people are denied the intimacy they deserve because they are entrenched in social structures that at times, suffocate them. Recognizing this is essential. Relational dynamics cannot be divorced from the historical wounds and sociopolitical forces.

The PRIDE model is a road map that I have offered to you for facilitating healing among marginalized couples. By inviting clients to pivot, rumble, imagine, develop, and evolve, you can truly help them to reclaim their lives and develop nurturing relational realities. Know that this model is not a one-size-fits-all approach. When incorporating the PRIDE model into your work, remember to collaborate with your clients and weave their unique stories and dimensions into the work.

In this work, I stressed that we cannot impose preconceived definitions of intimacy or healing on our clients. We must practice critical consciousness, prioritize our clients' actual realities, and move delicately through the imbalance of power that is often inherent in the therapeutic relationship. To do so, you must truly become the BIOME.

The GLITCH framework is a useful process to guide us practitioners when we engage this work as well. It solidifies the value of recognizing grief, embracing liminality, expanding imagination, engaging in experimentation, creating tools for healing, and honoring the complexities of every journey. We are called here to move outside of traditional therapeutic boundaries and construct spaces laden with creativity, empowerment, and authenticity.

The wider call in the field for the decolonization of therapy underlies much of the work in this text. It has penetrated my being for as long as I have been in the field. When we confront the damaging and dominant perspectives that stifle the voices of our clients, we help our clients and ourselves open pathways for growth. There is a deep joy that comes from this. However, as I have also realized, it can be terribly confusing and scary. This fear necessitates community. Remember this: the value of community. You need a sturdy nurturing community for this work. You cannot do it alone.

As we conclude, let us remember that this work is not simply about doing therapy. This is about justice. This is about wholeness. This is about a sense of restoration and belonging that marginalized people deserve. In this nonlinear messy work, let us also remember that our clients are resilient. They are powerful and strong. Celebrate their identities. Ensure that you find ways to elevate their voices and honor their paths.

Let us continue to build a world where love is boundless and where every person truly feels a deep sense of worth. Let us continue to build an environment where people can feel valued and experience intimacy that is safe, liberating, and blissful. Thank you for allowing me and this work into your space! I am humbled and grateful.

The journey continues, and it is one we walk together. Always.

REFERENCES

Albimawi, H., Tobroni, & Nurhakim, M. (2023). Human nature in the view of the Qur'an and Ibn Arabi. *International Journal of Health, Economics, and Social Sciences (IJHESS)*, 5(3), 270–277. https://doi.org/10.56338/ijhess.v5i3.3829

American Masters. (n.d.). *Toni Morrison on writing without the "white gaze."* PBS. https://www.pbs.org/wnet/americanmasters/toni-morrison-on-writing-without-the-white-gaze/14874/A

American Psychiatric Association. (2017). *Mental Health Disparities: American Indians and Alaska Natives*.

Alang, S. M. (2019). Mental health care among blacks in America: Confronting racism and constructing solutions. *Health Services Research*, 54(2), 346–355. https://doi.org/10.1111/1475-6773.13115

Baker, K. (2020). Cancer in LGBT populations: Differences, disparities, and strategies for change. *Cancer Epidemiology, Biomarkers & Prevention*, 29(12 Supplement), IA12. https://doi.org/10.1158/1538-7755.DISP20-IA12

Beckes, L., & Coan, J. A. (2011). Social baseline theory: The role of social proximity in emotion and economy of action. *Social and Personality Psychology Compass*, 5(12), 976–988. https://doi.org/10.1111/j.1751-9004.2011.00400.x

Boal, A., & McBride, C. A. (1993). *Theatre of the oppressed*. Theatre Communications Group.

Bodenheimer, D. (2018, November 27). When the clinical is political and the political is clinical. Walnut. https://www.walnutpsychotherapycenter.com/post/when-the-clinical-is-political

Bolger, N., DeLongis, A., Kessler, R. C., & Wethington, E. (1989). The contagion of stress across multiple roles. *Journal of Marriage and the Family*, 51(1), 175–183. https://doi.org/10.2307/352378

Butler, O. (1993). *Parable of the sower*. Grand Central.

Calhoun, D. M. (2018). *Race, rejection sensitivity, and identity centrality among young sexual minority women* (Doctoral dissertation, Old Dominion University). https://digitalcommons.odu.edu/psychology_etds/69

Comas-Díaz, L. (2006). Latino healing: The integration of ethnic psychology into psychotherapy. *Psychotherapy: Theory, Research, Practice, Training, 43*(4), 436–453. https://doi.org/10.1037/0033-3204.43.4.436

Dayton, T. (2015). *Neuro-psychodrama in the treatment of relational trauma: A strength-based, experiential model for healing PTSD*. HCI.

Dennis, M. F. T. (2022). *The impacts of identity centrality on mental health in Black Americans* (Master's thesis, Yale University). https://elischolar.library.yale.edu/cgi/viewcontent.cgi?article=2139&context=ysphtdl

Diemer, M. (2011). Critical consciousness: Current status and future directions. *New Directions for Child and Adolescent Development, 2011*(132), 41–49. https://doi.org/10.1002/CD.310

Downey, G., & Feldman, S. I. (1996). Implications of rejection sensitivity for intimate relationships. *Journal of Personality and Social Psychology, 70*(6), 1327–1343. https://psychology.columbia.edu/sites/default/files/2016-11/merp.pdf

Doyle, D. M., & Molix, L. (2015). Social stigma and sexual minorities' romantic relationship functioning: A meta-analytic review. *Personality and Social Psychology Bulletin, 41*(10), 1363–1381. https://doi.org/10.1177/0146167215594592

Du Bois, W. E. B. (2007). Of our spiritual strivings. In S. Edwards(Ed.), *The souls of Black folk*. Oxford University Press. (Original work published 1903)

Ecker, B., Ticic, R., & Hulley, L. (2024). *Memory Reconsolidation and the Psychotherapy of Transformational Change*. Routledge.

Emlet, C. A. (2016). Social, economic, and health disparities among LGBT older adults. *Generations, 40*(2), 16–22. https://www.ncbi.nlm.nih.gov/pmc/articles/PMC5373809/

Erickson, C. M., & Largent, E. A. (2024). Diagnosing preclinical and prodromal neurodegenerative diseases—the clinical is political. *JAMA Neurology, 81*(5), 439–440. https://doi.org/10.1001/jamaneurol.2023.5684

Fani, N., Carter, S. E., Harnett, N. G., Ressler, K. J., & Bradley, B. (2021). Association of racial discrimination with neural response to threat in Black women in the US exposed to trauma. *JAMA Psychiatry, 78*(9), 1005–1012. https://doi.org/10.1001/jamapsychiatry.2021.1480

Federal Reserve Survey of Consumer Finance. (2023). *Greater wealth, greater uncertainty: Changes in racial inequality in the survey of consumer finances.* https://www.federalreserve.gov/econres/notes/feds-notes/greater-wealth-greater-uncertainty-changes-in-racial-inequality-in-the-survey-of-consumer-finances-20231018.html

Feinstein, B. A., Goldfried, M. R., & Davila, J. (2012). The relationship between experiences of discrimination and mental health among lesbians and gay men: An examination of internalized homonegativity and rejection sensitivity as potential mechanisms. *Journal of Consulting and Clinical Psychology, 80*(5), 917–927. https://doi.org/10.1037/a0029425

Flores-Torres, L. L., & Ramirez, S. Z. (2006). Indigenous treatments: Dichos. In Y. Jackson (Ed.), *Encyclopedia of multicultural psychology* (pp. 250–251). Sage. http://dx.doi.org/10.4135/9781412952668.n126

Fragoso, S. (Host). (2020, November 15). How do we heal with Resmaa Menakem. In *Talk Easy with Sam Fragoso*. [Audio podcast episode]. Lemonada.

Fredriksen-Goldsen, K. I., Kim, H.-J., Barkan, S. E., Muraco, A., & Hoy-Ellis, C. P. (2013). Health disparities among lesbian, gay, and bisexual older adults: Results from a population-based study. *American Journal of Public Health, 103*(10), 1802–1809. https://doi.org/10.2105/AJPH.2012.301110

Frost, D. M., LeBlanc, A. J., de Vries, B., Alston-Stepnitz, E., Stephenson, R., & Woodyatt, C. (2017). Couple-level minority stress: An examination of same-sex couples' unique experiences. *Journal of Health and Social Behavior, 58*(4), 455–472. https://doi.org/10.1177/0022146517736754

Frost, D. M., & Meyer, I. H. (2009). Internalized homophobia and relationship quality among lesbians, gay men, and bisexuals. *Journal of Counseling Psychology, 56*(1), 97–109. https://doi.org/10.1037/a0012844

Goldberger, N. R., & Veroff, J. B. (Eds.). (1995). *The culture and psychology reader*. New York University Press.

Greenberg, L. S. (2010). *Emotion-focused therapy: A clinical synthesis*. York University, Toronto.

Haines, S. (2019). *The politics of trauma: Somatics, healing, and social justice*. North Atlantic Books.

Hammond, M. D., & Overall, N. C. (2013). When relationships do not live up to benevolent ideals: Women's benevolent sexism and sensitivity to relationship problems. *European Journal of Social Psychology, 43*(3), 212–223. https://doi.org/10.1002/ejsp.1939

Hardy, K. V. (2016). Mastering context talk: Practical skills for effective engagement. In K. V. Hardy & T. Bobes (Eds.), *Culturally sensitive supervision and training: Diverse perspectives and practical applications* (pp. 136–145). Routledge/Taylor & Francis Group.

Hardy, K. V. (2023). *Racial trauma: Clinical strategies and techniques for healing invisible wounds* (Kindle ed.). Norton.

Hartig, M. D. (2019). *Outness, social support, and well-being in gay and lesbian couples* (Doctoral dissertation). Rutgers University, Camden. https://rucore.libraries.rutgers.edu/rutgers-lib/60741/PDF/1/play/

Hemphill, P. (2021). The wisdom of process. In T. Burke & B. Brown (Eds.), *You are your best thing: Vulnerability, shame resilience, and the Black experience* (Kindle Edition). Random House.

Hill, S. A. (2005). *Black intimacies: A gender perspective on families and relationships* (Gender Lens, pp. 58–59). AltaMira Press.

House of Commons Library. (2020, August 10). *Insight: Which ethnic groups are most affected by ethnic inequality.* https://commonslibrary.parliament.uk/income-inequality-by-ethnic-group/

Hughes, M., Kiecolt, K. J., Keith, V. M., & Demo, D. H. (2015). Racial identity and well-being among African Americans. *Social Psychology Quarterly, 78*(1), 25–48. https://doi.org/10.1177/0190272514554043

Jones, T. W., Power, J., & Jones, T. M. (2022). Religious trauma and moral injury from LGBTQA+ conversion practices. *Social Science and Medicine, 305*, 115040. https://doi.org/10.1016/j.socscimed.2022.115040

Keisler-Starkey, K., & Bunch, L. N. (2020). *Health insurance coverage in the United States: 2019 current population reports.* https://www.census.gov/content/dam/Census/library/publications/2020/demo/p60-271.pdf

Kelley, A. & Marriott, S. (Hosts). (2023, June 6). Healing intergenerational and ancestral trauma with Linda Thai. In *Therapist Uncensored.* [Audio podcast episode]. Therapist Uncensored.

Kennedy, B. (2022). *Good inside: A practical guide to resilient parenting prioritizing connection over correction.* Harper Wave.

Khan, L., Saini, G., Augustine, A., Palmer, K., Johnson, M., & Donald, R. (2017, July 5). *Evaluation of the mind Birmingham up my street programme.* https://www.centreformentalhealth.org.uk/publications/against-odds/

Lavner, J. A., Barton, A. W., Bryant, C. M., & Beach, S. R. H. (2018). Racial discrimination and relationship functioning among African American couples. *Journal of Family Psychology*, *32*(5), 686–691. https://doi.org/10.1037/fam0000415

LeBlanc, A. J., Frost, D. M., & Wight, R. (2015). Minority stress and stress proliferation among same-sex and other marginalized couples. *Journal of Marriage and Family*, *77*(1), 40–59. https://doi.org/10.1111/jomf.12204

Levy, S. R., Ayduk, O., & Downey, G. (2001). The role of rejection sensitivity in people's relationships with significant others and valued social groups. In M. R. Leary (Ed.), *Interpersonal rejection* (pp. 251–289). Oxford University Press.

Meehan, K. B., Cain, N. M., Roche, M. J., Clarkin, J. F., & De Panfilis, C. (2018). Rejection sensitivity and interpersonal behavior in daily life. *Personality and Individual Differences*, *126*, 109–115. https://doi.org/10.1016/j.paid.2018.01.029

Menakem, R. (2023). *Monsters in love: Why your partner sometimes drives you crazy—and what you can do about it*. Central Recovery Press.

Menakem, R. (2022). *The quaking of America: An embodied guide to navigating our nation's upheaval and racial reckoning* (Hardcover). Central Recovery Press.

Mok, C. (2023). *Addressing mental health barriers in the community*. https://www.nami.org/asian-american-pacific-islander/addressing-mental-health-barriers-in-the-aapi-community/

Montero, A., Hamel, L., Artiga, S., & Dawson, L. (2024). *LGBT adults' experiences with discrimination and health care disparities: Findings from the KFF survey of racism, discrimination, and health*. https://www.kff.org/report-section/lgbt-adults-experiences-with-discrimination-and-health-care-disparities-findings/

Naidoo, D., Mkhize, N. M. C., & Leclerc-Madlala, S. (2023). Persistent police discrimination in South Africa: Experiences of the LGBT community. *Social Science and Medicine*. https://hdl.handle.net/10520/ejc-genbeh_v21_n2_a17

National Health Service. (2016). *Adult psychiatric morbidity survey: Survey of mental health and wellbeing, England 2014*. https://www.mind.org.uk/about-us/our-strategy/becoming-a-truly-anti-racist-organisation/facts-and-figures-about-racism-and-mental-health

National Indigenous Australians Agency. (2022). *Aboriginal and Torres Strait Islander health performance framework employment*. https://www.indigenoushpf.gov.au/measures/2-07-employment

National Indigenous Youth Education Coalition. (2024). *The school exclusion project*. https://www.niyec.com/the-school-exclusion-project

Ochieng, O. (2018). *Intellectual imagination: Knowledge and aesthetics in North Atlantic and African philosophy*. University of Notre Dame Press.

Ogolsky, B. G., Monk, J. K., Rice, T. M., Theisen, J. C., & Maniotes, C. R. (2017). Relationship maintenance: A review of research on romantic relationships. *Journal of Family Theory and Review, 9*(3), 275–306. https://doi.org/10.1111/jftr.12205

Osmetti, L. A., & Allen, K. R. (2024). Predictors of psychological well-being in transgender and gender diverse Australians: Outness, authenticity, and harassment. *Sexuality Research and Social Policy, 21*, 1047–1058.

Otis, M. D., Rostosky, S. S., Riggle, E. D. B., & Hamrin, R. (2006). Stress and relationship quality in same-sex couples. *Journal of Social and Personal Relationships, 23*, 81–99.

Pachankis, J. E., Goldfried, M. R., & Ramrattan, M. E. (2008). Extension of the rejection sensitivity construct to the interpersonal functioning of gay men. *Journal of Consulting and Clinical Psychology, 76*(2), 306–317. https://doi.org/10.1037/0022-006X.76.2.306

Pereira, H., & Esgalhado, G. (2021). Intimate dynamics and relationship satisfaction among LGB adolescents: The role of sexual minority oppression. *Children, 8*(3), 231. https://doi.org/10.3390/children8030231

Porges, S. W. (2011). *The polyvagal theory: Neurophysiological foundations of emotions, attachment, communication, and self-regulation* (Norton Series on Interpersonal Neurobiology) (1st ed.) [Kindle edition]. Norton.

Ramchand, R., Schuler, M. S., Schoenbaum, M., Colpe, L., & Ayer, L. (2021). Suicidality among sexual minority adults: Gender, age, and race/ethnicity differences. *American Journal of Preventive Medicine*. https://www.ajpmonline.org/article/S0749-3797(21)00443-8/abstract

Ratié, I. (2016). Utpaladeva and Abhinavagupta on the freedom of consciousness. In J. Ganeri (Ed.), *The Oxford handbook of Indian philosophy* (pp. 437–468). Oxford University Press. https://doi.org/10.1093/oxfordhb/9780199314621.013.27

Riley-Richardson, A. (2023, November/December). Reclaiming Black imagination: The PRIDE approach to healing. *Psychotherapy Networker*.

Ross, J., & Adams, A. (2016). *Your brain on ink*. Rowman & Littlefield.

Shulman, L. (2009). *Skills of helping: Individuals, families, groups, and communities* (6th ed.). Brooks Cole.

Siegel, D. J. (2020). *The developing mind: How relationships and the brain interact to shape who we are* (3rd ed.). Guilford Press.

Sloan, T. (2002). Psicologia de la liberacion: Ignacio Martín-Baró. *Interamerican Journal of Psychology, 36*, 353–357.

Somé, S. (1997). *The spirit of intimacy: Ancient teachings in the ways of relationships.* Berkeley Hills Books.

Smith, W. A., Hung, M., & Franklin, J. D. (2011). Racial battle fatigue and the miseducation of Black men: Racial microaggressions, societal problems, & environmental stress. *The Journal of Negro Education, 80*(1), 63–82. https://doi.org/10.2307/41341106

Taylor Shore, J. (2024). *Setting boundaries that stick: How neurobiology can help you rewire your brain to feel safe, connected, and empowered.* New Harbinger Publications.

Taylor Shore, J. (2025). *STAIR Level 2: Empowering clients to change their experiences through memory reconsolidation.* Academy of Therapy Wisdom. https://academy.therapywisdom.com/spaces/18659100/content

Stats NZ. (2021, October 27). *1 in 20 adults identify as LGBT+ in major social survey.* https://www.stats.govt.nz/news/1-in-20-adults-identify-as-lgbt-in-major-social-survey

Todosijevic, J., Rothblum, E. D., & Solomon, S. E. (2005). Relationship satisfaction, affectivity, and gay-specific stressors in same-sex couples joined in civil unions. *Psychology of Women Quarterly, 29*(2), 158–166. https://doi.org/10.1111/j.1471-6402.2005.00178.x

Trail, T. E., Goff, P. A., Bradbury, T. N., & Karney, B. R. (2012). The costs of racism for marriage: How racial discrimination hurts, and ethnic identity protects, newlywed marriages among Latinos. *Personality and Social Psychology Bulletin, 38*, 454–465. https://doi.org/10.1177/0146167211429450

U.S. Department of Health and Human Services, Office of Minority Health. (2025). *Mental and behavioral health—Black/African Americans.* https://minorityhealth.hhs.gov/mental-and-behavioral-health-blackafrican-americans

United Nations. (2024, April 17). *30 years on, South Africa still dismantling racism and apartheid's legacy.* https://www.ohchr.org/en/stories/2024/04/30-years-south-africa-still-dismantling-racism-and-apartheids-legacy

Yehuda, R., & Lehrner, A. (2018). Intergenerational transmission of trauma effects: Putative role of epigenetic mechanisms. *World Psychiatry, 17*(3), 243–257. https://doi.org/10.1002/wps.20568

Yunkaporta, T. (2020). *Sand talk: How Indigenous thinking can save the world.* HarperOne

Zuniga, M. E. (1991). "Dichos" as metaphorical tools for resistant Latino clients. *Psychotherapy: Theory, Research, Practice, Training, 28*, 480–483. http://dx.doi.org/10.1037/0033-3204.28.3.480

INDEX

Header note: Italicized page locators refer to figures; tables are noted with a *t*.

Abhinavagupta (Tantric master), 56
Aboriginal people (Australia)
 educational barriers for, 6, 16
 income inequality and, 16
Aboriginal worldviews, "protection" in, 25–26
acceptance, healthy psychological boundary and, 160
accountability
 power and deficiency in, 34–35
 status in the world and messages about, 24
 systemic trauma, path to intimacy, and, 19
Adams, A., 141
adverse health experiences, LGBTQIA+ people and, 15
affect, in VIMBASI method, 52
affection
 fear of public displays of, 18, 20
 shame and withholding of, 35, 76
affinity spaces, 27
affirmation cards, boundaries and, 162
affirmation jar, 137
affirmation stories, 141
affirming conversations, in identity and relational cherishing case example, 134–35
African Americans, lack of health insurance and, 14

agency, 62, 63
 building liberatory connections and, 130
 expanded sense of, 42
 family narratives and, 84
 intimacy and, 24
 reinstating, in client, 47
 relational terrain and, 80
aggression, 156
Akomolafe, B., 164
Alaska Natives, mental disturbance rates among, 13
Alexander, I., 21, 27
Alibey, R., 26
all-in-the-same-boat phenomenon, relational healing circles and, 126, 127
alphapoems, 141
American Indians, mental disturbance rates among, 13
American Psychiatric Association, 13
analogies, 79
ancestral art creation, intergenerational compassionate network and, 119–20
ancestral trauma
 responsible externalizing and, 94
 rumbling through, assisting clients in, 53–54
ancestral wisdom, PRIDE model and, 51
anger, 54
ANS. *see* autonomic nervous system (ANS)
anxiety, 12

LGBTQIA+ people and, 14, 15
 trauma survivors and, 54
Arabi, M. I., 56
art
 coming-out story and, 78
 family tree art, 87
 relational terrain and, 82
 survival habits and, 75
artistic vision boards, relational declarations and, 148
Asian Americans, barriers to support for, 14
assaulted sense of self
 BIPOC people and, 28–30
 LGBTQIA+ persons and, 30–31
 systemic trauma and, 28–32
attribution, threat mitigation and, 95
audio declarations, 148
authentic heart, engaging with, xxiii
authenticity, resilience and, 141
autonomic nervous system (ANS)
 functions of, 10
 two branches of, 11
 window of tolerance and, 12

beauty of your identity, cultivating space for discovery of, 132
Beckes, L., 39
behavior, in VIMBASI method, 52
belonging. *see* social welcoming and belonging

biome
  other human beings as part of, 39
  relational healing circles as, 126
  safe, lack of, 40
BIOME, becoming
  intentionality behind, 40
  path toward liberation and, 174
  pivoting and rumbling and, 55
  remaining for our clients, 59, 105
BIOME, the, xxii
  building liberatory connections and, 130, 132
  continuous trauma work and, 109–10
  finding exceptions trans throuple case example and, 121
  grief in the GLITCH model and, 166
  habits of survival and elements of, 71
  integration of, into relational curiosity, 62–63
  intention setting case example and, 103–5
  outcome of the rumble and, 53
  PRIDE model and presence of, 58
  relational curiosity overview and, 91t–92t
  relational healing circles and educating group about, 127
  responsible externalizing and, 97, 108
  setting of intentions and, 102
  see also GLITCH model; PRIDE model; VIMBASI method
BIOME, therapeutic
  bravery, 40, 40, 41–43, 49
  components of, 40, 40
  epistemic embracing, 40, 40, 48–49

intensity/intimacy, 40, 40, 44–45, 49
micro-liberatory movements, 40, 40, 47–48, 49
openness, 40, 40, 45–47, 49
practitioner's reflection on, 49
required stance in, 40
BIPOC people
  assaulted sense of self and, 28–30
  decolonizing the relationship for BIPOC couples, 153
  grieving process and, 96
  intergenerational trauma and BIPOC families, 83
  lack of access to support and, 14
  meaning of marginalization for, xxi
  rejection sensitivity and impact on, 32
  resilience and well-being of, 138, 141
  self-marginalization and, 47
Black bodies, exploitation of, 48
Black people, psychophysiological reality of, 12–13
Black women in UK, mental health challenges of, 14
bleaching of skin, 30
Boal, A., 65
boarding schools, 13, 29
boundaries
  containing, 155–59
  healthy, need for, 155
  in identity and relational cherishing case example, 135
  intimate relationships, systemic realities, and, 20, 30
  nurturing your creativity and, 161–62
  psychological, 155, 159–61
boundary check-ins, 161
boundary visualization, 161
boundary work, 132, 155–59, 163
Boyega, J., 32
brain, 10

genes and function of, 54
memory reconsolidation and regulation of, 113, 128
oppression and impact on, 65
racism and threat-inhibition networks in, 8
rumble and transformation of, 55
see also nervous system
bravery, 94, 110
  bidirectional relationship between openness and, 46
  coming-out story and, 91t
  critical consciousness and, 62, 73
  family narratives and, 84 92t
  habits of survival and, 70, 73, 91t
  in PRIDE model for exploring systemic trauma with marginalized couples, 57
  responsible externalizing and, 97
  in theater of oppression case, 67, 68, 69
  theater of oppression technique and, 91t
  in therapeutic BIOME, 40, 40, 41–43, 49
  see also courage
breath constriction, oppression manifesting as, 48
brown, a. m., 55, 149
Bryant, T., 6
Buddhism, imagination in, 55–56
building blocks, 142
Butler, O., 56

Canada, Indigenous children in residential schools in, 29
cancer, LGBTQIA+ community and, 15
cardiovascular disease, same-sex-loving women and bisexual women and, 15–16
case examples, methodology behind, xxii
celebration rituals, 137

Index

central nervous system, components of, 10
change, relationships as crucibles for, 129
chattel slavery, BIPOC bodies and, 48
cherishing
  future- and process-oriented statements and, 143
  in relational declarations case example, 145
  in trans throuple case example, 134, 135, 136, 137
cherishing letters, 137
chronic and pervasive systemic trauma, 7, 8t
clinical as political, 37, 47
clinical curiosity, 6
clinicians, critical consciousness practice and, 41–42. *see also* practitioner's reflection; therapeutic stance
Coan, J. A., 39
co-contacting and naming the harm
  in case example, 98
  responsible externalizing and, 94, 95–96, 108
collaborative resilience poetry, 141
collages
  collage images signifying boundaries, 161
  finding exceptions and, 124
  survival habits and, 75
collective wisdom, PRIDE model and, 51
colonialism
  erasure of non-White ways of being and, 29
  intergenerational trauma and, 53
coming-out story, 63, 64, 75–79
  case example, 76–78, 103–5, 150
  decolonizing the relationship case example, 150–53
  nurturing your creativity and, 78–79
  overview of, 91t

questions related to, 75–76, 91t
commitment
  as a dynamic force, 144
  relational declarations and, 143
  in relational declarations case example, 145, 146
community, remembering value of, 174
compassion, 44, 61, 154
  dialectical process and, 126
  relational healing circles and, 127
  rumbles and, 54, 55
  sending to ancestor, intergenerational compassionate network and, 114
  sending toward emotional learning, finding exceptions and, 121
compassionate gestures, in containing boundaries, 156, 158
compassionate letters, intergenerational compassionate network and, 120
confrontation, rumbling and, 53
connection and connectedness, 62, 102
  cherishing and, 137
  facilitating through one's systemic context, 24, 36
  protection and preservation of, 160
  reclaiming of narratives and, 149
  soundscapes of, 154
  see also liberatory connections, building; social welcoming and belonging
consolidation, definition of, 112
containing boundaries, 155–59
  case example, 157–59
  essence of, 155
  Shore's equation for, 156
containment, intention setting and, 105
continuous trauma work. *see* trauma work, continuous

conversations under the stars, 137
conversion therapy, 48
couple-level minority stress, 21–22, 35
couple-level shame, 35–36
courage
  "delicate," in relational declarations case example, 144, 147
  trying it out phase in GLITCH model and, 169
  see also bravery
creating, in the GLITCH model, 165, *165,* 170, 171, 172
creativity
  building liberatory connections and, 130
  GLITCH framework and, 59
  intention setting and, 101, 103
  trying it out phase in GLITCH model and, 169
criminal justice system
  as perpetrators of systemic harm, 6–7, 23, 39
  relational terrain and, 92t
critical action, 41, 42
critical consciousness
  bravery and, 62, 73
  definition of, 41
  family narratives and, 86
  habits of survival and, 70, 73
  path toward liberation and, 174
  practicing, 41–42, 50
  practitioner role in systemic oppression and, 41–42
  primary components of, 41
  in responsible externalizing example, 97
  systemic intentions and, 100
critical reflection, 41
culturally informed psychology, main question asked by, 6
cultural wisdom, relational healing circles and use of, 125
curiosity, 61. *see also* relational curiosity

Dagara people, on sacred intimacy of couples, 93
dance
  decolonizing the relationship and, 154
  relational declarations and, 148
  relational terrain and use of, 82
  theater of oppression and, 70
danger, dorsal vagal system and, 11–12
data sharing, relational healing circles and, 124–25
Dayton, T., 87
declaration collages, 148
declarations, power of, 142
decolonization
  in therapeutic space, active, 63
  of therapy, path toward liberation and, 174
decolonizing the relationship, 47, 48, 132, 149–54, 163
  case example, 150–53
  definition of, 149
  halting the dance of the stereotypes and, 153–54
  nurturing your creativity and, 154
  questions related to, 149–50
decontextualized trauma, 18
delicate courage, in relational declarations case example, 144, 147
demystifying the process, in intergenerational compassionate network case example, 116
depression, 12, 14, 15, 54
devaluation, psychological domination and, 28
development
  containing boundaries and, 157, 158
  in decolonizing the relationship case example, 151
  in identity and relational cherishing case example, 135

  in individual and relational resilience case example, 140
  path toward liberation and, 174
  in PRIDE model, 50, 56, 57, 58
  in relational declarations case example, 145, 146
diabetes, bisexual men and, 16
dialectical process, relational healing circles and, 126–28
dichos, "subversive strategies" provided by, 125
Diemer, M., 41
dignity, 61, 107
disability rates, LGBTQIA+ community and, 16
discernment, healthy psychological boundary and, 160
disconnection, threat and sense of, 11. *see also* connection and connectedness
discrimination, 9t, 166
  couple-level minority stress and, 21
  financial harm and, 16–17
  intimacy and, xxii
  intimate relationships, systemic realities, and, 20
  reclaiming identity and, 131
disenfranchised pain, systemic trauma and, 7
DNA (deoxyribonucleic acid), epigenetic regulation and, 54
dorsal vagal branch, 11–12
dorsal vagal system, threat, sense of danger and, 11–12
double consciousness, 29
dramatic tableaux, theater of oppression and, 69
drawing(s)
  boundaries and, 161
  co-contacting and naming the harm and, 95, 98
  finding exceptions and, 124
  survival habits and, 75

  theater of oppression and, 70
Du Bois, W. E. B., 29

ear, inner, autonomic nervous system and, 11
Ecker, 112
economic barriers, LGBTQIA+ people and, 16–17
economic structures, as perpetrators of systemic harm, 6, 23
educational system
  as perpetrator of systemic harm, 6, 23, 39
  relational terrain and, 92t
egalitarian and emancipatory ethos, cultivating, 46–47
embodied movement
  decolonizing the relationship and, 154
  intergenerational compassionate network and, 120
Emergent Strategy (brown), 55
emotional dysregulation, 53
emotional learning(s), 112
  dialectical process and, 126–27
  finding exceptions and activation of, 120
  finding exceptions and witnessing stance toward, 114, 120
  finding exceptions trans throuple case example and, 123
  initial, assessing for, 115, 121
  intergenerational compassionate network and activation of, 114
  in intergenerational compassionate network case example, 118, 119
  memory reconsolidation and activation of, 112–13, 128
  relational healing circles and, 127, 128
emotional memories, 112

Index

emotional regulation, systemic trauma *vs.* single-incident trauma and, 9t
emotion-focused therapy, 75
empathy, 134, 154
  finding exceptions trans throuple case example and, 122
  rumbles and, 54
employment challenges, LGBTQIA+ persons and, 16–17
empty-chair technique, 95
epigenetics, 54
epigenome (or epigenetic) markers, 54
epistemic embracing, 56
  building liberatory connections and, 130
  coming-out story and, 78
  containing boundaries and, 157, 158
  continuous trauma work and, 109
  in decolonizing the relationship case example, 150, 151
  family narratives and, 86, 92t
  habits of survival and, 73, 91t
  in identity and relational cherishing case example, 133, 134, 135
  imagination and, 102
  in individual and relational resilience case example, 139, 140
  in intention setting case example, 104, 106, 107
  in PRIDE model for exploring systemic trauma with marginalized couples, 57
  relational curiosity and, 63
  in relational declarations case example, 144, 145, 146
  relational privilege score and, 92t
  relational terrain and, 92t

responsible externalizing and, 97, 108
  in theater of oppression case, 66, 67, 68
  in therapeutic BIOME, 40, 40, 48–49
equality, yarning and, 61
ethical non-monogamy, 89
evolution
  containing boundaries and, 159
  in decolonizing the relationship case example, 152–53
  in identity and relational cherishing case example, 136
  path toward liberation and, 174
  in PRIDE model, 50, 56–57, 57, 58
  in relational declarations case example, 146, 147
exception journals, 124
exceptions, definition of, 120
exceptions, finding, 120–24, 128
  case example, 121–23
  nurturing your creativity and, 123–24
  steps in, 120–21
exhaustion. *see* fatigue and exhaustion
experimentation, trying it out phase in GLITCH model and, 169

facial muscles, autonomic nervous system and, 11
failure, trying it out phase in GLITCH model and, 169
family narratives, 63, 64, 83–87, 115
  case example, 84–86
  nurturing your creativity and, 86–87
  overview of, 92t
  questions related to, 83–84, 92t
  relational privilege and, 54
family tree art, 87

Fani, N., 8
fatigue and exhaustion, 5, 9, 12, 16, 28, 90
fawning, 26, 156
Federal Reserve Survey of Consumer Finance, 16
felt sense
  definition of, 112
  "psychological floor" and, 33, 79
fight or flight response, 11
financial barriers, mental health access and, 14
financial harm, 16–17, 23, 101
financial protection
  lack of, 27
  safety and, 25
financial security, intimate relationships, systemic realities, and, 21
Freire, P., 41
future-oriented statements, examples of, 143

gaslighting, therapeutic, defining, 49
gender identity, value of, being intimately aware of, 132, 133
generational story mapping, intergenerational compassionate network and, 120
genes, brain and nervous system function and, 54
genital mutilation, 48
genocide, intergenerational trauma and, 53
GLITCH model, 59
  as the chasm in your work, 165
  creating in, 165, 165, 170, 171, 172, 174
  grief in, 165, 165, 166, 171, 172, 174
  honoring the process in, 165, 165, 171, 172, 174
  imagination in, 165, 165, 168–69, 171, 172, 174
  liminality in, 165, 165, 166–67, 171, 172, 174

GLITCH model (*continued*)
  path toward liberation and, 174
  trying it out in, 165, *165*, 169–70, 171, 172
  see also BIOME, the; PRIDE model; VIMBASI method
Good Inside (Kennedy), 154
Greenberg, L., 33, 75
grief, 54, 59, 162
  as birthplace of imagination, 166, 168
  in the GLITCH model, 165, *165*, 166, 171, 172, 174
  intention setting and, 101
  responsible externalizing and, 94, 96, 108
  in responsible externalizing example, 98–99
"grounded learnings," 168
groundedness, expanded sense of, 42

habits of survival, 63, *64*, 70–75
  case example, 71–74
  definition of, 70
  nurturing your creativity and, 74–75
  overview of, 91*t*
  questions related to, 70–71, 91*t*
Haines, S., 142
hair discrimination, White gaze and, 29
Hardy, K., 28, 29, 30, 44, 46, 64
Hartig, M. D., 32
healing
  honoring the process in GLITCH model and, 171
  identity and, 57
  imaginal worlds and, 56
  see also BIOME, the: GLITCH model; PRIDE model; VIMBASI method
health care providers, LGBTQIA+ community and, 15, 16
heart rate, increased, oppression manifesting as, 48

Hemphill, P., 34, 155
heteronormative norms, decolonizing the relationship and impact of, 149–50
Holocaust, intergenerational trauma and, 54
homonegativity, internalized, 33
homophobia, 9*t*, 35, 66, 97, 139, 166
honoring the process, in the GLITCH model, 165, *165*, 171, 172, 174
hooks, b., 168
humility, 62
hyperarousal, 65
  in the window of possibilities, *13*
  in window of tolerance, 12
hypervigilance, 8, 8*t*, 9, 12
hypoarousal, 65
  in the window of possibilities, *13*
  in window of tolerance, 12

ICN. *see* intergenerational compassionate network (ICN)
identity
  healing and, 57
  reclaiming, 131, 174
  systemic trauma *vs.* single-incident trauma and, 9*t*
identity and relational cherishing, 132–37, 163
  case example, 133–37
  nurturing your creativity and, 137
  supporting clients with, 132–33
identity collages, 137
identity hearts, 137
images and imagery, 65
  psychological boundaries and, 160, 161
  in VIMBASI method, 52
imaginal worlds, creating, 56
imagination, 59
  building liberatory connections and, 130
  development as manifestation of, 56

epistemic embracing and, 102
  in the GLITCH model, 165, *165*, 168–69, 171, 172, 174
  grief as birthplace of, 166, 168
  intention setting and, 101
  in intention setting case example, 103, 106
  of others, LGBTQIA+ people trapped within, 149
  path toward liberation and, 174
  in PRIDE model, 50, 55–56, *57*, 58
  in relational declarations case example, 145
  relational healing circles and, 127
  in VIMBASI method, 52
immigrant families, intergenerational trauma and, 83
immobilization, 12
implicit memory system, memory reconsolidation and, 112
income disparities, race and, 16
Indigenous children, oppression of, 48
Indigenous people, intergenerational trauma and, 53
Indigenous students in Australia, systemic harm and, 6
individual and relational resilience, 132, 138–42, 163
  case example, 139–41
  definition of, 138
  nurturing your creativity and, 141–42
  protective factors and, 138
  questions related to, 138
individual-level minority stress, 21
integrity, yarning and, 61
intensity/intimacy
  coming-out story and, 91*t*
  in PRIDE model for exploring systemic trauma with marginalized couples, 57

Index

relational privilege score and, 92t
responsible externalizing and, 97
in therapeutic BIOME, 40, 40, 44–45, 49
see also intimacy
intentions
  definition of, 100
  types of, 100
  see also relational intentions; systemic intentions
intentions, setting, 59, 93, 99–108
  BIOME and, 102–3
  case examples, 103–7
  PRIDE process and, 101–2
  questions related to, 99–100
interdependence
  status in the world and messages about, 24
  systemic trauma, path to intimacy, and, 19
intergenerational compassionate network (ICN), 114–20, 128
  case example, 115–19
  nurturing your creativity and, 119–20
intergenerational trauma, 83
  examples of, 53–54
  relational curiosity overview, 92t
intimacy, 94
  context of, 24
  continuous trauma work and, 109
  embodied relational privilege and, 39
  fawn response and, 26
  habits of survival and, 72
  in intention setting case example, 103, 104
  pivoting and interrogating our stories about, 41, 42–43
  risky nature of, 24
  systemic trauma and disrupted path to, 17–22, 23
  in theater of oppression case, 67, 69

widening our understanding of, 23
see also intensity/intimacy; relational privilege
intimacy story, pivoting and interrogating, 42–43, 102
Islam, imagination in, 56

job market, LGBTQIA+ people and, 17
joy
  relational declarations process and, 147
  seeking in identity and relational cherishing case example, 134, 137
Joy, B., 35
justice, path toward liberation and, 174

Kennedy, B., 154
"kind intention," compassion as, 55
kindness
  containing boundaries and, 156
  rumbles and, 54

language barriers, mental health access and, 14
larynx, autonomic nervous system and, 11
Latinx community, psychological distress rates among, 13
Lavner, J. A., 21
letters
  cherishing, 137
  relational declarations and, 148
LGBTQIA+ bodies, genital mutilation and, 48
LGBTQIA+ community
  coming out and persons in, 75
  powerful cultural sayings within, 125
LGBTQIA+ people
  assaulted sense of self and, 30–31
  couple-level minority stress and, 22

criminal justice system and challenges faced by, 6–7
decolonizing the relationship and LGBTQIA+ couples, 150–53
fawning in LGBTQIA+ partnerships, 26–27
financial harm and, 17
grieving process and, 96
lack of access to support and, 14
loss of connection from religious communities and, 7
meaning of marginalization for, xxi
physical harm and, 15–16
rejection sensitivity and impact on, 32–33
resilience and well-being of, 138
self-marginalization and LGBTQIA+ clients, 47
suicidality and, 14
liberation
  GLITCH framework and, 59
  reflecting on the path toward, 173–75
liberation psychology
  epistemic embracing and, 48–49
  main question asked by, 6
liberation work, theater of oppression and, 65–66
liberatory connections, building, xxii, 47, 56, 57, 59, 129–63
  the BIOME and, 130
  boundary work, 132, 155–59, 163
  decolonizing the relationship, 132, 149–54, 163
  identity and relational cherishing, 132–37, 163
  individual and relational resilience, 132, 138–41, 163
  neurobiological underpinnings of, 131
  practitioner's reflection on, 162
  PRIDE model and, 130–31

liberatory connections, building (*continued*)
   psychological boundaries, 159–62
   questions related to, 130
   relational and systemic intentions and, 131
   relational declarations, 132, 142–48, 163
   techniques used for, 132, 163
liberatory connections, definition of, 129, 162
life mapping, habits of survival and, 74
liminality, 59
   definition of, 166
   in the GLITCH model, 165, *165*, 166–67, 171, 172, 174
   imagination and, 167, 168
living your truth, 64, 102
   "being out" and, 31–32
   building liberatory connections and, 131
   habits of survival and, 72
   openness and, 47
   as a privilege, 8
   relational privilege score and, 89, 90, 92*t*
   relational privilege score assessment for, 87, 88*t*
   in relational privilege wheel, 24, *25*, 28–32, 36, 87
lost spaces, reclaiming, 164–72
   GLITCH model and, *165*, 165–72
   intense turning points in, 165
love
   boundless, path toward liberation and, 175
   containing boundaries and, 159
   defining in decolonizing the relationship case example, 151–53

marginalization
   continuous trauma work and, 109
   intimacy and, xxii

   meaning of, xxi
marginalized people
   boundaries and, need for, 155
   denying validity of relationships between, 149
   epistemological assumptions of, honoring, 51
   lack of safe biome for, 40, 49
   lack of social welcoming and belonging for, 32–33
   protective factors in lives of, 138
   reclaiming imagination for, 55
   reclaiming their identities, 131
   reflecting on path toward liberation for, 173–75
   relational harm and, 17–23
   self-invalidation of, 7–8
   shame as experienced by, 34
   see also BIPOC people; LGBTQIA+ people
marriage
   same-sex, 1920
   slave marriages, 19
Martín-Baró, I., 48
meanings, in VIMBASI method, 52
medical professionals, LGBTQIA+ community and, 15, 16
memory reconsolidation, 112–13, 128
   in finding exceptions trans throuple case example, 121–23
   relational healing circles and, 124
Menakem, R., 18, 52, 129
metaphors, 65, 79
   mapping, family narratives and, 87
   psychological boundaries and, 160
   relational terrain and, 80, 81
   writing, 74
microaggressions, 7, 14
micro-liberatory movements, 56, 63

building liberatory connections and, 130
continuous trauma work and, 109
in decolonizing the relationship case example, 151
family narratives and, 84, 86
in identity and relational cherishing case example, 133
in individual and relational resilience case example, 139
in intention setting case example, 103, 104, 106
in intergenerational compassionate network case example, 116
in PRIDE model for exploring systemic trauma with marginalized couples, 57
in relational declarations case example, 144
relational terrain and, 80
responsible externalizing and, 97, 98, 108
in responsible externalizing case example, 97, 98
in theater of oppression case example, 69
theater of oppression technique and, 91*t*
in therapeutic BIOME, 40, *40*, 47–48, 49
mindfulness, 53
mind mapping, finding exceptions and, 124
misgendering experiences, 14
mismatch detection
   dialectical process and, 126–27
   finding exceptions and, 121
   finding exceptions trans throuple case example and, 122, 123
   intergenerational compassionate network and, 114–15, 116, 118, 119
   relational healing circle and, 128
Morrison, T., 29
movement, 48, 65

Index   193

habits of survival and, 74
intergenerational compassionate network and, 120
relational declarations and, 148
relational terrain and, 82
theater of oppression and, 70
see also micro-liberatory movements
multigenerational trauma, 53–54
muscle tension, oppression manifesting as, 48
mutual aid dynamics, relational healing circles and, 124–27

National Indigenous Youth Education Coalition School Exclusion Project (Australia), 6
neck, autonomic nervous system and, 11
nervous system
  attending to sympathetic and parasympathetic branches of, 53
  genes and function of, 54
  habits of survival and, 70
  hypervigilance and impact on, 9
  intention setting and, 102
  oppression and impact on, 65
  relational terrain and, 79–80
  systemic trauma *vs.* single-incident trauma and, 8*t*
  two major parts of, 10
  see also brain
network lability, 113, 118
New Zealand, health disparities for LGBTQIA+ people in, 14–15
nonbinary identity, celebrating, 134
non-monogamy, ethical, 89

Ogolsky, B. G., 94, 95
openness, 63
  bidirectional relationship between bravery and, 46
  coming-out story and, 91*t*
  family narratives and, 92*t*
  habits of survival and, 72, 73, 91*t*
  in intergenerational compassionate network case example, 116
  in PRIDE model for exploring systemic trauma with marginalized couples, 57
  relational privilege score and, 89, 92*t*
  relational terrain and, 80, 92*t*
  in theater of oppression case, 66
  theater of oppression technique and, 91*t*
  in therapeutic BIOME, 40, 40, 47–48, 49
oppression
  internalized, shame and, 34
  theater of, 63–70, 64
  unpleasant bodily sensations and, 48
Oschieng, O., 56
"outness," restricting levels of, 31–32

Pacific Islanders, barriers to support for, 14
painting
  relational declarations and, 148
  survival habits and, 75
parasympathetic nervous system (PNS), 11, 12, 53, 65, 131
passing privilege, 31
pause, in containing boundaries, 156
peripheral nervous system, components of, 10, *10*
personal change, relationships as crucibles for, 129
personal integrity words, 156, 157–58
physical harm, 15–16, 23
physical protection, 25
  femme presenting *vs.* masc presenting and, 31
  lack of, 27

picong, in Trinidadian culture, 125
pivoting, 61, 162
  becoming the BIOME and, 55
  coming-out story and, 76, 77, 91*t*
  family narratives and, 84, 92*t*
  habits of survival and, 71, 73, 91*t*
  intention setting and, 102
  in intention setting case example, 103, 105
  path toward liberation and, 174
  in PRIDE model, 50, 51–53, 57, 58, 91*t*
  relational curiosity and centrality of, 62
  relational healing circles and, 127
  relational privilege score and, 89
  relational terrain and, 80, 81, 82, 92*t*
  in theater of oppression case, 66, 67, 68
  theater of oppression technique and, 66, 91*t*
  see also rumbling
pivoting, four components of
  turning backward, 51, 52, 58
  turning forward, 51, 52, 58
  turning inward, 51–52, 58
  turning outward, 51, 52, 58
playback theater, coming-out story and, 79
Play-Doh crafting
  coming-out story and, 78
  theater of oppression and, 70
playfulness, trying it out phase in GLITCH model and, 169
PNS. *see* parasympathetic nervous system (PNS)
poetry
  collaborative resilience, 141
  coming-out story and, 78
  relational declarations and, 148

political efficacy, 41, 42
Politics of Trauma, The (Haines), 142
Polyvagal Theory, 11
Porges, S., 11
posttraumatic stress disorder (PTSD), 8*t*
postures, micro-liberatory movements and, 48
poverty, 9*t*
power
  deficiency in accountability and, 34–35
  harm committed in therapy and, 46
  in individual and relational resilience case example, 139
  reinstating, for minoritized clients, 47, 48
  risk taking in romantic relationships and, 24
practitioner externalizing
  responsible externalizing and, 94–95, 108
  in responsible externalizing example, 97
practitioners, redefining role of, 168
practitioner's reflection
  on the BIOME, 49
  on building liberatory connections, 162
  on PRIDE model, 58
  on relational curiosity strategies, 91
  on relational healing circles, 128
  on relational privilege, 36
  on relational risk taking, 45
  on responsible externalizing, 108
  on systemic trauma, 23
PRIDE model, xxii, 37, 49, 51–58, 59
  building liberatory connections and, 130–31, 132
  continuous trauma work and, 110, 113
  creating, reason behind, 149
  development in, 50, 56, 57, 58

evolving in, 50, 56–57, 57, 58
for exploring systemic trauma with marginalized couples, 57
finding exceptions and, 120
habits of survival and, 71
imagination in, 50, 55–56, 57, 58
integration of, into relational curiosity, 62, 63
intention setting case example and, 103–5
path toward liberation and, 174
pivoting in, 50, 51–53, 57, 58
practitioner's reflection on, 58
relational curiosity overview and stages in, 91*t*–92*t*
rumbling in, 50, 51, 53–55, 57, 58
what it is and what it is not, 51, 58
see also BIOME, the; GLITCH model; VIM-BASI method
PRIDE process
  intention setting and, 101–2
  responsible externalizing and, 96
process-oriented statements, examples of, 143
protection, 102
  boundaries and, 155
  connections and, 160
  habits of survival and, 72
  relational privilege score and, 89, 92*t*
  relational privilege score assessment for, 87, 88*t*
  in relational privilege wheel, 24, 25, 25–27, 36, 87
  safety *vs.*, 25–26
protective factors
  individual and relational resilience case example and, 139
  resilience and, 138
psychodrama, family narratives and, 87

psychological and emotional harm, 9–15, 23
psychological boundaries, 155, 159–62
  case example, 160–61
  central components of, 160
  definition of, 159
  healthy, establishing, 159–60
psychological floor, "felt sense" of the world and, 33, 79
psychological protection, 25
  femme presenting *vs.* masc presenting and, 31
  lack of, 27
psychosis, racial minorities in the United Kingdom and, 13
PTSD. *see* posttraumatic stress disorder (PTSD)

queer people, physical harm and, 15
queerphobia
  impact of, struggling with, 18–19
  internalized, high levels of, 14

race, income disparities and, 16
racial discrimination
  couples' relational health and, 21–22
  lack of social welcoming and belonging and, 32
racial identity, value of, being intimately aware of, 132, 133
racial minorities
  financial harm and, 16–17
  psychophysiological reality of, 13
racism, 9*t*, 18, 105, 141, 166
  impact of, struggling with, 18–19
  income disparities and, 16
  mental health challenges and, 13–14
  threat-inhibition networks in brain and, 8

Index

Ramchand, R., 14
Randai.i., U. B., 61
reciprocity, yarning and, 61
reflection prompts, decolonizing the relationships and, 154
regulation
  of brain, memory reconsolidation and, 113, 128
  emotional, systemic trauma vs. single-incident trauma and, 9t
  relational healing circles and, 127
rejection sensitivity, 32–33
relational curiosity, xxii, 53, 59, 61–92, 97, 101, 121
  BIOME framework integrated into, 61, 62–63
  co-contacting and naming the harm vs., 95
  PRIDE model integrated into, 61, 62, 63
  relational healing circles and, 127
  responsible externalizing and, 93, 94
  yarning and, 61
relational curiosity strategies
  coming-out story, 63, 64, 75–79, 91t
  family narratives, 63, 64, 83–87, 92t
  habits of survival, 63, 64, 70–75, 91t
  overview of, 91t–92t
  practitioner's reflection on, 91
  relational privilege score, 63, 64, 87–90, 88t, 92t
  relational terrain, 63, 64, 79–82, 92t
  theater of oppression, 63–70, 64, 91t
relational declarations, 48, 132, 142–48, 163
  changing, 147
  features of, 142
  questions related to, 143
  self discovery and, 148
  visual reminders for, 147
relational harm, 17–23

relational healing circles, 124–28
  all-in-the-same-boat phenomenon and, 126
  definition of, 124
  dialectical process and, 126–28
  discussing a taboo area and, 125–26
  moving through, steps in, 127–28
  nurturing your creativity and, 128
  practitioner's reflection on, 128
  sharing data and, 124–25
relational imagination, 47
relational intentions
  building liberatory connections and, 129, 131
  case examples, 103–7
  containing boundaries and, 157–58
  decolonizing the relationship case example and, 152
  definition of, 100
  in finding exceptions trans throuple case example, 121, 122
  in identity and relational cherishing case example, 136
  individual and relational resilience case example and, 139, 141
  intergenerational compassionate network case example and, 115
  in relational declarations case example, 144
  relational healing circles and, 127
  setting, 52
  supporting clients with, questions for, 102–3
relational intention words, 156
relational privilege, 3, 23, 64, 141
  clinicians' relational risks and, 44
  coming-out story and, 75, 78

  critical reflection and, 41
  definition of, 24, 36
  dimensions of, 24, 87
  embodied, defining intimacy and, 39
  family narratives and, 54
  habits of survival and, 71, 72
  intergenerational trauma and, 83
  openness and, 47
  our own, definitions of relationality and, 102
  practitioner's reflection on, 36
  reinstating, in client, 47
  theater of the oppressed case and, 66, 68
relational privilege score, 63, 64, 87–90
  case example, 89–90
  description of, 87
  overview of, 92t
  questions related to, 88–89, 92t
relational privilege wheel, 24, 25
  living your truth, 24, 25, 28–32, 36
  protection in, 24, 25, 25–27, 36
  self-worth in, 24, 25, 34–36
  social welcoming and belonging in, 24, 25, 32–33, 36
relational risk, 39, 63, 110
  family narratives and, 85
  finding exceptions trans throuple case example and, 121, 122
  grieving and, 96
  intensity and intimacy and, 44–45
  practitioner's reflection on, 45
  relational privilege score and, 90
  relational terrain and, 81, 82
  in theater of oppression case, 67, 68
relational terrain, 63, 64, 79–82
  case example, 80–82, 105
  nurturing your creativity and, 82

relational terrain (*continued*)
overview of, 92*t*
questions related to, 80, 92*t*
relational worlds, creating, 142
relationship, yarning and, 61
religious institutions, as perpetrators of systemic harm, 6, 7, 23, 39
residential schools, in Canada, 29
resilience, 63. *see also* individual and relational resilience
containing boundaries and, 156
definition of, 138
resilience mapping, 141
resilience rituals, 142
resistance, encouraging, coming-out story and, 77
responsibility, yarning and, 61
responsible externalizing, xxii, 59, 93–99, 101, 129
BIOME framework and, 97, 108
case example for, 97–99
client choices relative to, 108
co-contacting and naming the harm, 94, 95–96, 108
critical reflection and, 41
definition of, 93, 108
grieving, 94, 96, 108
practitioner externalizing, 94–95, 108
practitioner's reflection on, 108
PRIDE process and, 96
relational curiosity and elements of, 93, 94
three components of, 94, 108
responsiveness
status in the world and messages about, 24
systemic trauma, path to intimacy, and, 19
retreating, 156
role playing
boundaries and, 161
decolonizing the relationship and, 154

family narratives and, 87
finding exceptions and, 124
theater of oppression and, 69
roles, in theater of oppression, 64, 65, 68
romantic relationships, power in the world and risk taking in, 24
Ross, J., 141
rumbling, 61
becoming the BIOME and, 55
coming-out story and, 76, 77, 78, 91*t*
family narratives and, 84, 85, 92*t*
finding exceptions trans throuple case example and, 121–22
habits of survival and, 71, 73, 91*t*
intention setting and, 101
path toward liberation and, 174
in PRIDE model, 50, 51, 53–55, 57, 58
relational curiosity and centrality of, 62
relational healing circles and, 127
relational privilege score and, 89, 90
relational terrain and, 80, 81, 92*t*
responsible externalizing and, 96
in theater of oppression case, 67, 68
theater of oppression technique and, 66, 91*t*
trauma work as, 110
see also pivoting
ruptures, habits of survival and, 73

safety
individual and relational resilience and, 139, 141
protection *vs.*, 25–26
in relational declarations case example, 145

rumbling and, 53
same-sex marriage, delegitimizing of, 19–20
Sand Talk (Yunkaporta), 25
sculptural representations, relational declarations and, 148
self-acceptance, 141
self-compassion, 55. *see also* compassion
self-determination, yarning and, 61
self-hatred, relational harm and, 35
self-invalidation, 7–8
self-knowledge, relational health and, 30
self-marginalization, reducing likelihood of, 47
self-protection, shame and, 34
self-trust
facilitated by one's systemic context, 24, 36
lack of, intimate relationships and, 20
self-worth, 102, 110
reinstating, in client, 47
relational privilege score and, 89, 92*t*
relational privilege score assessment for, 87, 88*t*
in relational privilege wheel, 24, 25, 87
theater of the oppressed case and, 68
sensory reminders, boundaries and, 162
sex discrimination, lack of social welcoming and belonging and, 32
sexism, 9*t*
sexual identity
"being out" and, 31–32
value of, being intimately aware of, 132, 133
sexual minorities, financial harm and, 16–17
shame, 12, 31
definition of, 34
individual-level *vs.* couple-level, 35
self-marginalization and, 47

Index

withholding of affection and, 35, 76
Shange, N., 132
Shore, J. T., 33, 79, 155, 156, 159, 160
Siegel, D., 9, 10, 12
single-incident trauma, systemic trauma vs., 8t–9t
slavery
  erasure of non-White ways of being and, 29
  intergenerational trauma and, 53
  relational harm and, 19
slowness, in decolonizing the relationship case example, 150, 152
SNS. *see* sympathetic nervous system (SNS)
social baseline theory, 39, 126
social change, relationships as crucibles for, 129
social engagement systems, compromised, systemic harm and, 26
social justice in practice, PRIDE model as, 51
social location, transparency about, 45–46
social security "spousal" benefits, 20
social welcoming and belonging
  relational privilege score and, 89, 92t
  relational privilege score assessment for, 87, 88t
  in relational privilege wheel, 24, 25, 32–33, 36, 87
  theater of the oppressed case and, 68
  see also connection and connectedness; liberatory connections, building
somatic engagement, 47–48, 65
Somé, Sobonfu, 50, 57, 93, 130
Souls of Black Folk, The (Du Bois), 29
soundscapes of connections, decolonizing the relationship and, 154

South Africa
  economic inequality in, 16
  homophobic and transphobic violence in, 6
spinal cord, 10
Spirit of Intimacy, The (Somé), 50
STAIR (self-trust and integrated resilience) method, 33, 79
Stamps, K., 19
Stats NZ, 14
stereotypes, halting dance of, in decolonizing the relationship, 153–54
stories about intimacy, pivoting and interrogating our own, 41, 42–43
storytelling sessions, 137
stress crossover, 22
stress spillover, 22
substance abuse, LGBTQIA+ people and, 14
suicidality, LGBTQIA+ persons and, 14
sympathetic nervous system (SNS), 11, 65, 131
  limited relational possibilities and impact on, 26
  mindfulness and attending to, 53
  window of tolerance and, 12
systemic change, political efficacy and, 42
systemic harm, 46, 63
  challenging, relationship shifts and, 101
  perpetrators of, 6, 23, 26, 39
  PRIDE model and working with, 51
  as relational harm, 39
  undoing, 47
  unpredictable nature of, 7, 8
  see also systemic trauma
systemic harm, distress caused by, 9–23
  financial harm, 16–17, 23
  physical harm, 15–16, 23
  psychological and emotional harm, 9–15, 23
  relational harm, 17–23

systemic intentions
  building liberatory connections and, 129, 131
  case examples, 103–7
  containing boundaries and, 156, 158
  creating, invitation for, 105
  decolonizing the relationship case example and, 152
  definition of, 100
  in finding exceptions trans throuple case example, 121
  in identity and relational cherishing case example, 136
  intergenerational compassionate network case example and, 115
  questions related to, 100–101
  relational declarations and, 142
  in relational declarations case example, 144, 147
  relational healing circles and, 127
  relationship shifts and, 101
  setting, 52
  supporting clients with, questions for, 102–3
systemic oppression
  boundaries against, 155
  practitioner reflection on, 41–42
systemic trauma, xxii, 173
  addressing, liberatory connections and, 129
  assaulted sense of self and, 28–32
  assault on imagination and, 55
  chronic and pervasive nature of, 7, 8t, 12, 109, 167
  cultural wisdom and countering of, 125
  defining, 6, 23
  disenfranchised nature of, 7, 44, 125
  disrupted path to intimacy and, 19–22
  enduring nature of, 110, 111, 112

systemic trauma (*continued*)
  exploration of, 6–23
  family narratives connected to, 86–87
  features of, 7–9
  gentle pace in treatment of, 50
  GLITCH model and, 165
  grieving impact of, on relationship, 96
  imagination and, 168
  mental health challenges and, 12–15
  practitioner's reflection on, 23
  psychological boundaries and, 160
  ravages of, containing boundaries and, 156
  relational healing circles and, 124
  responsible externalizing and, 94
  single-incident trauma *vs.*, 8*t*–9*t*
  system induced nature of, 7
  unpredictable nature of, 7
  word "treat" in context of, 109
  see also systemic harm

taboo area, discussing in relational healing circles, 125–26, 127
terror and freeze response, 11
Thai, L., 6
theater of oppression, 63–70, 64, 97
  case example, 66–69
  nurturing your creativity and, 69–70
  overview of, 91*t*
  questions to ask about, 65, 91*t*
Theatre of the Oppressed
  coining of name for, 65
  stress spillover and, 80
therapeutic alliance, honoring the process in GLITCH model and, 171
therapeutic gaslighting, preventing, 49

therapeutic relationship, as a biome, 40
therapeutic stance
  becoming the BIOME and, 39–49, 40
  practitioner's reflection on the BIOME, 49
therapy
  decolonization of, 174
  GLITCH process and transformative approach to, 171
  redefining, 168
threat-inhibition networks in brain, racism and, 8
threats
  attribution and mitigation of, 95
  vagal tone and, 11
Torres Strait Islanders
  educational barriers for, 6, 16
  income inequality and, 16
traditional psychology, main question asked by, 6
transparency, about social location, 45–46
transphobia, 89, 121–23, 166
transportation barriers, mental health access and, 14
trauma
  decontextualized, 18
  intergenerational, 53–54
  loss of imagination and, 55
  narrowing of life outcomes and, 9–10
  see also ancestral trauma; intergenerational trauma; systemic trauma; trauma work, continuous
trauma-informed therapy, main question asked by, 6
trauma work, continuous, 109–28, 129
  aim and goals of, 111, 128
  the BIOME and, 109–10
  finding exceptions and, 120–24, 128
  how we see ourselves in, 110–11
  intergenerational compassionate network and, 114–20, 128

  memory reconsolidation and, 112, 128
  neurobiological underpinnings of, 112–14
  one-off work *vs.,* 110
  PRIDE model and, 110–11, 113
  questions related to, 109
  relational healing circles and, 124–28
Trinidad and Tobago
  homophobic and transphobic violence in, 6
  LGBTQIA+ people and health access challenges in, 15
  White ideologies and residing in, 29–30
Trinidad and Tobago Transgender Coalition, 26
trust
  status in the world and messages about, 24
  systemic trauma, path to intimacy, and, 19
trying it out, in the GLITCH model, 165, *165,* 169–70, 171, 172, 174
turning backward
  family narratives and, 85, 92*t*
  pivoting and, 51, 52, 58
  relational curiosity and, 62
  responsible externalizing and, 94
turning forward
  in intention setting case example, 103, 105, 106
  pivoting and, 51, 52, 58
  setting intentions and, 99
turning inward
  habits of survival and, 73
  neurological benefit of, 52–53
  pivoting and, 51–52, 58
  relational curiosity and, 62
  relational privilege score and, 90
  relational terrain and, 81
  in responsible externalizing example, 99

Index

theater of oppression technique and, 66
turning outward
  family narratives and, 85
  habits of survival and, 73
  pivoting and, 51, 52, 58
  relational curiosity and, 62
  relational terrain and, 81
  responsible externalizing and, 93
  in theater of oppression case, 66
  theater of oppression technique and, 66, 68
two-chair work or two-chair enactment, survival habits and, 75

United Kingdom
  race and income inequality in, 16
  racial minorities and psychosis in, 13
United States
  homophobic and transphobic violence in, 7
  race and income inequality in, 16

vagal tone, threats and, 11
validation and tending, for grieving, 96
values words, in containing boundaries, 156
ventral vagal branch, 11
ventral vagal tone, witnessing with kind intention and, 55
vibrations, in VIMBASI method, 52
VIMBASI method, 52

coming-out story and elements of, 77
finding exceptions and use of, 120
finding exceptions trans throuple case example and use of, 122, 123
habits of survival and, 71, 74
intergenerational compassionate network case example and, 116
relational healing circles and use of, 127, 128
relational terrain and elements of, 81
in responsible externalizing example, 99
sending compassion toward learning and elements of, 121
theater of oppression case and elements of, 67, 69
witnessing stance toward learning and use of, 114
see also BIOME, the; GLITCH model; PRIDE model
visibility, commitment to, 63
vision boards, decolonizing the relationship and, 154
visioning, intention setting and, 101–2
visual storytelling, coming-out story and, 78
voice
  autonomic nervous system and, 11
  creating for our clients, 47
vulnerability, 63

Walcott, D., 142

well-being, expanded sense of, 42
wellness, building liberatory connections and, 130
White gaze, omnipresence of, 29
White ideologies, dominance of, 29–30
wholeness, path toward liberation and, 174
window of possibilities, 9, 10, 12, 156
  being outside of, 53
  biome and opening of, 40
  habits of survival and, 70
  potentialities within, 12, 13
window of tolerance, 9, 10, 12, 65, 131, 156
"Wisdom of Process, The" (Hemphill), 34
witnessing mindset, developing, 52–53
witnessing stance
  deepening, in intergenerational compassionate network case example, 117
  toward learning, using VIMBASI, 114, 120
writing, metaphors, 74

xenophobia, 18

yarning (Aboriginal process)
  habits of survival and, 73
  relational curiosity and principles of, 61
Yoruban tradition (African), imagination ("ashe") in, 56
Yunkaporta, T., 25, 27

ABOUT THE AUTHOR

Akilah Riley-Richardson, MSW, CCTP, is a dedicated couples therapist, educator, and researcher. As a Certified Clinical Trauma Professional and STAIR Method certified clinician, she specializes in relational healing, focusing on the needs of couples and individuals all over the world. Akilah is passionate about supporting sexual and racial minorities, ensuring her practice is inclusive and culturally sensitive. She has worked with various organizations, providing healthcare training and community support, and is committed to advancing understanding around marginalized populations. Akilah has shared her expertise at forums such as Harvard Medical School, New York University, the Psychotherapy Networker Symposium, and the Black Mental Health Symposium. She served as a social work educator at the University of the Southern Caribbean from 2012 to 2025. As the founder of the Relational Healing Institute and creator of the PRIDE model, she is dedicated to promoting relational therapies and healing.